MW01231990

IT'S NOT ABOUT YOU

T. COLLINS

CROSSBOOKS

CrossBooks™
A Division of LifeWay
One LifeWay Plaza
Nashville, TN 37234
www.crossbooks.com
Phone: 1-866-768-9010

First published by CrossBooks 1/7/2015

ISBN: 978-1-4627-5610-0 (sc)
ISBN: 978-1-4627-5612-4 (hc)
ISBN: 978-1-4627-5611-7 (e)

Library of Congress Control Number: 2014922231

Printed in the United States of America.

This book is printed on acid-free paper.

Any people depicted in stock imagery provided by Thinkstock are models,
and such images are being used for illustrative purposes only.
Certain stock imagery © Thinkstock.

To my wife:

I pray I would love you as Christ loves the church; I would lift you up and encourage you; and you would know I am not me without you.

To Anna and Noah:

You have taught me more about the love of God than anything imaginable. I pray when the time comes this book will serve to guide you deep into the heart of God.

Contents

INTRODUCTION

Have you ever thought about what you would say if you wrote a book? How would you start it? What would it be about? I have thought about those things, and my answers were all wrong.

I have enjoyed writing since I was a kid. I remember writing humorous and nonsensical stories to pass the time when I was in elementary school. Later I enjoyed writing essays on various literary works I had read. Writing has never been a chore for me but rather something I have enjoyed doing. To think I would one day write a book was not a strange or silly idea for me, though I guess for a lot of people the idea of having to write a book is a scary prospect. To me, it's like running—it comes naturally. I have fun doing it. But to think the first book I would complete would be this one ... I would've never guessed it. It seems God had other plans.

For about a year and a half, the title for this book, *It's Not About You*, bounced around in my head while I mulled over the implications. The premise of the book was fairly simple, at least in theory: We, as humans, steal God's glory and find ways to make everything, even the best of things, about us. While this is a seemingly simple proposition, working through it in a meaningful manner is something completely different. It's hard. It's a huge, bitter-tasting pill to swallow. I know because I've been trying to swallow the pill for the last year and a half, and with the writing of this book, the pill seems to have only gotten larger. Some sections have poured out with practically no effort. Other sections have been difficult to work through. In the end, it represents a large amount of prayer and study, as well as feeling like I've been punched in the mouth by the words hanging out there in front of me on the computer screen.

It has been, and continues to be, a growth experience. I've had to let down the mask and take an honest look at myself—my motives, attitudes, and actions. It is my hope and prayer for anyone who reads this book that you too will be able to let down your guard and look honestly at yourself. If you don't feel like your toes have been stepped on in some way or other as you read it, then one of two things has happened: I have missed the mark or you haven't let down your guard and taken off the mask. However, I am confident if we are faithful to be honest with ourselves and with God, He is faithful to forgive us and help us to have a deeper, abiding faith in Him.

You may have noticed a couple of things about the cover of the book. First, my name is only included in the biographical information, and is not on the front cover or spine. From the outset of the writing of the book, I did not intend to use my real name because after all, it isn't about me. But a number of people with a lot more knowledge on book publishing advised me otherwise. My compromise was to refrain from putting my name on the cover, except in the biographical information, and not include my whole name. The other thing about the cover is it has a bathroom mirror on it. For the majority of us, our mental image of who we are—what we present to the world—is derived from what we see in our bathroom mirror. It's a place where we brush our teeth, comb our hair, shave or put on makeup. It's where we create an image we want the world to see, an image that may not be a true reflection of who we really are. This concept of the mirror comes from a chapter in the book where I talk about a guy who lives in my mirror who makes excuses for why he can't give up certain luxuries in life. We all have someone who lives in our mirrors. Sometimes we have a hard time getting a good look at the person in the mirror because he or she is hiding behind a mask, a mask no one seems to be able to see behind—or at least that's what the guy in my mirror thinks. Our mirrors represent a great opportunity for us to stop and honestly look ourselves in the eyes and see who we really are—to see the reality behind the mask we show the world. After all, God sees behind the mask. He knows what's in the heart of the guy in my mirror. He knows the good and the bad. He wants to help that guy take off the mask and be honest with himself—that is, with me. I want him to take off the mask and be honest with me too. But that's hard to do because it means letting down the guard and admitting there is something being hidden. It means admitting he's not, and I'm not, perfect. While this isn't news to God, sometimes it seems like it is news to us.

You will see this book is divided up into three sections. The first section, the largest of the three, deals with myriad ways we go about stealing from the glory of God. It deals with the nitty-gritty reality of what lies within us in places even we sometimes cannot see. This first section is where we get punched in the mouth, at least if we are brave enough to let down the masks. The goal is to bring us all to a place where we are forced to admit there are things we do to steal the glory from God, to put ourselves first. The first section is not designed to give you answers but rather to get you to look at yourself in an honest way—it's designed to be a spiritual mirror.

The second section of the book is about God's greatest blessing as viewed through the lens of Christ's Beatitudes from the Sermon on the Mount. As you will see, the Beatitudes can describe the spiritual metamorphosis arising from coming to faith in Christ. The Beatitudes serve as a bridge from the self-centered reality in which we live to the eternal transformation God brings about in us by faith in Christ.

The final section of the book works through how we, through the work of the Holy Spirit, can come to the place in our lives where it really is not about us. It is designed to turn our focus, all of it, to God. In short, the book represents the gospel. The first section makes us come face-to-face with our sinfulness; the second section describes the change that occurs as a result of faith in Christ; and the third section gives us the tools to live out the God-focused life to which Christ has called us.

A few months ago I was driving to work and listening to a great band called Cloverton. They had just released their first full-length CD, *Patterns*, and I was listening to the twelfth track on the CD, "God Help Me to Be." As I was listening to the song, I heard a line that said, "Now let me see with those same eyes that created me."[1] In that instant, I thought about something so profound as to be dumbfounding. Before God made me, or you, or the guy in your neighbor's mirror, He knew we would put ourselves first. He knew we would not love our neighbors as ourselves. He knew we would point at specks in the eyes of others though we have logs in our own. He knew all of those things, from the seemingly mundane to the most heinous. What's more, He knew that because of all of these things He would have to send His Son to die in our place. And you know what? He chose to make me anyway. In spite of all of that stuff, God made me anyway.

The ultimate goal of this book is to remind that guy, the one in my mirror—the one who God made in spite of all I have gotten wrong, continue to get wrong, and will get wrong in the future—that even when he thinks he has it all together, there is always the opportunity to grow in faith and to have a deeper relationship with God. It's about giving all of the glory to God, who is so overwhelming as to be indescribable. It's about the grace He pours out on all of us through Jesus Christ in spite of what we continue to keep doing wrong. It's about God.

Section I

It's Not About a Lot of Things

CHAPTER 1
IT'S NOT ABOUT YOUR IMPORTANCE

Have you ever tried to think about how great God is? Sure, we sing songs that say things like, "How great is our God," but have you ever actually stopped and tried to think about how great God really is? You can't do it. If you do, you've missed something—you've gotten something wrong. My favorite name for God comes from Daniel 7:9, "The Ancient of Days." There is something about that name I have always found to be, quite literally, awesome. God is the Ancient of Days because He has no beginning and no end. He is outside of time. He is completely infinite with regard to His attributes. This is our God, the one true God—YHWH.

Now, if I try to contrast what little bit of understanding I have of the greatness of the Lord Almighty against the lackluster guy who lives in my mirror, it's a ridiculous comparison. If I think of it in mathematical terms, infinity continues on forever; the numbers just keep going. If the guy in my mirror is equal to the number one, he's so far removed from infinity as to be nonexistent. Even if the guy in my mirror is really super and scores a one hundred, compared to infinity, it might as well be zero. So even on my best days, I am infinitely incomparable to the greatness of God. Unfortunately, we often somehow manage to forget the difference. It happened to Adam, and it's been happening ever since.

The first mistake we make, one inherent to our nature and nurtured by our culture, is to think we are important. We are groomed to believe we, as individuals, have a special place in the story of the world and by extension, the story of God. After all, God chose us, right? In the first chapter of Ephesians, we read that those of us who are believers were predestined to be adopted by God. So we must then be important or at least more important than nonbelievers. We must have had some great attribute or attributes that led God to want to adopt us. Otherwise why would He do such a thing? If God chose us in such a manner, it stands to reason we must be important to God's story. If we are important to God's story, then we are, by definition, important.

Our logic follows that since we are important, we must be deserving of good things: honor, peace, prosperity, security, or whatever else we may see as good. This sort of errant logic has been present since the dawn of mankind, and we see it played out throughout the Bible.

As Important as God

In the garden of Eden, Adam and Eve had everything they needed. They were at peace. They were prosperous. They had a task, which was tending the garden. They were honored to have a relationship with God so intimate that they spent time with Him in the garden. He walked with them in the garden. Think about that. God came into the garden, and they walked around and talked with Him. But as we know, this relationship with God did not last.

What was at the heart of Adam and Eve's turning from God? It's the same thing at the heart of all of our sins—pride. The serpent came to Eve in the garden and appealed to her pride. It was a simple scheme that worked fantastically and continues to work thousands of years later. Eve knew eating the fruit of the Tree of the Knowledge of Good and Evil was wrong. God had told her so. But Satan used her self-worth, her pride, against her, and she, and subsequently Adam, fell for it with remarkable ease.

Satan coupled Adam and Eve's adoration of God with their own self-worth and created a trap they jumped into. Satan knew Adam and Eve adored God. God is of such greatness and awe-inspiring wonder as to be completely immeasurable. Adam and Eve knew that firsthand from the time they had spent with God in the garden. They knew He was worthy of worship and adoration. So Satan took their knowledge, their correctly oriented worship and awe, and helped them turn it toward themselves. It is not hard to imagine Satan saying, "Think of how great God is. Isn't He the most amazing thing in all of creation? Wouldn't it be great if you could be that magnificent? You know ... There is a way." With that, he planted the seed in their minds and cultivated their egos to desire to assume an equal position with God. He led them to doubt what God had clearly told them. Then he told Eve, "For God knows that in the day you eat from it your eyes will be opened, and *you will be like God*, knowing good and evil" (Genesis 3:5 NASB, emphasis added).

If we really look at the third chapter of Genesis, it's hard to make a case that Adam and Eve consciously intended to supplant God. The line they bought was that they were going to "be like God." They knew God intimately. They were in awe of Him and wanted to be like Him. Satan used their desire to be like God and transformed it into something more. He told Adam and Eve they surely wouldn't die. They had nothing to worry about with regard to dying, he told them. In that moment, Satan planted in their minds the seed of thought that God was withholding something from them. You can imagine Adam and Eve asking, "Why would God withhold this from us? Why would He lie to us about dying if we will not? Don't we deserve to be like God?" Their desire to be like God grew into something more. They thought they were important enough to *deserve* to be like God. The overestimation of their importance was pride. That's where they made their mistake. Unlike Christ, Adam and Eve saw themselves as worthy of being equal with God. (Philippians 2:6) In that instant, they removed God from the throne of their hearts and placed themselves upon it. They became their own gods and established the model by which all of mankind has fallen ever since.

Glory and Individualism

God guards His glory dearly. When God wrote the Ten Commandments, He began with stating that He is God alone, and He is the only one worthy of honor, praise, and worship. In fact, in Exodus 20:5 God said, "For I, the LORD your God, am a jealous God" (NASB). He is jealous of anyone or anything that would seek to take away His glory. Why is that? Is it because God is self-centered and egocentric? That's a question originating from our own prideful hearts as we seek to make God like us.

God is all holy and all-powerful. He has all knowledge. God is perfection manifest. He is "all in all" (1 Corinthians 15:28). There is nothing greater than God (Hebrews 6:13). Because this is the case, God deserves all honor and all praise. God doesn't need worship, honor, and praise for His ego. He doesn't need validation from lesser things, which, as it turns out, is everything in existence other than God. When something else receives the honor and praise due God, it detracts from God's greatness. This doesn't really impact God, but rather it impacts everything else. God knows when something takes away from His glory destruction occurs, and that's not what He wants.

God doesn't need our praise. He allows us to experience something of Himself, and the response that follows is praise. But we take it to mean God needs us. We ignore that the throne of God is constantly being showered with praises from cherubim and seraphim, the latter of which fly around God continuously for all of eternity, crying out, "Holy, holy, holy is the LORD of hosts" (Isaiah 6:3 NASB). But the truth is God doesn't need us. He doesn't need us for His praise. He doesn't need us for His story, and this is where the pill gets hard to swallow.

We are *not* important to the narrative of God. The Bible is *not* a story about us. God does not need any of us for His story. He chooses to continually redeem defiled people in the story, but we as individuals are not important to it. God made us, yes. He created us "a little lower than the angels" (Psalm 8:5) indeed. But without God, we are nothing—always have been and always will be. God in us is important, but without Him, we are otherwise meaningless. Without us, God is still God in all of His glory, without the loss of anything—always has been and always will be.

We try to take from God what is not ours to possess. In our self-centeredness, we are convinced we deserve the peace, security, and prosperity of the garden—that those things are somehow owed to us. Along the way, we have been readily convinced we as individuals are important. This is played out in every arena of consumer marketing. We are told we deserve the luxury of a given item, whether it is an exotic car, a pricey perfume, or extra-absorbent paper towels. Whatever it is, we are told we deserve the best, and we buy into it without a second thought.

Our churches haven't done much to dissuade us from our self-centered thinking. While God is, without a doubt, glorified and honored in most of our churches, we are too. In the church we like to talk about the ninety-nine who were left for the one who was lost. We think about the widow frantically searching her house to find her lost coin—an image reminiscent of Gollum in *The Lord of the Rings* desperately trying to find his precious.[2] It makes us feel good to think about the great love the Lord has for us. We individualize it, and we revel in our importance as individuals.

Individualism is foundational in our American way of thinking. The ideals of individualism were written into the Declaration of Independence and the Constitution. We are all created equal, as individuals with unalienable rights. But this concept is recent in human history, especially with regard to it being viewed as a positive thing. The individual was important in Greek society, but such was not the case in monarchical societies like those found in Europe during the period of American colonization. Individualism was not an important part of social or political thought before the writings of John Locke, an influential seventeenth-century political philosopher.[3] The impact of Locke's philosophies on individualism can be seen clearly in our nation's founding documents. Since the founding of our country, Americans have held tightly to the concept of individual freedom, rights, and worth. It's where we get the ideals of personal achievement and autonomy. As a Western civilization, we operate under these Western premises. But that was not true for ancient Israel and the Jews.

The Jewish culture was based on the importance of the community. The family unit was the building block of Jewish society and culture, not the individual. When God called Abram to leave Ur in Genesis 12, He commanded Abram to leave his family. But we see that Abram took with him his wife, Sarai, and his nephew, Lot, along with a number of other people. So this call on Abram, though seemingly individual, was a call on a group of people, and Abram was the representative of the group. The individual was not the focus of society.

For as long as I can remember, people have told me (imagine this being said in a softly spoken, and perhaps slightly patronizing, Southern drawl), "Jesus loves you so much that if you were the only one, He would've come and died for you." That sounds really nice. Is it true? Where in Scripture does the Bible say anything like that? It makes me feel good, like I'm important. But is it true?

If we look at the parables in Luke 15, we see Jesus speaking to the Pharisees about why He was spending time with the tax collectors and the sinners. Jesus asked who among them would not leave ninety-nine sheep to go find one that was lost. This single sheep was then compared to one sinner who repents as opposed to ninety-nine who did not need to repent. Jesus was not magnifying the individual. He was saying He wants everyone to come to repentance. This is echoed in 2 Peter 3:9 when Peter wrote, "The Lord is not slow about His promise, as some count slowness, but is patient toward you, not willing for any to perish but for all to come to repentance" (NASB). The same is the case with the single lost coin out of the widow's ten coins. His point was about getting everyone into a right relationship with God, not just the one. The parables in Luke 15 are not about the single sheep or the lost coin. They are about the faithfulness of the shepherd and the woman to find them. Think about it from the perspective of Jesus trying to teach the Pharisees. He was saying, "Wouldn't you guys be faithful to go through the same trouble if you had lost a sheep or a coin? I'm doing this because God doesn't want anyone to perish."

When we look at Luke 15:11–32, we see the parable of the prodigal son. Superficially, we can say this parable is about everyone being glad when the lost son comes home. In truth, it's about considerably more. The lost son (played by the thieves and prostitutes in Jesus' day) demonstrated his self-centeredness and pride by demanding his share of the inheritance early—an inheritance he would normally have received when his father died. In effect, the son was saying to his father he would rather his father would die. The son ran off and squandered everything, defiling himself as he went, only to return when the money ran out to beg to be a servant at his father's house. The father, though, was ecstatic at the return of his son. He had been waiting, hoping, and longing for the day his son would return. When he saw him coming from a distance, the old guy took off running. He didn't tell his servants to go check out the scene. He didn't mount a horse and ride out to meet him as the lord of the estate. He ran.

A great celebration was arranged, and the older brother who had remained with his father the whole time (played by the Pharisees and religious leaders) became angry because the return of his wayward brother was being celebrated. The brother was consumed with jealousy over the ordeal and readily explained to the father why. He lashed out at his father and basically condemned his father's happiness regarding his wayward brother's return. In the end, the father sought to reconcile not only the son who had returned home but also the jealous brother. This parable too is about the faithfulness of the father. All three parables are about the faithfulness of God to bring everyone into reconciliation with Him. They are not about an individual. To this same end, regarding His reason for coming, Jesus said, "Of those whom You have given Me I have lost not one" (John 18:9 NASB).

We can say whatever we want to about a scenario wherein the Son of God would have come to earth to suffer and die to redeem me, or you, alone. But the fact is neither you nor I are the only one, just as Jesus said in John 18:9. Christ did not come to save just me, and so such a statement is a bit ridiculous. In fact, it's fantastical thinking because it's just not the way things are, and there is no way to prove or disprove how such a completely different scenario from reality would be played out.

Does this line of thinking make you uncomfortable? Does thinking that maybe you are not important get under your skin? It bothers me. I bristle at the suggestion that I'm not as important to God as I have always thought. What is it that compels us to feel that way? Pride. We are certain we are important as individuals. We have been trained to think that way since we were born.

While there is no place in the Bible to suggest Christ would have died for me alone, there are things in addition to the parables of Luke 15 that point to something in the story more important than individuals.

Every morning since I have been married, I have prayed I would "love [my wife] as Christ also loved the church," which is drawn directly from Ephesians 5:25. There have been times when I prayed, "God, help me to love her as You love her ..." But recently, when I was leading a Bible study through Ephesians, I began to meditate on this section of chapter 5. "Husbands, love your wives as Christ also loved the church and gave Himself up for her" (Ephesians 5:25 NASB). It does not say, "Love your wife as God loves her." There is a striking difference. As husbands, we are called, we are commanded, to love our wives "as Christ also loved the church, and gave Himself up for her." For me, if I really grasp what it is Christ did when He took on human flesh, lived a sinless life, and died on the cross on Golgotha to redeem His bride, this is the most difficult commandment in all of Scripture. Christ did all of those things for the church, not just me. In Revelation we read about the wedding banquet for Christ and His bride, the church. It is all a celebration of His redeemed church, which is much greater than me.

The most telling of Jesus' parables on the point that I am not as important as I think comes from Matthew 22, where He tells of a king who arranged a wedding celebration for his son. When none of the invited guests came to the festivities, the king ordered his servants to go out and tell the invitees that he, the king, had prepared a wonderful banquet and all they had to do was show up. Those who were invited scoffed at the servants, and as a result, the king ordered his armies to go out and destroy them. Then he commanded his servants to go out into the surrounding countryside and invite all they could find, "the good and the bad," to come to the wedding feast of his son. When everyone had arrived, the king found an attendee who was not dressed for the occasion, so the king had him bound, tied, and thrown out.

The secondary invitees, the ones who came from the highways and byways to the wedding banquet, were there on the invitation of the king. However, the banquet was not about the invitees. It was about his son and by extension, himself. This was a grand celebration to honor the marriage of the prince, and the individuals attending, as demonstrated by the ousting of the chap in ill-suited clothing, did not matter.

In the end, God has a much bigger plan than we can comprehend. It's not a plan for individuals but rather a plan for the Bride of Christ, which is the church. We as individuals are not important to the story except as we play a role within the framework of the church. It is there where we find our importance, not in ourselves and our own self-worth but in the position we have in Christ and the importance He gives us as a result.

CHAPTER 2
IT'S NOT ABOUT YOU PLAYING GOD

*AND IF ANYONE HEARS MY WORDS AND DOES NOT BELIEVE, I DO
NOT JUDGE HIM; FOR I DID NOT COME TO JUDGE THE WORLD BUT
TO SAVE THE WORLD. (JOHN 12:47 NKJV)*

In our society today, the church is all too often seen as judgmental, condemnatory, unloving, unaccepting, and hypocritical. Why? Is it because we are in the right and the world is in the wrong? Is it because people don't want to hear the truth of the gospel of Christ? Or could it be something different? Is there legitimacy in the assessment of those outside of the church?

In the Old Testament, when people had turned away from God, when they lived lives marked by sin, God chose prophets to speak to the people—to pronounce upon them the things they were doing that were wrong in God's eyes, and to warn them to turn from their sinful ways. After being chosen, the prophet would receive a message or messages from God, which often came via the angel of the Lord, who was likely a physical manifestation of God, as suggested by the words of the angel of the Lord in Genesis 22:12 when he was speaking to Abraham. It was the role of the prophet to convey God's message, which was quite often one of judgment upon the children of Israel.

Judgment Is God's Job

After Christ came, the task of speaking for God, whether in the form of convicting the world of sin or drawing unbelievers to the Lord, was given to the Holy Spirit. It is the Holy Spirit's role to judge the hearts of men and convict them of sin. In John 16:8, Jesus said when the Holy Spirit "has come, He will convict the world of sin, and of righteousness, and of judgment" (NKJV). It is the Holy Spirit's job to draw people to the Father through the Son, in accordance with Jesus' words in John 6:65:

"Therefore I have said to you that no one can come to Me unless it has been granted to him by My Father" (NKJV).

If given the opportunity to defend it, many people in the Western church who are seemingly well-intentioned will say it is our responsibility to tell people when they are wayward or "living in sin." They see this as being a light to the world, and "where there is light, the shadows will appear." Is that really what it is? Is it really an interest in exposing the sins of the world? If so, why isn't that light shining on all of the sins consuming our world and not just a select few hot-button items?

Look again at what Jesus said in the second half of John 12:47: "For *I did not come to judge the world* but to save the world" (NKJV, emphasis added). Jesus Christ, the Son of the Living God yet also God Himself, said He did not come to judge the world. Of all people in all of history, Christ was the one who could rightfully judge the world, yet He clearly said He did not come to do that. Further, He said He came "to save the world." Here the Lord separated the two completely; *judging* the world has nothing to do with *saving* the world. So if the one who had every right to judge the world said He did not come to judge the world, why do we feel the obligation to do so? Further, if it was Jesus' mission to save the world, if we are truly seeking to follow Him, why aren't we deeply engaged in that mission?

If you ask the average person in any given evangelical church if it is our responsibility to point out the errors of those nonbelievers who are living in sin, it seems, based on my nonscientific sample, they will almost all say it is an imperative task of a Christian to do so. They go back to being a light to the world. Somewhere along the line, it became seen as our role to inform people of the error of their ways. Where did that come from? It didn't come from Jesus. His purpose was to save the world, and to do so He loved the world.

In the fourth chapter of John, the story of the woman at the well gives us great insight into Jesus' approach to these situations. Jesus met the woman at the well, and at no time throughout the conversation did Jesus condemn the woman. He acknowledged she was living with a man who was not her husband, but beyond that, He did not say anything more regarding the situation, at least not that was recorded by John. He did not qualify it as right or wrong. Jesus looks on us and loves us, just as He did with the rich, young ruler in Mark 10:21.

Another great example of Jesus' lack of interest in judging people is recorded in the eighth chapter of John. I personally see this story of Jesus' actions as one of the greatest, dare I say coolest, in the whole Bible because it tells us something of Jesus' personality and what He was really about. I learn so much from it because I am both the woman and the Pharisees.

As a brief recap, there was a woman who was caught in adultery and was apprehended by the scribes and Pharisees, those people in Jewish society who were supposedly the ones who had their spiritual act together. They brought her to Jesus to have Him pronounce judgment on the woman. Imagine the scene. Jesus was in the street, most likely with a group of people. The scribes and Pharisees stormed up, undoubtedly making quite a ruckus as they pushed through everyone to get to Jesus, and then they threw the woman in front of Jesus. They launched into their description of the situation and how, according to Mosaic law, the penalty was for her to be stoned. Then they asked a feigned question in the hope of trapping Jesus. During all of this commotion, Jesus had bent down and started writing in the dirt of the street. What was He writing? We are not told. Some people have speculated He was writing various sins out in the dirt, but in reality we do not know. Nevertheless, this is an interesting scenario because in His action, Jesus demonstrated He was not interested in the Pharisees' judgment of the woman, neither was He interested in judging the woman.

Think of what must have been going through the Pharisees' minds. "Is this guy paying attention to us? Doesn't He realize who we are and that this is a matter of significant importance?" Not to be deterred, the Pharisees kept asking Jesus what He thought should be done about the matter.

Finally, Jesus "raised Himself up and said to them, 'He who is without sin among you, let him throw a stone at her first.' And again He stooped down and wrote on the ground" (John 8:7–8 NKJV). At His doing this, all of those Pharisees who had already condemned her in their hearts became convicted of their own sin and went away. But it's not over there. Jesus was still there drawing in the dirt, and everyone had left except for the woman. "When Jesus had raised Himself up and saw no one but the woman, He said to her, 'Woman, where are those accusers of yours? Has no one condemned you?' She said, 'No one, Lord.' And Jesus said to her, 'Neither do I condemn you; go and sin no more'" (John 8:10–11 NKJV).

Jesus didn't judge the woman. He was, for most of the story, just drawing in the dirt. When she came face-to-face with the reality of Christ, with the love and lack of condemnation, she didn't need the pharisaical approach to having her sin pointed out to her. After she had gone away, Jesus turned, undoubtedly to the disciples, who were probably standing there with their mouths gaping open at what had just happened, and He said, "I am the light of the world. He who follows Me shall not walk in darkness, but have the light of life" (John 8:12 NKJV).

If we really want to shed light in dark places, Jesus has given us the model to follow, so why don't we follow His approach? Why do we refuse to operate in such a manner? Why are we obliged to pass judgment? Is it because the Holy Spirit can't handle the job? Is it because God Almighty wouldn't be able to accomplish His task without me? Or is it something else we have packaged in a manner that seems acceptable to us?

If you ask one of the average evangelical churchgoers I mentioned earlier what sorts of people they think need to be informed they are living in sin, those churchgoers are almost always locked and loaded with a response. Certainly a hot-button topic of today is homosexuality. It is always first on the list of sins that must be openly and unabashedly condemned. Is it a sin? The Bible is pretty clear homosexual behavior is a sin. But there are a lot of other sins the Bible addresses more frequently than homosexuality. Why aren't we ready to jump to those sins and condemn the people who practice them?

According to the Center for Disease Control, as of August 2013, 35.7 percent of adults in the United States were obese.[4] That's not just overweight; that's obese. If we include overweight people in the numbers, 69.2 percent of American adults are overweight or obese. What does the Bible say about being overweight? Well, being overweight was a rare issue in biblical times, so there isn't a lot said specifically about it. But gluttony was definitely addressed in the Bible. Solomon addressed gluttony on three different occasions in Proverbs (23:2, 23:20–21, 28:7). Gluttony is a manifestation of a lack of self-control (one of the fruits of the Spirit), and a lack of self-control is definitely addressed in Deuteronomy 21:20, 1 Corinthians 7:5, 2 Timothy 3:1–9, and 2 Peter 1:5–7. All of these verses address the need for self-control and condemn the lack of it as sinful. So if more than two-thirds of adults in our nation are manifesting physical evidence of a lack of self-control, why aren't we condemning them? Why aren't we lobbying for legislation to stop this rampant sin? Could it be because we are among them?

Building Our Kingdoms

In Luke 12 Jesus told a parable about greed. Therein, He told of a man who had an abundant crop, but because all his barns were already full, he decided he would tear them down and build bigger barns to store all of his grain and goods with a plan to "take life easy; eat, drink, and be merry." God demanded the man's life and Jesus said, "So is he who lays up treasure for himself, and is not rich toward God" (Luke 12:21 NKJV). What about all of the people out there who are building bigger barns?

As it turns out, the average new home in the United States in 2009 was 2,164 square feet. In Italy, it was 872 square feet. In urban centers in China, it was 646 square feet, and in Hong Kong, it was 484 square feet.[5] Data are not even available on houses in places like Africa or Haiti. So if we have so many people building these bigger barns in the United States, why aren't we moving to stop it? Shouldn't we take a stand to end the rampant greed that is condemning our nation?

If one were sitting around in the evenings with nothing to do and happened to have cable television, one might occasionally flip through large numbers of channels, all of which seem to have nothing particularly worthwhile to offer. As it turns out, on several of those channels there are a host of pseudo-reality television options, some of which have to do with people foisting their children onto beauty pageant stages. Others center on people's escapades in remodeling their homes, and still others have to do with things like cold-water fishing. I am referring to it as pseudo-reality because the editors, producers, and executives at the given network manipulate it all so that it really isn't reality. This has become a pervasive television genre, presumably because there are a lot of people out there watching.

While flipping around the channels in the evening, I have seen some programs centered on self-storage facilities. I have never watched one of these programs, but from the advertisements I have determined there are people who make it their business to go around and buy the contents of self-storage units where the rent has not been paid or when they have been abandoned. Are there really so many storage units with contents that go unclaimed that businesses can be run off of them? Apparently there are.

Let's try to frame the numbers of the self-storage industry. According to the Self-Storage Association, there are about 59,500 self-storage facilities in the world, more than 48,500 of which are in the United States.[6] So we in the US account for 80.8 percent of the total self-storage facilities in the world. There are over 2.3 billion square feet of self-storage space in the United States, which translates to about 82.5 square miles of floor space. That's bigger than the city of Baltimore, Maryland—the entire city. Further, almost 9 percent of all American households rented a storage unit in 2012, and the industry generated more than $24 billion in 2013. Think about that—$24 billion to store stuff we aren't even using! There are ninety-one different countries around the world whose gross domestic product is less than what we spend on storing our unused stuff.[7] What compels us to hoard so much stuff? It's easy to think of people in distant lands bowing down to idols, but we don't see that happening here in the United States, at least not overtly. Are we building little kingdoms in those storage units, to the tune of about $120 per month in rental costs, to house what are effectively idols?

We all have excuses why we keep stuff we don't need. For instance, I have a Civil War–era musket my mother won at a Bicentennial celebration when I was a toddler. It's fascinating to look at, but it's obviously old and the barrel has a slight hint of rust on it from lack of cleaning. Reportedly it's worth some money, though I don't know. My mother gave that musket to me, and it now sits, untouched, in the back of a closet in our house. I have never fired it. I have no intention of ever firing it. I won't be hanging it on a wall or putting it in a display case. I suspect it will be given to one of my children at some point as a relic. Why do I keep the thing? I say it's because it has intrinsic value as something historic, or it's valuable to me because my mom gave it to me, or because you can't get them anymore. In my answer, I'm sidestepping the real question. What purpose does it serve in my life or the life of my family? If it were suddenly gone, would my day-to-day life be changed at all? It wouldn't. I wouldn't notice it at all. If I'm honest, I think I keep it because somewhere, in the back of my mind, it's worth money. Just like the baseball cards I have in some boxes in the garage, I think it has value to someone else who is willing to pay me for it. That gives me the sense that someday, if I want to, I can cash it in and then I'll have the money. Once I have the money, I have the power to do with it what I want. What would happen if we could let go of all of those things we are keeping around, those things we don't use, the things rusting in some storage unit? What if we let them go and gave the money to make an impact in the world, to help those who are dying from hunger, lack of clean water, or preventable diseases? Jesus said, "Do not lay up for yourselves treasures on earth, where moth and rust destroy and where thieves break in and steal; but lay up for yourselves treasures in heaven, where neither moth nor rust destroys and where thieves do not break in and steal. For where your treasure is, there your heart will be also" (Matthew 6:19–21 NKJV).

Greed is "an excessive desire to acquire or possess more than what one needs or deserves, especially with respect to material wealth."[8] Don't our large appetites for food, big houses, and full self-storage units point to our unbridled greed? Certainly when we think of greed as a concept, we think of the love of money. Paul told Timothy, "The love of money is the root of all kinds of evil" (1 Timothy 6:10 NKJV). Money can definitely become our idol. What is it about money that is so attractive to us? What does money provide us that we want? Those who have money have security and power. That's why we talk about the power of money. We want to be in control, and being in control requires power.

What does our love of money say about us with respect to God? For those with traditional jobs, you rush off to work for forty hours every week for what purpose? Let me put it this way—no matter how much you like your job, if your boss came in and said, "Hey, we can't pay you anymore, but you are free to continue working here indefinitely," would you keep going to work there? I am forced to say I wouldn't. So, let's go back to the question. Why do you go to work for forty hours a week? It's to earn an income, to make money. We have to do that. Sure, we can get enjoyment out of our work and contribute to society. We may feel God has called us to our job or profession, but it's an untenable situation if you don't get paid. The local grocer won't give you food just because you enjoy your job. Certainly there is a biblical mandate for working to earn a living. Paul said, "If anyone will not work, neither shall he eat" (2 Thessalonians 3:10b NKJV). Paul made tents to provide for his needs. But at what point do we go beyond what we are commanded to do—that is work to be able to provide for our needs—and make it something else? When does it become a love of money, and what does our love of money point toward?

In the end, isn't part of our love of money that it provides us with security? If I have money, I know I will be able to pay for the things my family needs, such as food, water, a place to live, etc. If I have enough money, I don't have to depend on anyone, including God, to take care of my needs because I've got it covered. With that in mind, if I strip it down to the most basic level, isn't it really because I don't trust that God will take care of me?

Jesus knew well this is a problem for us. He spoke to this point in the Sermon on the Mount in Matthew 6:25-34 when He warned against worry. Jesus said we should "seek first the kingdom of God and His righteousness, and all these things shall be added to you" (Matthew 6:33 NKJV). Jesus was basically saying if we are diligent to seek after God, to make everything we do about Him and His glory, God is faithful to take care of our needs—not necessarily our wants but our needs. When we are focused on God and not on ourselves, we receive God's true blessing. David wrote about this in Psalm 37:4 when he said, "Delight yourself also in the Lord, and He shall give you the desires of your heart" (NKJV). In the end, when we don't trust that God will take care of us and we seek security in money, we are proving we do not believe God is true to His Word. We are saying Christ is a liar, so we must depend on ourselves to maintain our security. Calling God a liar is the same thing Adam and Eve did in the garden.

The Deceitfulness of Riches

We have bought into the lie that if we have enough money, we can make of our lives exactly what we want, and we can readily convince ourselves it is for good reason. If I have enough money, I can buy the big house with the manicured lawn in the perfect neighborhood—because my family needs to be somewhere safe and we need enough space for our larger family to visit. If I have enough money I can buy the new Audi A5—because it's a safe and well-made car. If I have enough money I can buy a condo at the beach—because we want to make sure our family spends time together away from the hectic schedule we've created. In reality, isn't it that we've made it all about us?

We want to be able to have what we want when we want it. We are certain we deserve all of the things the marketers have told us we deserve, and we want to have it now. We need only look at the statistics on credit card debt to see this playing out across our nation. As of March 2013 nearly two out of every five American adults (37 percent) were carrying credit card debt from month to month.[9] The average debt per credit card that usually carries a balance was $8,220 in March of 2013.[10] Solomon, a man who had kept from himself no earthly pleasure, warned his son in Proverbs that, "Hell and Destruction are never full; so the eyes of man are never satisfied" (Proverbs 27:20 NKJV). The credit card statistics corroborate the lack of material satisfaction we have in the United States. Why aren't we demanding that credit card companies be forced out of business if we are really trying to shed light?

Jesus spoke about money often because He knew that how we handle it is a demonstration of our spiritual condition. If we have trouble with our handling of money, with where we direct our financial resources, it is an indicator we have a spiritual problem. Jesus said, "Where your treasure is, there your heart will be also" (Luke 12:34 NKJV). The Lord knew we would spend our money on what is most important to us. Given this fact, if we are putting God first, we should be spending our money on God, or at least His church, right? Giving money to the church was initiated in the Old Testament. Tithing—that is giving 10 percent to God—was first mentioned in Genesis 14 when Abram gave a tithe of his spoils to Melchizedek. Subsequently, giving to God in the form of tithing was a part of the Law of the Old Testament (Leviticus 27:30, 32; Numbers 18:26; Deuteronomy 14:22, 28; 2 Chronicles 31:5). Interestingly, all of the commanded giving in the Old Testament actually translated to about 23 percent of the people's total income.

There is some debate now as to whether tithing is necessary or not since we are under the New Covenant. Jesus didn't command us to tithe, but He also didn't command us *not* to tithe. We do know He said we should "render to Caesar the things that are Caesar's, and to God the things that are God's" (Mark 12:17 NKJV). Paul wrote in 2 Corinthians 9:7, "*So let* each one *give* as he purposes in his heart, not grudgingly or of necessity; for God loves a cheerful giver" (NKJV). Even though Paul was not speaking about tithing in the passage but rather a special collection for the poor, some have used this as the basis for not giving 10 percent of their income to the church. It's interesting that if given an opportunity to give whatever it is we think God has purposed for our giving, we so often come out on the lower side of 10 percent. Why?

How do we know we often come out on the lower side of giving 10 percent to the church? According to research published in the book *Passing the Plate*, the median annual giving for an American Christian is actually $200, just over 0.5 percent of after-tax income.[11] About 5 percent of American Christians provide 60 percent of the money churches and religious groups use to operate. According to the Barna Group, which studies sociologic, cultural, and religious topics, only 12 percent of born-again Christians, including evangelical and nonevangelical, gave 10 percent or more of their income to the church during 2012.[12] That means 88 percent of born-again Christians did not give at least 10 percent of their income. Why? Based on the teaching of Jesus, it's because we have a spiritual problem—we are focused on our own desires and not God's. How does this happen? If we, as born-again believers in Jesus Christ, know what it is we are supposed to do regarding our money, how do we end up far removed from doing it?

Where we spend our money is a direct indicator of what we hold most important in life. In reality, those of us who profess to believe in Jesus Christ know we are to give a portion of our income. But based on the data available, this doesn't happen in a meaningful way. In Mark 4:13–20 Jesus told the parable of the sower. In verse 19 He said, "the cares of this world, the deceitfulness of riches, and the desires for other things entering in choke the word, and it becomes unfruitful" (Mark 4:19 NJKV). It's a heart problem, and it's rampant in the church. Why aren't we making every effort to stop it? Why are we storing up treasures in our 401(k)s and not in the kingdom of God? Are we demonstrating with our finances that it's about us and not about God? Are we giving the amount we think is best, which as it turns out is highly likely to be lower than what God had required in the Old Testament, because we think we know what is best for us and our financial situation? Are we not removing God from the discussion and taking over the financial reins?

What about something more incendiary? What about something like adultery? It's right there in the big ten. Moses brought that one down off of Mount Sinai. Of sins, it's pretty legitimate. Jesus had a fair amount to say about adultery. In Matthew 5:28 Jesus said unequivocally that to even think lustfully is the same as committing adultery. Further, in Matthew 19 Jesus went so far as to say if a man divorces a woman, except in the setting of sexual immorality, he commits adultery. So why aren't we doing something about the 50 percent of people getting divorces in mainline evangelical churches? According to Scripture, if someone is divorced for any reason other than marital infidelity and then gets remarried, it constitutes adultery. That's living in sin. Why aren't we trying to stop that? Where's the boycott of companies that openly support remarried divorcees?

Why are we compelled to point out the shortcomings of certain people but not all of the other people who also fall short of God's glory? What about those who are "lovers of themselves, lovers of money, boasters, proud, blasphemers, disobedient to parents, unthankful, unholy, unloving, unforgiving, slanderers, without self-control, brutal, despisers of good, traitors, headstrong, haughty, lovers of pleasure rather than lovers of God" (2 Timothy 3:2–4 NKJV)? We talk about shining light in dark places, but it seems it's only those places that don't exist in our immediate proximity. Why would we do that? Why would we want to play the role of the Holy Spirit? Is it because we think the Holy Spirit can't handle the job? Are we convinced we need to take over? Why do we want to play the role of God?

Mankind has been trying to play the role of God since Adam and Eve sought to "be like God" in the garden by eating of the fruit of the tree of the knowledge of good and evil. From the very beginning, we have tried to divert the attention or blame to someone else. Look at Adam's response when God asked him how he knew he was naked in Genesis 3:11. God said, "Have you eaten from the tree of which I commanded you that you should not eat?" (NKJV). What did Adam do? His immediate response was, "The woman whom You gave *to be* with me, she gave me of the tree, and I ate" (Genesis 3:12 NKJV). Look at that. Adam tried to blame not only Eve but also God by saying it was the fault of the woman God had given him. Basically Adam said, "God, the woman made me do it, and if You wouldn't have given her to me in the first place, this would have never happened. So this is really sort of on You." Wow, that was bold. Then, when God asked Eve what she had done, Eve immediately blamed the serpent.

Mankind's trait of passing blame has been maintained across time. In the intervening eons, we have become increasingly adept at magnifying the shortcomings of others as a means of diverting attention from our own. It gives us a false sense of spiritual superiority. It feeds our pride and ego that we, like the praying Pharisee, are not like the tax collector (insert homosexual, drunkard, drug addict, harlot, murderer, etc., here) whose shame was so great he could not even lift his eyes heavenward as he begged God to have mercy on him (Luke 18:10–14). So we storm off to Washington to protest some issue or other. We condemn and pass judgment on those who fill the needed role of sinning differently than we do, and at the end of the day, we pat ourselves on the back for being defenders of the truth and protectors of God's glory.

What if our goal wasn't to condemn the world but to save the world? What if it wasn't about our ego and pride but truly about God's glory? Instead of trying to play, or more to the point *be*, God, what if we instead tried to *be like* Jesus Christ?

CHAPTER 3
IT'S NOT ABOUT YOUR RIGHTS

We in America love to talk about our "rights." As we touched on in the last chapter, the rights of the individual citizen framed the formation of our nation. This is clearly stated in the Declaration of Independence: "All men are created equal, that they are endowed by their Creator with certain unalienable Rights, that among these are Life, Liberty and the pursuit of Happiness." Based on this same ethos, the Constitution includes specifically outlined rights to be guaranteed to the citizenry in what became known as the Bill of Rights.

The rights of the individual are important to us. They make up the fabric of our country and what have historically given us all some bit of common ground. We hold them very dearly and defend them with the utmost fervor. As a member of the US military, at my commissioning, I swore to "support and defend the Constitution of the United States of America against all enemies, foreign and domestic," and that I would "bear true faith and allegiance to the same." I have pronounced my belief in the ideals of our Constitution and sworn to uphold those ideals, our rights, to the utmost. But why is it, on a fundamental level, that we as Christians are compelled to defend our personal rights with such vigor? Are we all afraid, as it has been said, if we don't defend our rights, they will be taken away from us? If that is our concern, then perhaps we have a poor understanding of what it means to be a follower of Christ.

We Have No Rights

When we become followers of Christ, we have become slaves to righteousness, as Romans 6:18 says, "And having been set free from sin, you became slaves of righteousness" (NKJV). What's more, according to 1 Corinthians 7:22, we have become "slaves to Christ." He is our Lord, meaning He has all authority over us. We do not get to retain a little bit of the authority. The part we keep allows us to remain comfortable or privileged. As slaves, all of our rights have been removed, and we are not our own. The nature of this relationship is what makes the idea of slavery so abhorrent to us now when we look back in our nation's history. Our individualism now looks at the founding documents of our country and questions how slavery could have existed if "all men were created equal with certain unalienable rights." We see what slavery was and how it was antithetical to our core beliefs. But if we are believers in Jesus Christ, we have relinquished our tightly held rights, whether we like it or not. We have no right to self-determination or direction. In Galatians 2:20, Paul proclaims the following:

> I have been crucified with Christ; it is no longer I who live, but Christ lives in me; and the *life* which I now live in the flesh I live by faith in the Son of God, who loved me and gave Himself for me. (NKJV)

We have died to ourselves. We have given up all of our rights. We are now under the direct, express authority of Jesus Christ. In this situation, I don't have a right to complain about someone being treated better than I am. I don't have the right to withhold giving to the poor because I want to maintain some level of comfort for myself; I don't have a right to comfort. The reflexive response we have when we consider the concept that we have no rights is to argue along the lines of, "If we don't defend our rights, they will be taken away from us!" That may well be true, at least for those who have rights. But if Christ is my Lord, I have no rights and this sort of argument is moot.

Why then do we insist on fighting for our rights? Why do we get inflamed over the politics and actions of nonbelievers? Why are we threatened by losing our rights or being discriminated against? Perhaps we feel threatened to defend our rights because having no rights means we have to deny ourselves as important, as worthy, as special, or as somehow deserving of God's favor. Maybe it's a fear that someone else is going to get ahead of us or get something we will not. We want everything the world has to offer, don't we? To maintain our rights, privileges, comfort, position, and power, we deny the very nature of our relationship with Jesus and seek to please the world in the hope we will get all of those things. What is the driving force behind it? James gave a stern warning in James 4:1–4 that gives us insight to the question.

> Where do wars and fights *come* from among you? Do *they* not *come* from your *desires for* pleasure that war in your members? You lust and do not have. You murder and covet and cannot obtain. You fight and war. Yet you do not have because you do not ask. You ask and do not receive, because you ask amiss, that you may spend *it* on your pleasures. Adulterers and adulteresses! Do you not know that friendship with the world is enmity with God? Whoever therefore wants to be a friend of the world makes himself an enemy of God. (NKJV)

The last part of verse 4 is challenging. If we make ourselves friends of the world, we are enemies of God. Why then do we chase after the things of the world? Why do we demand rights we no longer have? In truth, we want to have it both ways, don't we? Aren't we looking to maintain our rights and have a grand old time in the world but still be able to maintain our promise of heaven? In Revelation 2:4, Christ said to the church at Ephesus, "You have lost your first love." When there is anything more important than our love and obedience to the Lord, we have lost our first love.

In 1 John 2:15 we are told, "Do not love the world or the things in the world. If anyone loves the world, the love of the Father is not in him" (NKJV). If we consider that verse from 1 John and couple it with John 13:35 where Jesus told the disciples, "By this all will know that you are My disciples, if you have love for one another" (NKJV), then we see the interplay of love for others and our witness to the world. If we do not love the world, we have the love of the Father in us, and having His love allows us to love others, which then leads to the world knowing we are disciples of Jesus Christ. But if we love the world, we don't have the love of the Father and the world will not know we are Jesus' disciples. Does my need to maintain my rights and desires supersede my love? If so, does the world know I am a disciple of Jesus Christ? It is not likely.

Slaves to Unrighteousness

In John 8:34, Jesus said, "Whoever commits sin is a slave of sin" (NKJV). This was echoed by the apostle Paul in Romans 6:20 when he spoke of believers having been "slaves to sin" before they came to faith in Christ. Stop to think about that. People who do not have a saving faith in Jesus Christ are slaves to sin. They have no option but to sin. Even if they know what righteousness is, they are slaves to sin. They are in bondage to unrighteousness. Yet, filled with righteous indignation, how often do we condemn and rail against them to prove our own righteousness? We expect them to understand righteousness and to follow along with what the Holy Spirit has revealed to us, even if we carry out that expectation without love.

Frankly, for us as believers to expect nonbelievers to act in a righteous manner is ludicrous. How can we expect slaves to unrighteousness to understand righteousness or be accepting of it? That's absolute lunacy because they have no choice when we consider their spiritual situation. We would benefit and our mission to spread the gospel of Jesus Christ would benefit if we would stop to realize but for the grace of God and the Holy Spirit's working in our hearts, we would be in the same shape. This should lead us to a spirit of thankfulness that God's grace has been poured out on us, and it should also move us to have pity on their spiritual condition.

We want to fight about our rights with people who are slaves to sin. It's much easier to war against someone who isn't like us. It's easier to condemn someone in whom we do not see ourselves. When we see it's only by God's grace we aren't still slaves to sin, our enemy becomes someone we can actually love. Once we love them, the Holy Spirit can use us in a meaningful way to impact their lives for Christ. When that happens, we won't have to worry about fighting for the rights we have given up under the lordship of Jesus Christ.

Denying Ourselves and Our Rights

In Luke 9:23–25, Jesus was very direct in addressing the subject of our rights. There He gave us perhaps the greatest instruction on how to follow Him. In verse 23 the Lord addressed the group and said, "If anyone desires to come after Me, let him deny himself, and take up his cross daily, and follow Me" (NKJV). This is one of the most instructive verses in Scripture as it pertains to following the Lord.

When Christ said "deny," the word used in the Greek text is *aparneomai*, which means *to affirm that there is no acquaintance with someone*,[13] or to forget one's self-interest. Jesus was saying that, in a real sense, we are to forget we even exist. To do so is to crucify ourselves; all things directed at ourselves are to be disregarded. This doesn't mean we are to deny the talents or personality God has given us. Instead, it is the denial of those things directed toward our own autonomy, our own glory, and ourselves. It is the relinquishing of our rights. Perhaps it would be better if I said I am to crucify my own rights and desires every day. If I am living this out, every day I am to forget that I as an independent person even exist. My entire identity is to be found in Jesus Christ. As such, whatever He wants for me and my life is what I am to want, without question or exception. What I think may be my mission in life may not be His mission for me. Those things I think I was made to do may not really be what He made me to do. I have no right to impose my will on my life, for it belongs to Christ.

Matthew also recorded Jesus' instruction found in Luke 9. However, in Matthew's version, the one difference is the lack of the word *daily*, which we find in Luke's recording. I have always been fonder of Luke's version because I think the word *daily* here is instructive and important. The Lord knew we wrestle with pride and self-interest. He knew this is an ongoing battle for us, a daily battle. It is something we all deal with; if we don't think we deal with it, then our problem is much greater than most. Jesus knew we do and admonished the disciples, and us, to undertake the act of self-denial in an ongoing, daily fashion. Otherwise, we will never be able to accomplish such a task.

In several of Paul's letters in the New Testament he referred to himself as a servant or slave of Christ. The Greek word used in those instances is *doulos*, which can be translated as either servant or slave but carries the essence of one being devoted to another to the disregard of one's own interests. This is someone who has no rights but is focused solely on his or her master or lord. Paul used this word intentionally for this purpose. He saw himself absolutely as Christ's slave, and he celebrated it.

24

Paul had a pretty rough go of serving the Lord. He recounted in 2 Corinthians 11:24–27 the adversities he had faced up to that point.

> From the Jews five times I received forty *stripes* minus one. Three times I was beaten with rods; once I was stoned; three times I was shipwrecked; a night and a day I have been in the deep; *in* journeys often, *in* perils of waters, *in* perils of robbers, *in* perils of *my own* countrymen, *in* perils of the Gentiles, *in* perils in the city, *in* perils in the wilderness, *in* perils in the sea, *in* perils among false brethren; in weariness and toil, in sleeplessness often, in hunger and thirst, in fastings often, in cold and nakedness. (NKJV)

To say Paul had suffered for the sake of Christ is an understatement. He faced things we cannot really imagine, and yet what was his response? He kept on serving the Lord. How could he do that? That is, where did get his strength to keep serving the Lord through those circumstances? When we think of having the strength to do something difficult, we often are drawn to recall Philippians 4:13: "I can do all things through Christ who strengthens me" (NKJV). This is a great and powerful verse. But in reality, it's not the entire picture. In fact, what is more telling occurs immediately before Philippians 4:13. What Paul had to say in Philippians 4:10–12 is monumental in our lives if we consider it within the context of being a slave to Christ.

> Not that I speak in regard to need, for I have learned in whatever state I am, to be content: I know how to be abased, and I know how to abound. Everywhere and in all things I have learned both to be full and to be hungry, both to abound and to suffer need. (NKJV)

How could Paul be content in any situation? He wrote Philippians somewhere around AD 62, which was after he had written 2 Corinthians. He was speaking of being content in all of those terrible circumstances he had suffered before, in addition to the ones that had occurred since he recounted the events in 2 Corinthians. How could he be content? Paul had relinquished all of his rights—he was a slave to Jesus Christ. In that regard, he did not have to concern himself with mistreatment or not having things go easily for him. He didn't have to concern himself with comfort or privilege.

To Live Is Christ

To Paul, "To live is Christ and to die is gain" (Philippians 1:21 NKJV). Having arrived at such a place spiritually, he could be content because he knew that in all of those situations, he was doing the will of the Lord. It doesn't mean he was overjoyed by the situation but simply that he was content. When we are content, we aren't complaining or seeking to improve the situation. We are satisfied with the situation in which we find ourselves. Can I say that about my day-to-day life? If I were thrust into a prison cell, beaten, shipwrecked, lost at sea, or otherwise in danger for my life, could I say I was content with Jesus Christ alone and really mean it? Could you?

Denying ourselves so we may become satisfied is completely counterintuitive to our natural, or carnal, way of thinking. It's hard to understand how we could give up ourselves, how we could completely forget about our own existence outside of Jesus Christ and somehow be satisfied. Such a proposition makes no sense to us, but it is exactly what Jesus was talking about when He said, "For whoever desires to save his life will lose it, but whoever loses his life for My sake will save it. For what profit is it to a man if he gains the whole world, and is himself destroyed or lost?" (Luke 9:24–25 NKJV). This teaching by Jesus was recorded in three of the four gospels because it is fundamental to following Christ. (In addition to the Luke passage, it is found in Matthew 16:25–26 and Mark 8:35–36.) Without really grasping what He was saying there and making it real in our lives, we are not following Him and He is not living in us.

In John 15 Jesus described Himself as the true vine and told the disciples they were the branches. He told them that God maintains the vine and branches to make sure fruit is being borne out. Then Jesus said, "Abide in Me, and I in you. As the branch cannot bear fruit of itself, unless it abides in the vine, neither can you, unless you abide in Me" (John 15:4 NKJV). We don't often use the word *abide* in our general conversation, but it carries a sense of remaining in or waiting for. Jesus was telling the disciples they must remain in Him and wait on Him if they wanted to produce fruit.

How often do we feel the need to rush into action to prove our fruitfulness? That's the opposite of what Jesus instructs us to do. What happens if we abide in the Lord? Later in the chapter Jesus instructed the disciples to abide in His love and keep His commandments. In verses 12 and 13 He told them, "This is My commandment, that you love one another as I have loved you. Greater love has no one than this, than to lay down one's life for his friends" (John 15:12–13 NKJV). When Jesus talked about the disciples laying down their lives for their friends, He was talking about surrendering their self-interest. He was talking about subjugating themselves for others; that's His example of what real love is. It's the same image He portrayed when He washed the disciples' feet. This is also the image of a slave that Paul used. In fact, immediately after telling the disciples that laying down their lives was a demonstration of the greatest love, Jesus spoke about no longer calling them servants in verse 15. The word translated as servant is *doulos*, the same word we discussed earlier that is usually translated as *slave*.

Our pride and self-interest are always there lurking and must be crucified daily or even minute by minute. How often have I been obedient to the Lord's call to deny myself, only to turn around and put myself first five minutes later? Jesus knew this is our nature and addressed it in Matthew 6:3 when He said, "But when you do a charitable deed, do not let your left hand know what your right hand is doing." If we are not careful, it is easy to do something with the greatest of intentions and then seek to get the glory for it. When we do, we are stealing the glory from God. In Matthew 5:16, Jesus said, "Let your light so shine before men, that they may see your good works and glorify your Father in heaven" (NKJV). There was no mention of the disciples receiving glory for their good works. The glory was to go to God. This is the essence of denying ourselves. It is the process of making everything we do ultimately about God's glory. When we are focused or centered on God, we forget about ourselves, even that we exist. We become contented in Jesus Christ alone. This is the spirit of the denial Jesus was talking about.

CHAPTER 4
IT'S NOT ABOUT WORSHIPPING YOUR WAY

*DO NOT WORSHIP ANY OTHER GOD, FOR THE **LORD**, WHOSE NAME IS JEALOUS, IS A JEALOUS **GOD**. (EXODUS 34:14 NIV)*

The Ten Commandments were God's first articulated laws. According to Romans, God gave us the law so we might recognize sin. In a real sense, the law does not protect us from sin but rather exposes us to what it really is. To this point, Paul wrote, "Therefore no one will be declared righteous in God's sight by the works of the law; rather, through the law we become conscious of our sin" (Romans 3:20 NIV). In fact, he said the law not only showed us what sin is, but the law also magnified sin: "The law was brought in so that the trespass might increase" (Romans 5:20a NIV).

Knowing our nature, that we seek to put idols before God, it should come as no surprise that the first commandment God wrote on the stone tablets in Exodus 20:2–3 was, "I am the Lord your God, who brought you out of Egypt, out of the land of slavery. You shall have no other gods before Me" (NIV). Later, in Exodus 34:14, God specifically addressed worship when He said, "Do not worship any other god" (NIV). God rightly established Himself as the only one to be worshipped. Later, in Deuteronomy 6:5, God gave Israel the commandment, "Love the Lord your God with all your heart and with all your soul and with all your strength" (NIV). It was this commandment Jesus referred to as the "first and greatest commandment" (Luke 10:27).

God knows the hearts of mankind and knows we were created to worship. In Isaiah 43:21 the Lord referred to Israel as, "The people I formed for Myself that they may proclaim My praise" (NIV). God knew that it was imperative for Israel to realize He was the one true God, and He was the only one to be worshipped. Since God created us for worship, it follows that it is inherent in the nature of man to worship. We were created for God's glory according to Isaiah 43:7. However, in our sin nature, we are prone to misdirect our worship. This is why the first commandment given dealt with God's sole position as the one to be worshipped. He knew it was a problem.

It is no coincidence that the first and second commandments dealt with having no other gods and the making of idols. Moses hadn't even gotten the tablets delivered by the time the children of Israel had violated the first two commandments. Think about what was going on when the Ten Commandments were actually being written out on those stone tablets. The people of Israel were at the bottom of Mt. Sinai waiting on Moses. Previously, in Exodus 20:19, they were so awestricken by the thunderings of God around Mt. Sinai that they said to Moses, "Speak to us yourself and we will listen. But do not have God speak to us or we will die" (NIV). They knew who God was. They knew His awesomeness and revered Him to the point of being afraid for Him to speak to them. Yet when Moses went up to Mt. Sinai while God was giving him the Ten Commandments, the children of Israel became impatient. So they approached Aaron and said, "Come, make us gods who will go before us. As for this fellow Moses who brought us up out of Egypt, we don't know what has happened to him" (Exodus 32:1 NIV). How quickly they forgot! God knew they would do so *before* He wrote the Ten Commandments. He knows how quickly our hearts turn away from Him. The children of Israel had proven how quickly we turn away from the Lord even while the Ten Commandments were being written. Our devotion is but fleeting.

Why is our commitment and worship of God fleeting? Is it not our own flesh, our pride, that rises up within us to seek our own way? In reality, we want a god we can control. We want a god we can see and touch, something tangible—something that bends to our desires. God—YHWH—is a loose cannon. He is certain to require more of us than we are willing to give. He is certain to impose upon us His desires instead of what we think is best. Even though the children of Israel had seen the miraculous things God had done to bring them out of Egypt, and even though they saw and heard His presence on Mt. Sinai, they wanted something they could look upon and reach out and touch. We are no different today. We may have a difficult time admitting it, but we are the same. We fancy ourselves as being so much more devout and having come so far spiritually over those people back there in the desert thousands of years ago. We've just become more discreet in the idols we worship. Idols take every possible form, and we have mastered disguising them as noble, worthwhile, and even God-honoring things.

Destroying God's Church in the Name of Worship

There has been a debate raging in evangelical churches for several decades regarding the format the worship service should take. The church my wife and I were in after we married had just celebrated their hundredth anniversary of existing as a body of believers. It was a well-established church. The membership could be referred to as mature. As we looked at the church, the average age of members must've been about seventy years, and that's not really an exaggeration. My wife and I saw it as an opportunity for gathering great wisdom from those who had a wealth of experience living with God. However, the worship service was very much in keeping with a traditional service. A typical service would include about four grand old hymns that were set to piano and pipe organ accompaniment. The pipe organ often seemed to be played in a minor key, giving it all a sense of Puritanical foreboding. Music that surely at some point in history was uplifting was to us rather depressing and did not move us to pouring out our hearts in worship. It was music from the eighteenth and nineteenth century, and though the message in the poetry of the hymns was outstanding, the music was a distraction to us and to almost everyone in our age group—the age group the church needed most if it was to survive.

As background on my inclination toward worship music, I was raised in a very small church in a little town. The biggest our church ever got while I was growing up was probably 110 people, but we hovered around 70 active attenders my whole life. The worship service was certainly traditional. We sang hymns from the Baptist hymnal, and mostly we stuck to a certain subset of hymns. We had a piano and an electronic organ. At Christmas the choir would perform a cantata that included what could be called near-contemporary music, which was already probably about ten to fifteen years past its date of publication.

When I was around twelve-years-old, we started to have a youth choir, and we would sing more contemporary praise choruses. Until that point, I really didn't know anything other than the hymns in the Baptist hymnal existed. When I first sang "Lord I Lift Your Name on High," I was shocked to think there was church music that was more upbeat and didn't have the distant reminiscence of a saloon piano piece. It wasn't until I was in my late teens that I heard a Michael W. Smith song on a radio station. Where I lived, there was just no exposure to contemporary Christian music. Once I got to college, I began to experience contemporary worship through campus Christian organizations. In those intimate settings, we all sang out in worship. We joined our voices and praised the Lord in those moments. We didn't meditate on the words of the songs so much as we lifted up the name of God and praised Him. To us, doing so was worship. Our services were full of college students praising God and developing deep and meaningful relationships with each other, and it seemed like a model that was translatable to other settings.

A couple of years after my wife and I were married, our pastor asked the church to submit to him what we thought was God's vision for the church—the one with an average age of over seventy years. I had been considering the progressive decline of the church and how the worship service, among other things, could be retooled in an effort to try to reach more young adults, the ones the church desperately needed, at least from a strategic standpoint. As is my tendency, when I have something to say, I write it, and I did the same with my thoughts on God's vision for our church. I outlined all of the reasons it was important to consider changing the worship format to a more contemporary style. I put a lot of thought and prayer into the writing of that letter. In it I noted that nowhere in Scripture is there a place wherein God gave people the vision to keep doing things the way they were doing them and felt compelled to point out that the grand old hymns had at some point been new or what might be called contemporary. Unfortunately, the pastor received it poorly and blew it off because "contemporary services are watered down and short on doctrine." That pastor eventually left the church, and a new pastor, who insisted on changing a host of things, came. The new pastor discounted the value of the older members' thoughts and experiences, and it led to a great schism in the church, one many churches have experienced during the decades while this debate has been ongoing. It was heart-wrenching to see and be a part of.

There was an event that happened one particular Sunday I might never forget. It was at once funny but also horrifically sad and telling. One of the older men in the church was staunchly opposed to anything that wasn't an old hymn or a responsive reading. He had been quite vocal about his disdain for the attempts at bringing the worship service into the twentieth century, never mind that this set of circumstances actually occurred in the early 2000s. So, one morning he showed up to the service with a large set of blaze orange earmuffs, the kind used at firing ranges to protect your hearing. He sat in his usual seat in the sanctuary with his arms crossed and a grimace on his face as choruses of "Shout to the Lord" rang out in the sanctuary. What would lead a man, presumably a godly man, to behave in such a manner?

The debate, or what in some churches has sadly become a war, over the style of the worship service has been raging in churches across the country, and it has left deep wounds in a lot of people. Why is that the case? Why do people feel so strongly about the style of worship? After all, aren't we called to present "[our] bodies as a living sacrifice, holy and pleasing to God—this is [our] true and proper worship?" (Romans 12:1 NIV). Paul here in Romans said worship is something we should be doing with our lives. Our whole lives should be directed at the purpose of worshipping God and Him alone. It's not about four songs on a Sunday morning. It's about living a life that reflects glory to God. In Colossians 3:23, we read that in "Whatever you do, work at it with all your heart, as working for the Lord, not for human masters" (NIV).

If we look at the sides of the debate on traditional versus contemporary worship styles, there are strong, often emotional points on either side, and mostly they are smokescreens to the real issue. The traditionalists have time on their side—they can point to the centuries the hymns have been tested and tried, time they have been shown to be beneficial. The traditionalists argue that the hymns are more reverent and meaningful. The theology in those hymns is great, and those of us who have experienced them as an integral part of our Christian experience can point to important spiritual truths we understand as a result of them. These hymns are accompanied by the piano and organ and oftentimes more sophisticated accompaniment, such as orchestral instruments. It is not uncommon for hymns to be lifted up as somehow sacred—they are often spoken of in reverent tones as holding some mystical, Scripture-like power. Those who hold tightly to the hymns see them as unassailable, as if they were written by the hand of God and brought down from on high. In the mind of the traditionalists, it seems, the grand old hymns are what are sung by the seraphim that fly around the thrown of God. In fact, Isaiah 6 clearly says the seraphim cry out, "Holy, holy, holy *is* the LORD of hosts; the whole earth *is* full of His glory!" Some might even say Isaiah 6 is a clear nod to the Baptist hymnal, which for years had "Holy, Holy, Holy," as the first song, at least until 2008.[14]

Traditionalists also posit that contemporary services are less intellectually rigorous than more traditional services. It is assumed because hymns written in Elizabethan English are used in traditional services, the service must therefore be godlier. This is an argument not far removed from bygone debates over Bible translations. It is uncertain why a given pastor, were he to be removed from a worship service utilizing traditional hymns and placed into one with a modern music style, would suddenly lose any ability to preach or teach in an intellectually and spiritually rigorous manner; however, this argument has definitely been made.

On the contemporary side of the debate, proponents want to bring in a more up-to-date worship style, often with drums, electric guitars, and other instrumentation that lead to a rock feel, the likes of which might be heard on any number of radio stations. This music style is claimed to possess more relevance to unchurched people—it has more approachability and authenticity. Contemporaries want to come to worship and be moved by the music, to dance or sing or shout. There is often an element of the charismatic in contemporary services, an element the traditionalists find frankly ungodly. The songs sung in contemporary services are often drawn from the Bible just like hymns, usually representing direct quotes or paraphrasing of various verses from Psalms. The rock concert feel that is often a part of contemporary worship services can be distracting. It's unclear how an electronic light show puts the focus of our worship on God. I am not certain why we need to pump a layer of smoke onto a stage to help us worship God. If God wants smoke in the service, He will produce it just like He did in 2 Chronicles 5:13.

With regard to intellectual and spiritual rigor, the contemporaries find no value in the argument that meaningful teaching is lacking because they recall that Christ said the Holy Spirit would "teach you all things and will remind you of everything I have said to you"(John 14:26 NIV). In either situation, the contemporaries would suggest, it is the Holy Spirit who teaches, and the words of man, no matter how eloquent, fall short of what God seeks to work in our hearts. Contemporary services are geared toward being seeker friendly, so if unchurched people attend, they do not feel completely lost in the subject matter; they can understand what is going on. Interestingly, this is where someone could use the verse from John 14:26 to levy a counterargument to say it is the Holy Spirit who will take care of that task. Those with traditional views also suggest that contemporary worship services are geared toward making the unchurched people who might attend the focus, as opposed to God, who is the one we are there to worship in the first place.

If we take a moment to stop and consider the circumstances surrounding the debate over worship style, we should recognize how disappointing the whole thing is to God. In this circumstance, we have people who are reportedly seeking what God wants for their churches. They are on a mission to make sure God is worshipped as they see fit. So, here we have two groups of people from the same body of believers who are now divided over a few songs to be sung during a fifteen- to twenty-minute period on Sunday mornings. People are belittling each other, and deep divides are being cut into the church and the people, and somehow we think the whole scene honors God. Somehow we have convinced ourselves God wants us to tear apart His church over the musical format. At some point we have been convinced of one of the grandest of lies—this is for the sake of true worship. God demands we live out our lives as our worship. How oxymoronic is it to wage a war with each other in our churches and claim it is for the sake of worshipping God?

In Spirit and Truth

Does God prescribe the style of worship He requires? Yes and no. In the Old Testament, worship was fastidiously prescribed. If specific rituals were not strictly adhered to, God's wrath would be poured out on the children of Israel. However, in the New Testament, Jesus changed those requirements, or at least our understanding of them. When He was speaking to the Samaritan woman at the well, the woman asked Jesus about the appropriate place to worship, whether on a hill in Samaria called Mount Gerizim or in Jerusalem. This was an important question in the Jewish and Samarian cultures because of the specific requirements of how and where God was to be worshipped in the Old Testament. Jesus responded by telling the woman the following:

> A time is coming when you will worship the Father neither on this mountain nor in Jerusalem. You Samaritans worship what you do not know; we worship what we do know, for salvation is from the Jews. Yet a time is coming and has now come when the true worshipers will worship the Father in the Spirit and in truth, for they are the kind of worshipers the Father seeks. God is spirit, and His worshipers must worship in the Spirit and in truth. (John 4:21–24 (NIV)

Here Jesus removed the idea that God was only to be worshipped in a certain setting under certain conditions. However, He was introducing a new concept—God must be worshipped in spirit and truth. This then is the new prescriptive component of worshipping God in the New Testament. What's more, worship isn't something isolated to the setting of a temple or church building. It's something we are to do with our entire lives (Romans 12:1).

What does it mean to worship God in spirit and in truth? The word used there for spirit is *pneuma*, which carries multiple definitions, but means the soul and emotions. It's the part of mankind that makes us more than a bunch of cells running around. To worship in spirit means we are worshipping in the very core of our being. There is no pretense or hidden part of us not fully engaged in the worship of God. A vital part of worshipping in spirit is to be free from any conflict with others. In Matthew 5:23–24, Jesus said, "Therefore, if you are offering your gift at the altar and there remember that your brother or sister has something against you, leave your gift there in front of the altar. First go and be reconciled to them; then come and offer your gift" (NIV). How hard is that? Jesus' command means we can't hold grudges or be upset or offended by someone else. In fact, Jesus takes the command a step further. He says it is a problem if someone has something against us. Our lives are to be above reproach to the point others do not have any issue with us. If we have some form of conflict with our brother, or he with us, then it bars us from worshipping God. Our spirit is distracted from the purpose of our worship, which is God, and if our whole spirit isn't in it, it's not worship, at least not according to Christ.

Worshipping in spirit also means to worship via the Holy Spirit. It is the Holy Spirit who brings our hearts into a right position to truly worship God. Without the Holy Spirit, we cannot worship God in any meaningful way. In his book *The Purpose of Man*, A. W. Tozer wrote the following:

> It is impossible to worship God acceptably apart from the Holy Spirit. The operation of the Spirit of God within us enables us to worship God acceptably through that person we call Jesus Christ, who is Himself God. Therefore, worship originates with God, comes back to us and is reflected from us. That is the worship that God accepts, and He accepts no other kind.[15]

Notice our worship is the same as our faith—it comes from God. We can't claim credit for it at all.

Worshipping God in truth requires us to know what the truth is. The word used for truth here is *alētheia*. It includes objective components such as would be seen in something that is true in any setting. It also carries subjective components, such as being without pretense, falsehood, or deceit. To worship God in truth then carries with it both components. To start with, it is knowing God is the one true God—that is true. Worshipping in truth must be informed by the truth of the Bible. We are to know the Word of God, meditate on it, and be open to being changed by and through it. We also must be free from any untruth in our being. This brings in part of the discussion on worshipping in spirit. If there is deceit or conflict in our hearts, we cannot worship in truth. If we are harboring unconfessed sin in our lives, we cannot worship in truth. Therefore, we cannot worship at all. If we are focused on getting out of the worship service in time to have lunch, go to the lake, or watch a football game, we are not worshipping in truth, at all. For that reason, we aren't worshipping at all. Instead, we are simply wasting time, both God's and our own.

Our Comfort with Worship

If we think about the contemporary and traditional worship service styles, one style seems to be more focused on worshipping in spirit, while the other seems to be more focused on worshipping in truth. Is there some of both in each style? Absolutely. But to really worship, it must be equal parts spirit and truth. As it turns out, worship must by necessity be 100 percent spirit and 100 percent truth. The nature of worshipping in spirit is worshipping without reservation, without holding anything back—100 percent of our hearts and souls worshipping. If it isn't 100 percent, it isn't worshipping in spirit. The nature of worshipping in truth is that if we hold anything back, it is a form of deceit and dishonesty, and therefore it isn't truth. So again, to worship in truth requires 100 percent truth. Whatever the worship style, it must be in spirit and in truth, or it is unacceptable to God.

While the debate continues to go around and around, as it has for decades, in the end, both sides seem to have merits and weaknesses. Ultimately though, they are both smokescreens for the real heart of the issue. The more you press people on the point, the more something else begins to come to the front. The discussion begins to move to one of what makes the participants comfortable, what they are used to, or what helps them feel like they can hear the Lord. It's about meeting our needs, not about God or the unchurched or the person across the aisle from them with blaze orange earmuffs.

We talk about certain types of music hindering us from worshipping God. We are uncomfortable with a worship service when it takes a different form than what we think it should, be it traditional or contemporary. To certain groups of people, God only receives praise in Elizabethan English, and all of the other people in the world, the ones who praise God with drums or shouts of praise in Swahili or some other tongue, must obviously be damned. To other groups, God can only be praised if we come to the service wearing sandals, torn blue jeans, and our meticulously mussed hairdo while raising one hand in praise and using the other hand to hold our mochaccino—and those who don't must not care about the poor, downtrodden, and unchurched and must obviously want to condemn them to eternal damnation. Truthfully, in the end, isn't it really about what makes us comfortable in worship?

If you put the gloves down and stop defending why you are right over it, isn't it really about what you want to get out of the worship service? It's not really about worshipping God then, is it?

In 1 Corinthians 9:19–23, Paul described the changes he made to win people to the Lord. He summed it up in 9:22 when he said, "To the weak I became weak, to win the weak; *I have become all things to all people so that by all possible means I might save some*" (NIV, emphasis added). Paul echoed the same sentiment in 1 Corinthians 10:33 when he said, "Even as I try to please everyone in every way. For I am not seeking my own good but the good of many, so that they may be saved" (NIV). To Paul, his life, his living worship, was the subjugating of his own desires, will, and comfort so souls would be saved. In our struggles to advocate for a given type of worship style—our type of worship—through which we have alienated entire generations of people, *have we become anything other than comfortable?*

Have you ever been offensive to God because you didn't worship Him in the way He wanted, in spirit and in truth? I have. I have been in a worship service and felt the need to stand up but didn't because everyone else was seated. I have looked around at everyone else standing, clapping, and shouting and felt in that moment the need to sit quietly. At times I have succumb to the scrutiny of everyone's opinion and ignored what I knew to be the way I should have been worshipping. Have you had that experience? Have you ever imposed your designs of worship on others, expecting them to follow along with what makes you comfortable, perhaps so you would feel justified in what you were doing? When we worship our idols, there is no feedback on how we should worship. When we worship God, things change. We are changed as we have a real encounter with the living God.

I remember a scene from my youth I think I will never forget. One Sunday a lady came to visit our church. She appeared to be of limited financial means, as her clothing was not particularly new and she was slightly unkempt. As we sang a hymn, the lady stood up—everyone else was sitting comfortably in our pews maintaining proper decorum—and began waving her arms in the air while she sang. Suddenly, an older lady seated a couple of rows behind her sprang into action to return things to the acceptable state. She reached forward over the intervening row to grab the back of the visiting lady's dress so she could pull her back down into her seat. The lady who was standing would not give way and continued praising God as the would-be sergeant at arms looked on in horror. Watching that scenario play out was a clear demonstration to me of what it means for someone to worship in spirit and truth and what it means for someone to do otherwise.

Our worship is important to God, not because it does anything for Him but rather because it puts us in a right position relative to Him. God knows He is the greatest entity there is, not out of conceit but as a matter of fact. He realizes when we worship Him in spirit and in truth, it brings our hearts into a position to hear from Him and know Him more. It is through hearing from the Holy Spirit and knowing Christ more that we grow to be more like Christ, which is the greatest possible outcome for us. It is the outcome the Holy Spirit is working to manifest in us, the thing God wants for us. So God has a keen interest in our worshipping Him for this reason.

In Philippians 2 Paul addressed becoming more like Christ, and apropos the topic of worship style, his words are striking.

> Therefore if you have any encouragement from being united with Christ, if any comfort from his love, if any common sharing in the Spirit, if any tenderness and compassion, then make my joy complete by being like-minded, having the same love, being one in spirit and of one mind. Do nothing out of selfish ambition or vain conceit. Rather, in humility value others above yourselves, not looking to your own interests but each of you to the interests of the others. In your relationships with one another, have the same mindset as Christ Jesus: Who, being in very nature God, did not consider equality with God something to be used to his own advantage; rather, he made himself nothing by taking the very nature of a servant, being made in human likeness. And being found in appearance as a man, he humbled himself by becoming obedient to death—even death on a cross! (Philippians 2:1–8 NIV)

In the end, the goal is for us to be more Christlike, which means we have to be less like ourselves. Presenting our lives in living worship to God will open us up to being molded by the Holy Spirit to this end. Anything standing in the way of us truly worshipping God is an idol, no matter how seemingly holy, right, or noble. Ultimately, it's evil in our hearts that creates the conflicts. We disguise our own self-centeredness in a debate about worship styles when it's really about what we want, what makes us comfortable. In that very moment, we would just as soon see someone condemned to eternal separation from God than to bend on a genre of music used during a twenty-minute span of a service one day a week.

It is in our nature to worship. We become distracted easily and focus our worship on things other than God. We may be well meaning and the things we are focused on may be, in some regard, God-honoring. To what extent have we made the focus of worship ourselves rather than God?

CHAPTER 5
IT'S NOT ABOUT SERVING WHEN IT SUITS YOU

JESUS, KNOWING THAT THE FATHER HAD GIVEN ALL THINGS INTO
HIS HANDS, AND THAT HE HAD COME FROM GOD AND WAS GOING
BACK TO GOD, ROSE FROM SUPPER. HE LAID ASIDE HIS OUTER
GARMENTS, AND TAKING A TOWEL, TIED IT AROUND HIS WAIST.
THEN HE POURED WATER INTO A BASIN AND BEGAN TO WASH THE
DISCIPLES' FEET AND TO WIPE THEM WITH THE TOWEL THAT WAS
WRAPPED AROUND HIM. (JOHN 13:3–5 ESV)

Washing feet was a dirty job. It was the lowliest job for the lowliest servants. People like to recount how dusty the roads were in the time of Christ. They always remember how much dirt was on the feet of the disciples when Jesus washed their feet in John 13. However, there was more to it than a layer of dust.

In the world at the time of Christ, animals were led through the streets of cities. They pulled carts with goods, or they were being led to market, or they were transportation for the people. With animals come their waste products, usually in large quantities. So the streets were certain to have had significant amounts of urine and feces in them. There were no sanitation departments. There were no well-organized animal excrement clean-up crews. The stuff was just out there, in the streets. The disciples weren't wearing waterproof galoshes; their shoes were sandals that were essentially soles, usually of leather, attached to their feet with lashings. Anything on the ground was on their feet, not just the sandals. As they walked along, they were certain to walk through whatever coursed along the ground in the streets. Thus, when the Lord washed the disciples' feet, He wasn't just washing off some dust. He was washing off the foulest material you can think of—and He chose to do it!

In the church we often talk about the body of Christ. When writing to the church at Corinth regarding spiritual gifts, Paul described us as "the body of Christ and individually members of it" (1 Corinthians 12:27 ESV). As members of the body of Christ, we all serve different purposes. In the analogy of the body, the body of Christ is like any normal body with a certain number of given parts. A body doesn't need six legs or five eyes. We as humans were designed with two ears, so having only one wouldn't be good. This is to say, as Paul did, each member has a given role to play in the body of Christ, and not everyone is given to the same task, by necessity. Each believer's role is important to the body of Christ and has been determined by God through the Holy Spirit.

> To each is given the manifestation of the Spirit for the common good. For to one is given through the Spirit the utterance of wisdom, and to another the utterance of knowledge according to the same Spirit, to another faith by the same Spirit, to another gifts of healing by the one Spirit, to another the working of miracles, to another prophecy, to another the ability to distinguish between spirits, to another various kinds of tongues, to another the interpretation of tongues. All these are empowered by one and the same Spirit, who apportions to each one individually as he wills. (1 Corinthians 12:7–11 ESV)

But there is something about being assigned a role that bristles against our American sensibilities. As a nation, we have historically been one of believing it is our right to determine our own destiny—something we discussed in chapter 3. We like to think of those who have pulled themselves up by their bootstraps to become something greater than they were. We believe it is our individual right to determine what we want to do. But out of what sort of heart does that line of thinking come? Is it not our pride that says to us, "You have the right to be whatever you so desire"? We have convinced ourselves if there is something in the world we desire, we should be able to have it. If there is something we want to be or do, then that is within our rights. However, Paul cautions against those who seek to be something other than what God has created them to be.

> If the foot should say, "Because I am not a hand, I do not belong to the body," that would not make it any less a part of the body. And if the ear should say, "Because I am not an eye, I do not belong to the body," that would not make it any less a part of the body. If the whole body were an eye, where would be the sense of hearing? If the whole body were an ear, where would be the sense of smell? But as it is, God arranged the members in the body, each one of them, as he chose. If all were a single member, where would the body be? As it is, there are many parts, yet one body. The eye

cannot say to the hand, "I have no need of you," nor again the head to the feet, "I have no need of you." On the contrary, the parts of the body that seem to be weaker are indispensable, and on those parts of the body that we think less honorable we bestow the greater honor, and our unpresentable parts are treated with greater modesty, which our more presentable parts do not require. But God has so composed the body, giving greater honor to the part that lacked it, that there may be no division in the body, but that the members may have the same care for one another. (1 Corinthians 12:15–25 ESV)

Paul, knowing our hearts, wrote that we are not to seek the positions in the body considered to be of great honor, but rather we are to accept the position the Lord has chosen for us and to which we have been appointed. It is our corrupt hearts and pride that lead us to seek to be something other than what the Lord has directed, and in so doing, we make the body of Christ weaker.

Dirty Jobs, Important Service

The truth is, almost all of us want to be something glamorous. We want to feel like we are important to the body, but only in so far as it brings us attention. If there were a form to be completed giving us the option of being an eye, the tongue, an ear, the spleen, or the anus, no one would check the box that says, "I want to be the anus in the body of Christ." The majority of people would probably choose an eye or the tongue because those seem important.

Many people in the church have already decided they must have been chosen to be the tongue because a lot of people speak out about the wrong others do. They believe it is their responsibility to point out the sins of others. But it seems like there are more tongues in the body of Christ than there are hands or feet, for instance. Why? Because being the one who gets to speak on behalf of God is glamorous. It gives us honor to hold such a high position. It means we are right up there alongside God, and He's giving us direct feed as to what He is thinking. But the math does not add up. For a given body, you don't need two or three or twelve tongues. You need one. The church has way too many people doing the talking.

What about the other end of the list of possible assignments? What about the idea of being the anus? The thought that there could be an anus in the body of Christ is probably shocking, and even offensive, to some people. If that's the case, keep reading and it will make sense why there not only is but in fact *must be* an anus in the body of Christ.

The human body is an amazing creation. The complexity of the interworking of multiple biochemical systems to produce and maintain a healthy human body is tremendous. The more we learn about the complexity of these systems, the more incredible it becomes. A significant part of the amazing nature of the human body comes from the instructions contained in our DNA. Those instructions act like the blueprints for each person, and there are thousands of instructions. Before our mothers knew we were in there growing in their wombs, our blueprints had been written out, and as a result specific chemical signals were occurring to tell different cells to migrate here or there to become a toe or an artery or a muscle to help us smile. Those signals are of the utmost importance in determining how we formed during our fetal life. When those signals go awry, even just one of them, birth defects can occur.

As you can imagine, with thousands of signals being sent out directing the building of a little human, there are all sorts of possibilities for error in the communication. Sometimes the signals are not as important, and a child might end up with a patch of white hair in the middle of the rest of his brown hair. At other times, the signals are much more important and can result in things like severe malformations of the heart, or other things—things that are of such importance as to be life-threatening.

Children can be born blind and still have very productive lives. They can be born deaf and still lead essentially normal lives. Some can be mute, and they can still accomplish many things. A person can even be blind, deaf and mute, as in the case of Helen Keller,* and can accomplish things almost beyond human comprehension. However, if a child is born without an anus, unless immediate surgery is performed, the child will die. The condition is called anal atresia, and it is a dire circumstance unless a surgical anus is created. So in a biological sense, all of the things we think of as being glamorous in the body of Christ may not be nearly as important as we think, and those things we think of as less honorable may in fact be lifesaving.

I have a friend whom I have come to think of as the anus in the body of Christ. The first time I told him, "Paul, I think of you as the anus in the body of Christ," he was shocked to hear it. Thankfully, he let me explain myself instead of punching me in the nose. But to me, Paul is an indispensable part of the body. He does the jobs no one else ever wants to do. If there is a really crummy or disgusting job, if there is something completely inconvenient or a time sink, if there is a task that will by no means be glamorous, Paul is the one who volunteers to do the job. He does those jobs because he wants to serve the Lord, and he knows those jobs are of the utmost importance in the bigger picture of the gospel. Theologians can sit in their ivory towers and contemplate dispensationalism or the exegesis of Revelation, and we think they must be so close to God because God has given them a high degree of knowledge and they are the ones who speak to the church. But without those theologians, the gospel still goes out. It was

---

* *Helen Keller was not born deaf and blind but rather suffered an illness in early childhood resulting in her loss of sight and hearing. Nevertheless, she was thereafter blind, deaf, and mute.*

proclaimed through uneducated fishermen, tax collectors, and a tentmaker. But without the Pauls of the church, the ones who are willing to do the thankless and dirty jobs critical for church survival, the gospel falls flat.

Believe it or not, there are those of us who do the dirty jobs of the church who struggle with their service becoming an idol. We as carnal humans have the aptitude of being able to take just about anything God-honoring and turn it into something about us. Piety is no different. This gets back to the previous discussion regarding the right hand not knowing what the left hand is doing. If I am taking the crummy jobs or giving lots of time and money or living in a rundown part of town in an effort to be a living example of Jesus Christ, all of that is rubbish if I am glorified in it. If I do all of those things but then complain about it or go on and on about what a great sacrifice I have made, I am taking the glory that should be going to God and am pointing it toward myself. In my sacrifice, I am trying to increase myself in someone else's eyes. In the end, if I am not highly vigilant, I can make it about improving my position instead of improving the kingdom of God.

Helping Ourselves or Others

Barnes & Noble is the largest retail bookstore chain in the United States. They have stores across the country, and the average store carries around one hundred thousand titles. So Barnes & Noble carries a lot of books. In an effort to help customers find the genre of book they are looking for, bookstores have organized books into different sections. For instance, if I am looking for a book on cycling, I know to go to the sports section. If I want a biography on President Andrew Jackson, I would look in the biography section. Interestingly, if I am looking for a biography written about a cyclist, I still look in the sports section and not the biography section, which I don't understand. Nevertheless, the bookstore has set up these sections to help us find what we are looking for. Further, if you know the title of the book, Barnes & Noble has kiosks you can use to find the exact location of your desired book in that given store.

These days, the self-help or self-improvement section is a major section of any bookstore. In the latter third of the twentieth century, the publication of self-improvement materials increased markedly. In 2012 more than forty-five thousand self-help titles were in print, and the self-improvement industry's estimated annual US market share was $12 billion.[16, †] Taking the US population of approximately 317 million people, the average annual spending on self-improvement per person (men, women, and children) in the United States about $37.85—for each person! If

---

† *According to the World Health Organization, it would cost $11.4 billion annually to provide the entire world with clean water and sanitation. Clean water would prevent the water-borne illness–related deaths of millions of people every year. I think that there is a book about this topic available in the others-help section in your local bookstore.*

all of this self-improvement is working, why is the industry growing? Why haven't we improved to the point of not needing the self-improvement?

Just like Barnes & Noble, if you walk into a Christian bookstore, you will find a self-help section. Whether it's positive thinking or weight loss or beating depression, there are a host of self-improvement books in Christian bookstores. Does that not strike you as odd? More to the point, why are there no "others-help" sections in our bookstores? Why don't we have row after row of books designed to give us the tools to help others?

Someone might say we have to first help ourselves before we can help others. At best that is ludicrous, and at its heart, it is a vicious lie. It is in the helping of others that we find help, in the loving of others we find love. Unfortunately, we often do not embrace the example of Christ in this regard. He washed the disciples' feet. Think about the context of that situation. The Lord was on the verge of not only being abandoned by his closest friends; of being ridiculed, mocked, and beaten; and of suffering the most cruel form of death the Romans, masters in the art of painful death, could come up with, but He was also on the verge of, for the first time in all of eternity, being separated from God the Father. He knew full well what lay immediately before Him; in a sense He was already experiencing it, which would shortly thereafter lead Him to pray with sweat drops like blood (Luke 22:44). In those moments of being in the midst of the mental torment the near-future held, Jesus served the disciples in the most abased manner of the time—He washed their feet. It was not glamorous. It was lowly and disgusting and thankless, and it was the most important thing in the world to Him at that moment. Self-help was not on His mind when He served them and loved them.

Why then do we focus on self-improvement? As with everything else, it seems to boil down to a matter of pride, of putting ourselves first. We want to be complete. We use verbiage that comes out of the self-improvement movement like "reaching our full potential" and "being who we were meant to be." The difficult thing about self-improvement strategies is they hold truth. We should all seek to reach our full potential, absolutely. God has given us talents and abilities. In the end, He expects us to use those talents and abilities. According to Christ's parable of the talents in Matthew 25, we will be held accountable for what we do or do not do with what God has given us. So in a real sense, we are obligated to reach our full potential. However, the issue lies in the object of our striving. For what reason do we want to reach our full potential? What is our purpose in it?

Our problem arises when the goal of our self-improvement is purely for the sake of improving ourselves. That may sound ridiculous, but take a moment to consider it. The goal of any endeavor for self-improvement should be to better ourselves for the service of the Lord. If we are striving to improve for any other reason, our endeavors are in vain and could even be argued to be idolatry.

Whatever the reason for improving ourselves, there should be some tangible evidence it will have a positive impact on the kingdom of God. Otherwise we are simply serving ourselves; we are attempting to increase or improve something in ourselves to bring us glory.

CHAPTER 6
IT'S NOT ABOUT YOUR ANXIETY AND FEELINGS

AND DO NOT SEEK WHAT YOU SHOULD EAT OR WHAT YOU SHOULD
DRINK, NOR HAVE AN ANXIOUS MIND. (LUKE 12:29 NKJV)

A ccording to the National Institutes of Health, in any given year, 18.1 percent of adults in the United States are affected by anxiety disorders.[17] That equates to over 40 million people in the United States who are affected by significant anxiety issues every year. Anxiety is a substantial problem in our society. People in the church are no different; anxiety exists there too. In fact, if one out of every six adults has a problem with anxiety every year, then during a four- or five-year period, it is likely half of all adults in the United States will have had an issue with anxiety. Unless we as individuals are completely isolated from other people, then anxiety has an impact on all of lives.

What is anxiety? Anxiety can be defined as *distress or uneasiness of mind caused by fear of danger or misfortune.*[18] So anxiety is the tension in our minds that comes from fear. Anxiety is the mental manifestation of our fear, whether rational or irrational. Anxiety is hard-wired into our physiology; it drives the conscious part of our fight-or-flight response to danger. It is supposed to push us to action. Unfortunately, instead of pushing us to action, it can leave us paralyzed in a state of inaction and fear.

Søren Kierkegaard was a philosopher and Christian author whose contributions to theological thought are regarded highly. He wrote extensively on anxiety out of his own experience, including his books *Fear and Trembling*, and *The Concept of Anxiety*. Many people have turned to the works of Kierkegaard to find encouragement about their own anxieties. Kierkegaard argued that anxiety was not intrinsically sin but rather the internal conflict arising from dealing with the freedom to make a choice in a given circumstance. Ultimately, Kierkegaard's personal experience of wrestling with anxiety in his own life shaped his understanding of anxiety.

Is being anxious inherently sinful? Based on the account of Jesus praying in the garden of Gethsemane, it would seem it is not. Clearly on the eve of His crucifixion and separation from God the Father, Jesus "began to be sorrowful and deeply distressed" (Matthew 26:37 NKJV). In fact, Jesus was in such distress that, "His sweat became like great drops of blood falling down to the ground" (Luke 22:44 NKJV). On three occasions that night Jesus prayed, if it was God's will, the cup, which was His upcoming crucifixion and separation from God, would pass from Him. He was anxious over the thought of what He faced. However, Jesus did not sin. So anxiety is not, in and of itself, sinful, but rather it is what we do with our anxiety. In Jesus' case, it drove Him to pray and to submit Himself to the Father. He trusted God, and His anxiety moved Him to pray. If His anxiety were to manifest as fear, worry, and doubt as a result of a lack of faith, it would've been a different story.

What if we looked at what Jesus said about worry and doubt? How would His teachings inform our understanding of it? In Matthew 6:25–34, Jesus addressed worry. Beginning in verse 25, Jesus said,

> Therefore I say to you, do not worry about your life, what you will eat or what you will drink; nor about your body, what you will put on. Is not life more than food and the body more than clothing? (NKJV)

What all was the Lord saying in this verse? There's a lot there. First, it is notable that this isn't a suggestion Jesus made. He said, "Do not worry ..." That's a command. If we accept that Jesus is God, then if we violate His commands, we sin. Therefore, the case could be easily made that to worry is to sin. But there is a bigger concept Jesus was addressing in this verse, which He raised in the question at the end: "Is not life more than food and the body more than clothing?" In reality Jesus is pointing toward where we put our priorities, what things in life we make the most important. Effectively, Jesus was telling the disciples, and us, the thing or things we value the most are going to be where we concentrate our concerns, and if those things are anything other than God and His kingdom, we are misguided in doing so.

Ultimately Jesus was addressing idolatry in verse 25 and in this passage. Those things we put first in our lives are going to be the things we fear losing. If we are afraid of dying from starvation then we will worry about how we will get food. If our focus is on Jesus Christ, we can say, as Paul did, "For to me, to live *is* Christ, and to die *is* gain" (Philippians 1:21 NKJV). So when we are met with anxiety, fear, and worry, it represents an opportunity for us to admit we have room to grow.

In verse 27 Jesus asked a rhetorical question when He said, "Which of you by worrying can add one cubit to his stature?" (Matthew 6:27 NKJV). Jesus is being pragmatic in telling the disciples that worrying will be of no practical benefit to them.

It's a waste of time and energy. So why do we do it? This is Jesus' next question as He addresses the ultimate reason we should not worry:

> So why do you worry about clothing? Consider the lilies of the field, how they grow: they neither toil nor spin; and yet I say to you that even Solomon in all his glory was not arrayed like one of these. Now if God so clothes the grass of the field, which today is, and tomorrow is thrown into the oven, *will He* not much more *clothe* you, O you of little faith? (Matthew 6:28–30 NKJV)

Jesus told the disciples they had nothing to worry about because God would provide for their needs. Do we believe Him today? Aren't we more sophisticated today? Medical researchers have proven there are chemical imbalances in our brains when we suffer from conditions like anxiety. So we can't really help being anxious; it's a part of our makeup, right? Such a line of reasoning could be entertained as long as we suppose that Jesus Christ, who was God incarnate, was totally unaware of the physical processes in His own creation and how those processes go awry. But what if instead of trying to explain it away, we strip away the justifications, the diagnoses, and the biochemical explanations we have for our fears and doubts? If we do, does it come down to us doubting that God will do what He says He will do? Does it come down to us believing He is not good?

In the fall of 2007, my wife was pregnant with our second child, a little boy. We were eagerly looking forward to his birth at the end of the year. That Halloween we took our daughter trick-or-treating around the neighborhood without incident—for the record, she was Snow White. The following night, my wife had a sudden severe pain, leaving her nearly incapacitated. She mustered enough strength to walk my daughter across the street to one neighbor's house to stay while she went next door to the house of our friends, Paul and Nancy (the same Paul about whom you read in chapter 5) to ask if Nancy could take her to the hospital. They roared away toward the hospital and stopped at our church praise team practice only long enough to tell me what was going on before tearing off to the hospital. In that moment, I don't recall being worried. I was just thinking that our son was about to be born two months ahead of schedule, but otherwise I didn't give it much thought.

By the time I arrived at the hospital, the emergency cesarean section was almost finished. Our son had just been delivered, and he was immediately placed on a ventilator to help his breathing before being whisked away upstairs to the NICU. After some period of time that I don't recall because I was calling everyone to let them know of the early arrival, my wife was taken to a hospital room, and I got to see her. Shortly afterward, I had the opportunity to visit the NICU to see my little boy—by little I mean an ounce under three pounds. The remainder of the night is a vague memory of frequent dressing changes for my wife and the discomfort of the hospital chair-bed for me.

The next morning, because my wife had continued to need dressing changes, and because she had some changes in her vital signs, her doctor rightly decided to take her back to the operating room to see if she had some issue going on in her abdomen. Then my experience began to change. I went from calm, cool, and collected, which tends to be my usual personality, to being afraid—afraid of losing my wife.

At that point in our marriage, my wife and I had been married for six great years. We had started out in a little apartment and then had gotten an even littler house when I started my residency training and she started dental school. We had seen the birth of our daughter and moved across the country for my fellowship—more training for me. She meant the world to me, and suddenly I was faced with the distinct possibility I could lose her. I was an emotional wreck.

In that situation, I was presented with a fear I could not control. I didn't know what or how to pray. I wanted what was best for her, and I knew God would do that—I knew He was somehow actively doing it right then. But I didn't want to pray for what was best for her because I was terrified of what it could possibly mean for me if I lost her. I told God outright that I couldn't do it; I couldn't keep going and take care of the kids and do what I thought I was supposed to be doing without my wife. Ultimately I admitted to God that I couldn't pray in faith and that I had to trust in Him. Even in that situation I was terrified. What was the origin of my gripping fear? I was afraid God would take my wife from me. I was afraid God would do something to devastate me. Here my wife was in an operating room on the brink of death after losing two-thirds of her blood volume due to all of the blood that had leaked into her abdomen overnight, and I was afraid for me. Even though I wanted to trust God, in truth I didn't. I was paralyzed by my own fear and selfishness. It was a manifestation of the fact I didn't believe God was good; I didn't trust Him to do what I thought was right; and I put myself ahead of Him, not to mention my wife.

It is really difficult for us to admit we think God is not good, that He doesn't have the best in mind for us, and that He doesn't care for us. But in reality, isn't that what we are doing when we harbor fear and worry? Instead of denying we don't trust God, what if we instead admitted we are, as Jesus called us, "of little faith"? If you are having a hard time believing we could think God is not good, compare Matthew 6:26, 30, and 32. In all three verses, Jesus reiterates God's goodness. He was impressing upon the disciples that God is good and He cares for us. If there weren't a problem in our believing God is good, Jesus wouldn't have said it three times.

There are people who wrestle mightily with anxiety and fear. There are those who have prayed for years to be released from those troubles and have questioned if their faith is strong enough. The problem is one of missing the heart of the matter. If we admit we don't trust God, then the Holy Spirit will work in our lives to change our lack of faith. If we are simply praying to be relieved of anxiety and fear, it does not move us in our relationship with God. It doesn't get at the real underlying issue. It's like praying that God would make me skinny when I was overweight instead of praying He would work in me to resolve my addiction to food and lack of exercise. Being overweight wasn't the problem—*it was the manifestation of the problem*.

What is the key to being free from worry and fear? At some point or other, someone with the greatest of intentions has probably recited to us Paul's words from Philippians.

> Be anxious for nothing, but in everything by prayer and supplication, with thanksgiving, let your requests be made known to God; and the peace of God, which surpasses all understanding, will guard your hearts and minds through Christ Jesus. (Philippians 4:6–7 NKJV)

Those are two powerful verses with great potential to change our lives, that's for certain, but they don't give us insight into the heart of our problem. Is there a place where we look to what Jesus said or did for an answer? How about the fourth chapter of the Gospel of Mark?

One evening after Jesus had spent a good amount of time teaching, He and the disciples got into a boat to cross the Sea of Galilee. Sometime thereafter, while they were out in the water, a big storm blew up and started tossing the boat about. This must have been a major storm. How can we infer so? Four of the disciples—James, John, Andrew, and Peter—were all professional fishermen. They had spent their lives out on that water in boats. They knew how to handle themselves in the weather on the Sea of Galilee. How did they respond to the particular storm that evening? They freaked out! As the boat was being tossed about and filled with water, the disciples were anxious and doubtful, afraid they were going to die.

Where was Jesus during all of the tumult—at the oars with them freaking out? No. He was asleep in the back of the boat! Asleep! Did Jesus not know this great tempest was about to come? Of course He knew. Was He anxious about it? No, He was asleep. He must've been a heavy sleeper given that the boat was wracked with waves and filling with water. It must've been a really great pillow He had. What did the disciples do? "They awoke Him and said to Him, 'Teacher, do You not care that we are perishing?'" (Mark 4:38 NKJV). The Greek word translated as *perishing* there means *to be destroyed* or *killed*. The guys thought it was all over. How did Jesus respond to them? He spoke and the tempest dissolved into stillness. Then Jesus asked them, "Why are you so fearful? How *is it* that you have no faith?" (Mark 4:40 NKJV). To Jesus, their fear was a lack of faith;

they didn't trust Him to save them. They didn't see the long-term outcome. They didn't trust that God had a plan for them.

What would've happened to the disciples if the boat had sunk? There are three potential options we could entertain. The first is Jesus could've raised the boat back up out of the water—a pretty awesome thing to behold. The second is Jesus could've given the disciples the ability to walk on the water to the other side, as Peter later did in Matthew 14—another amazing possibility. The third option is they could have all died and would've suddenly been in heaven. Whichever way you go, the disciples would've been involved in a mind-blowing miracle. But they didn't see those things as possibilities. They saw themselves dying in the waves and their God sleeping in the back of the boat.

God allows us to come into faith-testing situations. In this manner, God is able to remove those things that are not faith, the impurities. Peter spoke to this in 1 Peter.

> In this you greatly rejoice, though now for a little while, if need be, you have been grieved by various trials, that the genuineness of your faith, *being* much more precious than gold that perishes, though it is tested by fire, may be found to praise, honor, and glory at the revelation of Jesus Christ. (1 Peter 1:6–7 NKJV)

In these situations, when we are tried and are overcome with fear or doubt, we need to press into Jesus Christ and trust Him. That's hard, especially if we try to hide from the truth that we lack trust and that we doubt that God is good. Often our words will be left wanting, and we won't know what to say or how to say it. Thankfully, in this situation we have the Holy Spirit who "helps in our weaknesses. For we do not know what we should pray for as we ought, but the Spirit Himself makes intercession for us with groanings which cannot be uttered" (Romans 8:26 NKJV).

Our feelings can drive our thoughts and actions. They alter how we perceive the world and the way we interpret what is going on around us.[19] How we perceive reality, in fact, what we think *is* reality, is greatly dependent on our feelings and emotions. Our feelings, which according to psychologists are our interpretation of our emotions, and our perception of the world, which is the interpretation of the information we receive from our senses, combine to produce our experiences.[20] Unfortunately, our society has given too much credence to our feelings and emotions. We allow the way we feel in a given situation to determine the course of action we should take. We do "what feels right."

A lot of the interactions we have with others are geared toward protecting the feelings of others, making sure they have a happy emotional experience with the interactions. Certainly we don't typically set out with the mind-set that we are going to make someone feel bad as a result of the interaction we have. It's no fun to hurt someone's feelings. However, this concern about feelings seems to have taken center stage in our society. When was the last time you were able to have a meaningful conversation without being concerned that somehow you would say something over which someone might be able to be offended? There is a hypervigilance in our society oriented toward the importance of our feelings. The militants of political correctness roam about seeking ways they can be offended on the behalf of others. Feelings are on everyone's radar, especially their own feelings.

Some people have difficulty understanding the effect our emotions and feelings have on our ability to make a reasoned and balanced assessment or decision. If our feelings change what we perceive in the world and what we perceive in the world changes our feelings, it follows that using our feelings to determine if something is real or true is a dangerous proposition—it's a feedback loop that races out of control. When we allow feelings, which are readily subject to change, to determine what we think is reality and truth, we have nothing firm upon which to stand. Brownlow North was an English evangelist who understood such a perilous scenario when he wrote *Six Short Rules for Young Christians*. The last of his rules was as follows:

> Never believe what you feel, if it contradicts God's Word. Ask yourself, "Can what I feel be true if God's Word is true"? And if BOTH cannot be true, believe God and make your own heart the liar. (Roms. 3:4. 1 John 5:10-11).[21]

In today's society, it seems the norm is to believe what we *feel* to be correct, irrespective of what God's Word says. The sad thing is, this is true among Christians. In 2002, the Barna Group conducted a study on moral relativism among Americans. In the study, people were asked if they believe in moral absolutes.[22] The results are staggering. Two-thirds of all adults (a full 75 percent of those eighteen to thirty-five years-old) said they believe truth is always relative to people and their situations, whereas 83 percent of teenagers said the same. Among born-again Christians, the numbers were not particularly encouraging, with only 32 percent saying they believe in moral absolutes. We have come to trust in our feelings as a moral compass. Overlooking real truth, we look at what our emotions and experiences, which are so easily distorted, tell us. We have come to trust our hearts, ignoring the words of God in Jeremiah.

> The heart *is* deceitful above all *things*, and desperately wicked; Who can know it? (Jeremiah 17:9 NKJV)

Our moral relativism has led us away from God's absolute truth. We trust our hearts, which are filled with fear and anxiety, over His Word. What sort of sense does that make?

Our culture has certainly continued a trend toward moral relativism since the work of the Barna Group in 2002. We now live in a culture that bases what is right or wrong on emotions and feelings instead of on absolute truth. Following our feelings may make us feel better about ourselves because we don't have to face the truth, but this approach to morality has left us "tossed to and fro and carried about with every wind of doctrine, by the trickery of men, in the cunning craftiness of deceitful plotting" (Ephesians 4:14 NKJV). Following our feelings only serves to make us feel better, but it does not make us better.

If we do not trust God is good, do we believe Him at all? If I doubt God's goodness and faithfulness to take care of me to the point where I am worrying and anxious over temporary circumstances in my life, do I really believe He will save me from my sins and eternal damnation? It seems like a mutually exclusive scenario. Either I trust God to take care of everything, or I don't really trust Him to take care of anything. Either He is true to His Word to care for me, as Jesus said in Matthew 6:25–34, or He is not. If I do not believe God on this point, then the words of John suggest I do not believe God at all.

> He who believes in the Son of God has the witness in himself;
> he who does not believe God has made Him a liar, because he
> has not believed the testimony that God has given of His Son. (1
> John 5:10 NKJV)

Thankfully, God is always faithful. No matter what my heart tells me is true, or how far from truth we stray as a society, God remains faithful. He doesn't weigh our unbelief and go back on His Word and promises. He remains true.

> For what if some did not believe? Will their unbelief make the
> faithfulness of God without effect? Certainly not! Indeed, let God
> be true but every man a liar. (Romans 3:3–4a NKJV)

It is possible for the trend toward worry and moral relativism in the church to change. We have to prioritize our lives so God is first; we have to trust He is who He says and will do what He promises. When we worry about ourselves, about our outcomes, about how we have been wronged or how we feel about something, we are effectively saying we do not trust that God is good and will take care of us, and we are putting ourselves first. We have to admit our lack of faith. In so doing, we open ourselves up to the Holy Spirit's working in us to grow our faith in deeper ways. If we begin to focus on God and meditate on Him, our perspective changes. We see our hearts as what they are—deceitful. We will see

His truth, and our fears and anxieties will begin to subside. Paul spoke directly to this in the fourth chapter of Philippians.

> Finally, brethren, whatever things are true, whatever things *are* noble, whatever things *are* just, whatever things *are* pure, whatever things *are* lovely, whatever things *are* of good report, if *there is* any virtue and if *there is* anything praiseworthy—meditate on these things. The things which you learned and received and heard and saw in me, these do, and the God of peace will be with you. (Philippians 4:8–9 NKJV)

CHAPTER 7
IT'S NOT ABOUT YOUR CHURCH AND WHAT YOU THINK IT SHOULD BE

In the New Testament, the word translated as *church* is the Greek word *ekklēsia*. This word referred to an assembly of people, and in the Christian sense it was a group of people assembled to worship. The word *ekklēsia* is a compound word made from two words: *ek*, which means *out of* and *kaleō*, which means *to call*. So, *ekklēsia* really is *a group that has been called out*. As the church, we are to be a group that has been called out by God to worship and serve Him. As a group, we are supposed to be as diverse as the human body but yet come together to compose a functioning organism. Paul wrote about this in 1 Corinthians 12:27 when he said, "Now you are Christ's body, and individually members of it" (NASB).

As individual believers in Jesus Christ, we are all *called out* to be part of the body of Christ, which is the church. Because the church is a collection of individual people, it is then a reflection of the attitudes, aptitudes, and actions of those people. Whatever is in the people will manifest itself in the church. Our attitudes will become the character of the church. When people outside the church—nonbelievers—look at the church, they will see the attitudes of the believers. If one person's attitude begins to get off track, it can quickly spread to others, and soon our church as a body will get off track. That attitude will then be what is reflected to those who are watching us. In speaking to this idea, Paul wrote to the church at Corinth, "If one member suffers, all the members suffer with it" (1 Corinthians 12:26a NASB). If we are not careful, we can be fully off track and really not even realize it because all of those around us suffer from the same thing. If you don't think it can happen, look only as far as all of the writings of Paul in the New Testament. Every book Paul wrote was either to a church that had gotten off track or about a church that had gotten off track. If those believers did it then, we are certainly not immune to such a fate now.

It's hard to consider that we might have missed the mark. If you have been paying attention to this book so far, you have likely come across one or two things that made you stop to consider if your attitudes and focus have gotten off track; I certainly have as I have been writing it. So if we accept the premise that not only can we get off course, but we are all likely to be off course somewhere in our lives, how does that manifest in the church today? How do our own desires to glorify ourselves instead of glorifying God show up in the church? What are some of the things we do that are not a reflection of the attitude Christ wants in His bride? What does the church look like in our present culture, what I like to refer to as "the culture of me"?

First Church

First things first ... In the most famous scene in Shakespeare's *Romeo and Juliet*, Juliet asks, "What's in a name?" This was in the midst of pondering why the love between the title characters was forbidden solely on the basis of their names. So what is in a name? In Jewish culture, from ancient times until today, the naming of a child has been something done with great care. In Proverbs 22:1, Solomon wrote, "A *good* name is to be more desired than great riches" (NASB), a reflection of the attitude toward the naming of a child at the time. The child's name revealed something of the story of the child, as well as the sort of character the family wanted for the child. For instance, Abraham's son Isaac was so named because it means *he laughs*. When Sarah heard God tell Abraham they would have a son, though they were nearly one-hundred-years-old, she laughed (Genesis 18:12). The name Isaac was a reminder of God's faithfulness in what would otherwise be seen as a laughable circumstance. In biblical times, the name defined the person as much as the person defined the name.

People acquainted with me know my name. They also know something about me as a person. If someone were to make a list of character traits about me, the people who know me would be able to identify me without having my name at the top of the list. In this regard, my name doesn't define me, but rather I define my name. When people hear my name, they think of all of those traits, and it informs their mental image of what my name represents. If I started walking around calling myself Elvis Presley, people would think I had lost my mind, but they would also know I am not, in fact, Elvis. My name represents who I am but doesn't define who I am.

Going back to Juliet's question, what is in a name? For churches today, this is a valid question. Think about the names of churches around you. Those names are supposed to reflect something about the church; they help identify the church in some form or fashion. What do the names tell us? If we look around the country, we find certain church names that spring up in almost every city and town. Which church names can you think of that are common across the country? The one that jumps out at me first is "First (Insert-favorite-denomination-here) Church." I suspect there are more "first" churches in the United States than any other church name. In fact, though I cannot find any firm data to prove it, I am suspicious that all of the "first" churches added together may represent a very sizable percentage of the total churches in the country. "First" churches are everywhere. Whether in large cities, small towns, or the middle of nowhere, the "first" churches are there. I've been to a lot of places where I wondered why instead the name Only Baptist Church wasn't chosen. What's so important about being the first Baptist or Presbyterian or whatever church in a given town?

Presumably those "first" churches were literally the first church of that given denomination to spring up in that particular location. In some cities, over time more churches from given denominations may have coalesced, which gave rise to "second" or "third" churches—New Orleans has a Sixth Baptist Church. Those "first" churches still hold on to their titles of being "first." What does that name really mean though? In reality, it means those churches have had the longest time to make the most difference in their city or town, or their middle of nowhere. In fact, it means they have had the responsibility to set the example of what a church is supposed to be in their locale. Have they done something with that time? Can they point to the fruits of having stuck their flag in the dirt as the first? Other than "we got here first," what does being the "first" church convey to others?

There's something about being first, isn't there? If we are in a competition, being first means we are the best. We have performed better than everyone else and have been declared the winner. It makes us feel great about ourselves because we have been recognized for our hard work and effort. We have earned the position of first and deserve what comes with it. Does that sort of thinking sneak into our churches? I can say I have seen it. If we keep in mind the attitude of the church is a reflection of the attitude of the believers in the church, why would we think the desire to be first wouldn't be something manifesting in our churches? What's so important about being first? Does being the first church glorify God in some real way? Perhaps it sets the members apart, at least in their minds, as being special, as being glorified in some way. Could it be it is a point of pride to be first?

The desire to be first is really the opposite attitude of what Jesus said we are to have. In speaking to our desire to be first, to be glorified, Jesus said the following:

> But it is not this way among you, but whoever wishes to become
> great among you shall be your servant; and whoever wishes to
> be first among you shall be slave of all. (Mark 10:43–44 NASB)

Does the name "First (Insert-favorite-denomination-here) Church" convey something to nonbelievers other than, "Yeah, we were first"? Do people know us by our works, our attitudes, and our love? Do they know us by the impact we make on the community? If we stripped away the name of our church, would people in the community be able to identify us? Would they be able to tell of the way we are or are not being the hands and feet of Jesus in our locale? If not, our name is irrelevant.

Churches don't want to be irrelevant. In more recent years, churches have gone away from being the first or even from including a denominational association in their names. In an attempt to get away from what may be construed as names that are stodgy or carry some sort of image they want to avoid, churches are now taking on names they hope point toward something meaningful, hip, or catchy. Think about it for a minute. How did those connotations become associated with a certain church type or denomination? What is it that has led to a pushback from those sorts of names? Doesn't that sort of movement indicate we have something wrong?

Churches Searching for Relevance

Being relevant is important these days. *Relevant* is a big buzzword in Christian circles. Every church, which really translates to *every church's paid staff*, wants to be relevant to the church members and the general public, to unsaved or unchurched people in the community. That's become a goal of so many churches in recent years, to the point where there is a cottage industry on the topic, complete with websites and publications.

What does being relevant really mean? If we look at the dictionary, we find *relevant* is an adjective meaning: *bearing upon or relating to the matter in hand*; *pertinent*; *to the point*.[23] So the goal of relevance is to relate to some given matter. Which matter? Any matter, it seems. We just want to be able to relate to people out there who are not believers in Jesus Christ, right? Isn't that what we want? How do we go about doing it? What are the ways we see churches being relevant or trying to be relevant?

If we take a step back and look at the big picture, is the problem we have before us—our search for relevance in today's culture—not a problem of our own doing? How does someone or something become irrelevant? Irrelevance occurs when what is being said or offered by a person, group, or thing is not pertinent to or related to the matter at hand. This begs the question that if we have a problem with being irrelevant, is it not because we have made what we are offering or saying impertinent to nonbelievers?

Think about the way we usually approach trying to get people to come to our churches. We will often try to sell them on something great, whether it's some sort of program for kids, a chance to be involved in a softball league or a "rocking" worship service. We want them to come to a building to meet certain people and hear the gospel. Is that what we are called to do? Is that the example Jesus set for us? What if we changed things up a little bit? What if we got ridiculous and did things the way Jesus did them? What would that look like?

When I think about the way Jesus went about making an impact on people, I don't think of Him standing at a pulpit and preaching. Sure, there are accounts of Jesus teaching in the synagogue, but those occasions were rare. Jesus wasn't inviting people to come to a certain physical address for an hour or two a week. He was going to the people. Jesus was out there among them. That's the first thing He did differently with regard to His approach to being relevant. He was in the lives of the people and making a difference there. In a bigger context, this is the way the entire story of the gospel is played out. God doesn't wait for us to come to Him. He came to us. Emmanuel—God with us—came to live among us and save us where we are.

Jesus' approach to drawing people to God was different. He inserted Himself into humanity. He came to meet us where we were and are. Ultimately, Jesus offered something people needed. He offered the one thing everyone needs—love. That's how Jesus was relevant then, and that's how He is relevant today. In a world with misguided principles and failed morals, in a place where people are hurting and alone, love has been and always will be relevant.

Why do we love God? Is it because He is God? Is it because we are so spiritually enlightened that we have come to the place where we are compelled to love God because we know He deserves it? No. The reason we love God is not because of any of those things. "We love Him because He first loved us" (1 John 4:19 NKJV). If we want people to love God, we first have to show them that He loves them.

If the church is seeking to be relevant, it is because the church has become irrelevant. If we are irrelevant, it is because we have failed to follow the example of Christ—that is, we do not love people. The love of Jesus Christ is a power so great as to have overcome death and hell. That love is at our disposal if we will tap into it. Why don't we tap into that source? Why do we instead chase after fads and programs in an attempt to get people to come to where we want them, to a building?

The love of Christ is beautiful and irresistible. What would happen if we stopped wasting time on programs to cater to some superficial, temporal, or perceived desire and instead spent our time investing in, truly pouring our hearts and souls into, the people who are hurting and dying without Christ? If we stopped worrying about budgets and programs, buildings and marketing, and instead began going out into the world and started loving people with the love of Christ in a no-holds-barred, all-or-nothing, going-for-broke manner, then we wouldn't have to concern ourselves with relevance. Once people experience the love of Jesus Christ, they are changed and are compelled to experience more of it.

People in this world are hurting and alone. In fact, research has shown that loneliness is increasing in the United States, and about 20 percent of the US population feels lonely.[24] People are feeling more and more isolated and alone in spite of the promise of increased connectedness that social media offers. People want acceptance and seek approval. Ultimately though, they are seeking to be loved and will go to great lengths in an attempt to find love. What if we took it to them? What if the church followed the example of Christ and was out there loving people where they are? If we did, the world would be changed.

The truth is, we don't rush out there and love the world like Jesus did. Instead, we like for people to have to work for our love and acceptance, don't we? When it comes to God's love, we create even more barriers for people. Don't we try to place stipulations on people's coming to God? We say we want people to come to faith in Christ. We say we want them to come to our church. But isn't there some sort of stipulation we put on it? If you're an alcoholic who beats his wife or a woman who has fallen into a place where you have become involved in prostitution, we don't get too excited about those folks coming into the church. Don't we want them to clean up their act before they come to Christ? Aren't we prone to withholding our friendship, support, and love in those situations?

Let's make this a little more real. If you were told you had to have lunch with someone you had never met, would your likelihood of going to lunch be affected by knowing something about the person? For instance, would knowing the person was of the same gender, ethnic background, and financial standing as you are make you feel uncomfortable? It probably would not. Now, suppose instead you were told the person was of a different gender and ethnic background, and what if the person was also a known methamphetamine addict? Would you be more likely or less likely to go to the lunch than you would be to go with the person who was just like you? This seems like a silly question, perhaps, but it is extremely important, or relevant, to the discussion. We all have preconceived notions and expectations of people. We want people to come to us on our terms, on terms with which we are comfortable. Whether it is sharing lunch or sharing the love of Christ, these expectations or demands get placed on people, and we somehow convince ourselves we are justified by saying things like, "I'm just not comfortable going to lunch with that person," or "I don't think it would be safe for me to help that person." Thinking back to previous chapters, what right do we have to think like that? Haven't we already seen the fallacy of the comfort argument?

When we withhold the love of Christ, we do not realize the spiritual ramifications of our actions. In withholding the love of Christ, are we not demonstrating we believe a particular person is unworthy of His love? To act in such a way reveals the darkness in our hearts. When we act that way, have we not, in our hearts, condemned the person to an eternal hell apart from God's love? When we decide someone is unworthy to receive the love of Christ, have we not taken God's place as judge and determined the person's fate? In that moment, in our hearts, we have not only cast God from His throne, but we have also sentenced someone to eternal damnation. How much more arrogant and loathsome can we possibly be? Yet we are the ones withholding God's love. I'm pretty sure if I got up at my church and said, "Just to let you know, I routinely try to dethrone God ... oh, and I condemn people to hell at the same time," the folks in the church wouldn't be too excited about having me participate.

These same attitudes that live in our hearts, the ones that put us above someone else, manifest in the church. These attitudes and the withholding of Christ's love are what the world sees when they look at us. We like to convince ourselves it is because we are in the right, but it's our hypocrisy that makes us irrelevant.

In 2013 the Barna Group conducted a survey of self-identified Christians to determine the Christlike actions and attitudes we have.[25] In the survey, there were ten statements representing "Christlikeness" actions or attitudes and ten statements representing "Self-righteousness" actions or attitudes. Participants were asked to determine how well they agreed with each particular statement. The results were telling. The majority (51 percent) of Christian Americans surveyed had self-righteous actions and attitudes; only 14 percent had Christlike actions and attitudes. The remainder was split between Christlike attitudes with self-righteous actions (21 percent) and self-righteous attitudes with Christlike actions (14 percent). When the participants were broken out into the categories of evangelical, born-again, nonevangelical, notional, practicing Catholic, and practicing Protestant, the numbers were not any more encouraging. The group with the lowest self-righteous actions and attitudes and highest Christlike actions and attitudes were evangelicals, but even in that, the numbers were disappointing at 38 percent self-righteous and 23 percent Christlike, which is certainly not a victory. So if we are harboring these sorts of actions and attitudes, how are we being viewed by the outside world? If we are, by our own admissions, self-righteous hypocrites, what must the world think of us, and why would they be interested in being like us?

If we stop to look at what the church is offering the world, it's not the love of Christ; it's a set of rules and regulations, dosed with a strong helping of judgment and condemnation and topped with self-righteousness. We are offering dos and don'ts. People are lonely, hurting, and in need of love, not dos and don'ts. How did Jesus approach them? Did He bang them over the head with a set of regulations? No, He didn't. In fact, if we look at Jesus' summation of the entirety of the law, He said we should love God and love others. Ultimately, Jesus said we are to love.

We are supposed to be Jesus Christ to the world. He tells us to love; we set up rules and regulations. He pours out grace and mercy; we create restrictions and withhold grace like the unforgiving servant in Matthew 18:21–35. Jesus went out into the world to where the sinners are; we build buildings and tell them to come to us. Jesus advised us we should not judge the world; condemnation roils out of us at every opportunity. Are we really living up to our role of being a reflection of Jesus Christ to the world? Nonbelievers look at what we are selling and realize they cannot live up to it, not realizing we don't live up to it either. They decide they want nothing to do with the Jesus we are supposedly representing or with us, and that's how we become irrelevant. The love of Jesus Christ has never been and never will be irrelevant. Loving people with His love and pouring out the grace on people that has been poured out on us is the way we become and stay relevant.

First Corinthians 13 is often referred to as the love chapter. In it, Paul outlines the characteristics of love. That chapter is read at more weddings than any other passage of Scripture. We like to take it and apply it to our marriages and romantic love. My wife and I have a copy of it framed and hanging in our kitchen. But to take that chapter and apply it only in such a manner is taking it completely out of context. We have previously touched on some of the contents of the twelfth chapter of 1 Corinthians, but for a broader context with regard to love, it is important for us to consider what Paul was doing in the book. He was writing to the church at Corinth to help them solve some issues with which they were obviously having problems. Based on chapter 12, it's pretty clear they were not unified, they had issues with who had which gifts, and they were having problems with glorifying some gifts over others. Paul corrected their misunderstanding of the situation and then told them he would "show you a still more excellent way" (1 Corinthians 12:31b NASB). With that, he launched into chapter 13. That's when he told them about the importance of love and the position love has relative to all of the gifts, the ones they had been fighting about. The first three verses of chapter 13 apply directly to the discussion of the church's need to love each of its members and "the least of these."

> If I speak with the tongues of men and of angels, but do not have love, I have become a noisy gong or a clanging cymbal. If I have *the gift of* prophecy, and know all mysteries and all knowledge; and if I have all faith, so as to remove mountains, but do not have love, I am nothing. And if I give all my possessions to feed *the* poor, and if I surrender my body to be burned, but do not have love, it profits me nothing. (1 Corinthians 13:1–3 NASB)

Paul basically told the people at Corinth they needed to stop arguing over their individual spiritual gifts and who was greater than whom, and they needed to focus instead on love. Without love, Paul said, it doesn't matter what we know or what great things we can do. Without love, it's all wasted energy and meaningless.

When we love people and they experience that love, it gives us an opportunity to speak truth into their lives through the relationship we form with them. Running around beating people over the head with a big, heavy Bible and an accompanying set of rules and regulations is not the way to bring people into a relationship with Jesus Christ. In Matthew 28:19–20a, Jesus gave the disciples the Great Commission when He told them, "Go therefore and make disciples of all the nations, baptizing them in the name of the Father and the Son and the Holy Spirit, teaching them to observe all that I commanded you" (NASB). The Greek wording in verse 19 is better translated as "as you are going." This action of making disciples is then to be undertaken as we are going—that is, in our daily lives. Jesus had demonstrated to His disciples day in and day out for three years what it meant to make a disciple. He had come alongside each of them, loved them, invested in them, and spoken truth into their lives. Jesus was intentional with making His disciples. He loved them where they were, and then He taught and shaped them into what they were to be. We have been commanded to do the same thing. If we do not love people, we will not have the opportunity to speak into their lives. If we do not love people, they will not care what we have to say to them.

It's not uncommon to meet people in the church who think it is not their responsibility to be active in witnessing to nonbelievers or making disciples. Some people are even so brazen as to say, "It's the responsibility of the church staff to witness to others or make disciples." Somehow those people are convinced that if they throw some money into an offering plate, they are then absolved of Jesus' direct commandment to go out and make disciples of all nations. Other people may not be quite so bold in their statements. Instead, they say things like, "That's not my gift," or "I just don't think that it's my place to tell people what I believe." Somewhere along the way, we have taken verses like Matthew 5:16, which says, "Let your light shine before men in such a way that they may see your good works, and glorify your Father who is in heaven" (NASB), and we have decided it somehow means we can just go about our lives, in a somewhat unintentional manner and still make an impact for the kingdom of God. This idea of letting our lives be our witness is quite popular currently in the American church. In truth, why wouldn't it be? It doesn't take any effort on our part. We think we can just float along being a bunch of nice guys without ever speaking truth into someone's life. It is a fallacy to think that letting our lives be our witness is good enough to lead people to Christ. At some point, people have to hear the truth. In Romans 10 Paul deals with the need for people to be told about the gospel.

> How then will they call on Him in whom they have not believed? How will they believe in Him whom they have not heard? And how will they hear without a preacher? How will they preach unless they are sent? Just as it is written, "How beautiful are the feet of those who bring good news of good things!" However, they did not all heed the good news; for Isaiah says, "Lord, who has believed our report?" So faith *comes* from hearing, and hearing by the word of Christ. (Romans 10:14–17 NASB)

In our current culture, this idea of not actively speaking the truth into people's lives has become an increasingly common opinion among believers. As our culture becomes less and less accepting of Christian morals and the idea of absolute truth, nonbelievers are increasingly prone to tell us it's not our place to tell them what is right or wrong or how to live. If people are telling us that, it's because we haven't followed the example Christ set, the model of loving people first. When we love them first, we develop a real, meaningful relationship with people, and then we have earned the right to speak truth into their lives. Further, we will want to do it not because of a sense of obligation but rather out of our love for them. That will be real to them, and they will be interested in hearing from us because they know we love them.

The argument that some of us are not called to go out into the world and be living, breathing representatives of God is poorly contrived but remarkably well accepted. The church is here to make an impact on the world. The world is to know the living God and His Son Jesus Christ because of us. We are supposed to be a microcosm of the world around us in that we should be a diverse collection of people from all walks of life; however, there is the major exception that we have been changed by the Holy Spirit and have come to faith in Jesus Christ. We have been set apart for a purpose.

Peter wrote specifically about our being set apart in his first epistle. He was writing to believers in churches scattered around Asia Minor and who had come under persecution. In the second chapter, he encouraged those churches and reminded them they were set apart.

> But you are a chosen race, a royal priesthood, a holy nation, a people for *God's* own possession, so that you may proclaim the excellencies of Him who has called you out of darkness into His marvelous light; for you once were not a people, but now you are the people of God; you had not received mercy, but now you have received mercy. (1 Peter 2:9–10 NASB)

What was the reason for our having been chosen, called out, and made a royal priesthood? According to Peter, God did it so we might proclaim His praises. When the world sees us, they are supposed to see a people who are about glorifying God. When the world around us thinks about Christians, does the image of a people who have obtained mercy and are proclaiming the praises of God come to their minds? We've already covered the answer, and it's not what we want to hear.

Peter's encouragement to those Christians to whom he was writing is completely transferable to us today. In 1 Peter 2:4–5, Peter says we are "living stones" that were all rejected by men but have been accepted by God, and we are now "a holy priesthood, to offer up spiritual sacrifices acceptable to God through Jesus Christ" (NASB). We are all supposed to be serving in the capacity of royal priests for God. Why do we refuse to do so? Is it fear of rejection? In the end, is it not our pride keeping us from being God's representatives?

What do God's representatives look like to the world? The easy answer is Jesus Christ. But carrying on with Peter's words in chapter 2 of 1 Peter, we see we are to have our "behavior excellent among the Gentiles, so that in the thing in which they slander you as evildoers, they may because of your good deeds, as they observe *them*, glorify God in the day of visitation" (1 Peter 2:12 NASB). This is clearly a reflection on the words of the Lord in Matthew 5:16 when He said, "Let your light shine before men in such a way that they may see your good works, and glorify your Father who is in heaven" (NASB). In both places, we see the common theme that the world will see our "good works," which will result in their glorifying God. These good works aren't things we are doing in the misguided hope of earning forgiveness, but rather they are the outgrowth of our faith. Neither Christ nor Peter say that the world will hear our good words, well-worded arguments, condemnations, or hypocritical attitudes. They say the world will see our good works, those works representing self-sacrifice and love for our fellow man, and this will lead them to glorify God. It doesn't say they *may glorify God*, it says they *will glorify* Him. If the world around our churches isn't glorifying God because of our good works, it's because we aren't doing good works.

What then are good works? Do we really have to ask that question? We all know what good works are. James says true religion is to care for the widows and orphans (James 1:27). Jesus says it is taking care of the least of these—those who are hungry, thirsty strangers, those who are naked, sick, and imprisoned (Matthew 25:34–40). But we do that, don't we? Aren't we out there making a difference in the lives of the world? If that's the case, we should be able to open our churches' checkbooks and look at where our money is spent. Unfortunately, if we do so, we find we aren't spending our money on the least of these.

In chapter 2 I mentioned the book *Passing the Plate*, wherein the statistics of giving by American Christians were studied in detail. In 2005, Americans who considered themselves "strong" or "very strong" in their faith earned $2 trillion dollars. Let's lay that out … $2,000,000,000,000! If all of those people were a country, it would've been the seventh-highest-grossing country in the world—only six countries had a bigger economy. A total of $103 billion was given to houses of worship and denominational organizations. How much of the $103 billion was used to minister to non-Christians? The authors found only about 3 percent of donations to church or parachurch organizations actually went to helping non-Christians.[26] Is this in keeping with the command of Christ? In Matthew 5 Jesus addressed our tendency to love those who love us and care for those who care for us.

> "You have heard that it was said, 'You shall love your neighbor and hate your enemy.' But I say to you, love your enemies and pray for those who persecute you, so that you may be sons of your Father who is in heaven; for He causes His sun to rise on *the* evil and *the* good, and sends rain on *the* righteous and *the* unrighteous. For if you love those who love you, what reward do you have? Do not even the tax collectors do the same? If you greet only your brothers, what more are you doing *than others?* Do not even the Gentiles do the same?" (Matthew 5:43–47 NASB)

How can we legitimately say we are trying to carry out the command to go out and make disciples, to make an impact on "the least of these," when 97 percent of the money we give is spent on ourselves? We aren't giving to "the least of these." We aren't going out there and making an impact as individuals or as the body of Christ. These are the good works the world is supposed to be seeing and as a result glorifying God. Instead, we spend billions of dollars on our programs, our buildings, and ourselves. The attitudes and actions of the church are a reflection of the attitudes and actions of the people. What do they say about us?

Ambassadors for Christ

What if we took to heart this call to do good works? What if we let down our façades long enough to really embrace the truth—if it were not for the grace of God every one of us would be "the least of these"? Instead, solely by His grace God has made us into new creations. "For we are His workmanship, created in Christ Jesus for good works, which God prepared beforehand so that we would walk in them" (Ephesians 2:10 NASB). We have been given grace and have been reconciled to God so that we may go out and give grace and help bring about reconciliation in others.

> Therefore if anyone is in Christ, *he is* a new creature; the old things passed away; behold, new things have come. Now all *these* things are from God, who reconciled us to Himself through Christ and gave us the ministry of reconciliation, namely, that God was in Christ reconciling the world to Himself, not counting their trespasses against them, and He has committed to us the word of reconciliation. Therefore, we are ambassadors for Christ, as though God were making an appeal through us; we beg you on behalf of Christ, be reconciled to God. He made Him who knew no sin *to be* sin on our behalf, so that we might become the righteousness of God in Him. (2 Corinthians 5:17–21 NASB)

What a wonderful passage from 2 Corinthians! We are made new—completely and totally new. Because of Jesus, we as believers have been reconciled to God. Now, as Christ's ambassadors, we are to tell the world about the reconciliation God offers to everyone who will come to Him. We have become the righteousness of God in Christ! How awesome is that? What are we doing with it?

When I was growing up, I was involved in the Royal Ambassador (RA) program at my church. It was basically like a Christian Boy Scouts program. I went to RAs every Wednesday night from the time I was about seven or eight years old all the way into high school. Being involved in Royal Ambassadors was tremendously important in my development of faith, learning biblical truth, and building of friendships. As we met, the fact we were to be ambassadors for Christ was never lost from what we were studying, constructing, or doing. In fact, as a teen in the Pioneer component of RAs we had to memorize 2 Corinthians 5:20, which says we are ambassadors for Christ. It was a foundational verse for the RAs, for good reason. It's what we are all supposed to be about, what we are supposed to be doing.

How often do we embrace this idea of being an ambassador for Christ? What does being an ambassador really even mean? If we look at the actual definition, we find the following:

> Ambassador: a diplomatic official of the highest rank, sent by one sovereign or state to another as its resident representative[27]

An ambassador is sent to a foreign land to be the official representative of the governing authority under which the ambassador serves. If we think of a king sending out an ambassador to another land, the king gives his authority to the ambassador. When the ambassador arrives in the foreign land, he is effectively to be the embodiment of his king in that land. He has the authority to undertake whatever business necessary to uphold the interests of the king. To the people in the foreign land, the ambassador is the face of the king; he essentially *is* the king. This is what God has called us to be, His ambassadors. We have been given this great task to be the ambassadors for the One True God, to share His good news with the world.

Go back and read the excerpt from 2 Corinthians 5:17–21 again. When we read it, we should be overwhelmed by God's grace in our lives, excited about what it means, and resolute in being the embodiment of Christ to the world. Perhaps we have difficulty with the task of being ambassadors because we have lost the joy of our salvation, as David had when he wrote Psalm 51 and asked God, "Restore to me the joy of Your salvation and sustain me with a willing spirit. *Then* I will teach transgressors Your ways, and sinners will be converted to You" (Psalm 51:12–13 NASB). As the body of Christ, as His church, when the world looks at us, are they seeing Christ? Are they seeing the joy of God's salvation and the love of Jesus? What comes to mind when people outside the church look at us?

The Church's Schizophrenia

When the world looks at the church, instead of the love and grace they should be seeing, what we frequently portray are contentiousness and divisions among ourselves and judgment and condemnation for those outside of the church. Divisions among the members of the church go back to the time of Jesus. James and John wanted to be seated at either side of Jesus in heaven. They wanted to put themselves ahead of all the other disciples, which was clearly divisive (Mark 10:35–41). Peter tried to tell Jesus He wasn't going to be crucified (Matthew 16:21–23). In both cases, Jesus stopped the divisive attitudes immediately. He saw the attitudes as what they were: misguided and self-centered. In both situations Jesus responded by telling the disciples they must deny themselves, place themselves last, and be willing to die. Jesus stopped the division at its root, before it could cause a problem.

Paul and Barnabas were great missionaries. They were truly ambassadors for Christ and worked as an exemplary team to share the gospel. We see these two as greats in the Christian Hall of Fame. However, as we read in Acts 15:36–41, Paul and Barnabas got into an argument over bringing John Mark along on the trip. John Mark had effectively abandoned them on their first trip and Paul wasn't inclined to forgive him for it. In verse 39 we read, "And there occurred such a sharp disagreement that they separated from one another" (NASB). Paul and Barnabas, these greats of the New Testament church, let contention drive them apart. They made up later, and God used their separation to increase their effectiveness. But the fact remains that division and contention are long standing in the church. It continues to this day in a host of forms.

Churches have split down through the ages. A. W. Tozer said, "Problems in the church are nothing new, and there are really no new problems."[28] Some splits have been doctrinal in nature. Perhaps a group within a church became convinced they had been enlightened by God and gained some special knowledge, which thus compelled them to break away from those who hadn't received the revelation. Similarly, there are divisions that arise from one group being convinced their understanding of given passages of Scripture is the one and only true interpretation. These two examples tend to be the origins of denominations. Then there are other issues that arise, such as whether women should wear dresses; should we have the fried chicken social on the second or third Wednesday night of each month; what color should the carpet be in the sanctuary; or how long is too long for the sermon on Sundays. These sorts of personal preferential items tend to be the things people get offended by and over which feel compelled to leave a given church.

A terrible truth in the church is that divisions occur. A large part of the writings of Paul was devoted to dealing with things dividing the churches, things that were causing contentions. The response to the contention and division was always to bring reconciliation among the members. It was to take people's focus off of themselves and bring it back to where it was supposed to be, on God. In 1 Corinthians 3:3, Paul addressed the church on the divisions among them and said, "For you are still carnal. For where *there are* envy, strife, and divisions among you, are you not carnal and behaving like *mere* men?" When we are dealing with divisions, no matter how we are trying to spin it, it's the manifestation of sin in our own hearts. We are putting our own thoughts, attitudes, and actions ahead of the body of Christ. In that, we steal the glory from God and devalue the church to the world. How are we supposed to reconcile sinners to God if we cannot reconcile things among ourselves?

The Greek word for being divided is *schizō*. It's the root word from which we get schizophrenia. Sometimes people confuse schizophrenia with something called dissociative identity disorder, or what used to be called multiple personality disorder, but this is not what schizophrenia is. Schizophrenia is better thought of as a mind divided against itself. The person who suffers from schizophrenia cannot distinguish between what the mind is creating and what is reality. Consequently, when these people hear voices or see things, they do not know if they are real or a product of their minds. They are divided against themselves and in most cases lose the ability to function well.

I worked as a nursing assistant in a nursing home one summer when I was in college. I remember the first day I showed up at the nursing home for orientation. There were all of the residents going about whatever activities they were going about, shuffling to and fro, playing cards, or sitting in a corner talking. We walked through a common area, and one lady caught my eye. When I saw her I was immediately uncomfortable, and frankly a little afraid. I knew whatever the case I didn't want to have to be assigned to her. As you might imagine, that's eventually exactly what happened. Her name was Helen. She was in her sixties, and she had schizophrenia. Helen would roll around the facility in her PVC rolling chair and make all sorts of noises and sounds. If you asked her a question, if she recognized you were there, she would usually respond with unintelligible whoops, whistles, or clicks. I began to try to talk to Helen, to see if I could get to know the person who lay behind what I was seeing and hearing. As it turned out, when she was in her thirties, before schizophrenia ravaged her mind, Helen had been a successful, top-level accountant. When I knew Helen, she couldn't feed herself or hold a conversation. I would look into her eyes and see a blank, glazed stare. Every day that I worked with her, I would try to talk to Helen. Unfortunately, most days my efforts were unfruitful, but there were rare occasions when a switch would flip and suddenly Helen was a thoughtful and articulate woman who was, if only for two or three minutes, in control of her faculties. Then, just as quickly as it came, it would be gone. It was delightful and heartbreaking at the same time. This was a mind divided against itself.

When we allow strife and contentions to divide the church, it's not dissimilar from schizophrenia. Take a minute to think about what it looks like for someone outside of the church who is looking for truth, for the answers Jesus Christ gives. If they look at the church, what do they see? According to the Hartford Institute for Religion Research, they see that there are over two hundred denominations in the United States that claim to be Christian.[29] If we have the answer, why are there so many versions of the answer? Somewhere deep inside her embattled mind, Helen knew accounting inside and out. The truth of accounting was in there. But her mind had become so distracted by the dividing voices and sounds that the truth of accounting was lost. No one would ever think it was a good idea to give his financial work to Helen—it would be financial suicide. Yet as the divided church, that's what we are asking of nonbelievers. They look at us and see all of the denominations, divisions, and factions and see a schizophrenic church. Why would they trust their eternity to such a group?

In the seventeenth chapter of his gospel account, John records Jesus' prayer for Himself, the disciples, and all future believers, which includes the church today. There, John recorded Jesus' prayer and desire for the church on the night before His crucifixion. Of all the things Jesus could have prayed for us, the church, what did He pray?

> That they may all be one; even as You, Father, *are* in Me and I in You, that they also may be in Us, so that the world may believe that You sent Me. The glory which You have given Me I have given to them, that they may be one, just as We are one; I in them and You in Me, that they may be perfected in unity, so that the world may know that You sent Me, and loved them, even as You have loved Me. (John 17:21–23 NASB)

Jesus knew divisions would come. This was His last prayer of intercession with all of the disciples, and He prayed for unity among them and within the church. The King of glory on the night before His crucifixion was praying that we would be one. The word translated *one* there is very simply the Greek number one. It doesn't carry some deep and profound extraneous meaning. It is not implying agreement or solidarity. Jesus prayed that we, His church, would be a single entity. In the same sense that God the Father, Jesus Christ the Son, and the Holy Spirit are all one, Jesus prayed we would be one. So when we bring dissention and division into the church, we are working directly against the desire of Jesus Christ, to the detriment of the world coming to know Him.

What brings division in the church—what is the root of the problem? Did James and John want seats by Jesus because they wanted to sit right there beside Him for eternity, or was it because of a desire for position, prestige, and power? Was Paul right to refuse to take John Mark along on the second journey, or was he harboring resentment and a lack of forgiveness motivated by pride? Did Peter's denunciation of the Lord's impending death come from a place of victory, or was he speaking out of fear for himself? The truth is, when division comes, there are always at least two sides to the story. Both sides usually have strongly held beliefs based on some interpretation of Scripture, be that interpretation accurate or not. In an effort to defend our suppositions and ourselves, we alienate each other and offer no opportunity for reconciliation. Our ability to love one another is so easily overtaken by our ability to love our own ideas, opinions, and desires that we leave no hope to resolve the conflict and we go our separate ways—proudly.

CHAPTER 8
IT'S NOT ABOUT YOUR NUMBERS

In certain denominations, some churches have grown to such sizes as to become known as megachurches. What is the definition of a megachurch? Supposedly, a megachurch is a church with a weekly attendance of two thousand people or more.[30] What characterizes a megachurch?

In churches with two thousand or more members, there are a large number of resources available to the members, which can be great. There are great opportunities for meeting people just like you. In some megachurches, for example, if you are a single businessperson between the ages of twenty-eight and thirty-four years, there's a group of people just like you whom you can meet with and get to know. That way you can feel comfortable and have common things to talk about, and this, according to people who make it their jobs to promote church growth, will facilitate the development of a sense of community among attendees, which will ensure continued attendance. It seems the more tailored the group is to your specific needs, the more likely you are to feel a connection to the group.

Is this phenomenon of tailored groups the fault of the churches? No. Megachurches are megachurches because they have people who know what people want. In the business world, it's called marketing. The goal is to convince the consumer that the product being promoted is what the consumer really needs. Whether that is the truth or not is irrelevant. If the consumer is convinced he needs the product, then it becomes his reality. If he thinks he needs it, he will buy it. If it fulfills some need he has been convinced he has, he will tell his friends of how great the product is, and they will then be compelled to buy it as well. It's the same with some church growth strategies. It's marketing.

If you were given the task of attracting self-centered people to join a group of other people, how would you go about it? Would you create a diverse group of people from all walks of life, all socioeconomic groups, all educational levels and ethnic backgrounds? Would you put together a group that stretches people beyond their comfort zone by exposing them to types of people with which they aren't familiar?

Or would you create a tailored group just like your target audience, one that says, "You are so important, we have created this special group just for you"?

Now let's consider a different question. If you were going to try to put together a team of people who could accomplish any task that might arise, how would you go about it? Would you put together groups of people who are exactly alike, isolate them in silos, and keep them from intermingling with people not like them? Or would you put together a group of the most diverse people you could find? God wants the body of Christ to be able to handle any eventuality. He wants a diverse body with all of the necessary skills to get the job done. In this regard, the church should be like a well-stocked toolbox. Unfortunately, in some churches, there are only hammers or saws. Sure, there is every type of hammer you could think of; but if you need a screwdriver, a hammer will not get the job done.

For the first five years of our marriage, my wife and I lived in a city with several megachurches. One of the churches was far and away the largest in the city. In fact, it is one of the largest churches in the United States. For the sake of the discussion, let's call the church Big Church. At the time when we lived in the city, the membership of Big Church was around thirty thousand. Did you get that? Thirty thousand people are on the rolls of the church! Now, that by no means is indicative of the people who were actually involved in Big Church. Nevertheless, even if only half of the membership is actually involved on a regular basis, that's still fifteen thousand people. So, Big Church easily had enough members to be a respectable town.

Big Church sits on a large tract of land immediately off of the interstate on the eastern border of the city. The facilities are impressive; the first time I drove by Big Church, I thought it was a college campus. In fact, the truckers refer to it as Fort God. There are a number of buildings and a large number of manicured sports fields, not to mention acres of parking. They even have a little tram that drives around the parking lot to shuttle people to the main building—it's like Disneyland for Jesus.

As it turns out, Big Church has enough members that their sports teams don't have to play games against other churches or organizations. They have *their own leagues*. They have their own bookstore with a requisite self-improvement section. They have their own coffee shop and movie theater and cafeteria and … You get the idea. Big Church has been able to develop an environment that caters to its members and people just like its members. They come in on Sunday morning, receive a map of the facility, are directed to one of the many coffee and donut tables, and are then ushered to one of four or five groups of people just like themselves, out of forty or fifty groups meeting at that particular time. This way, attendees can come to church and feel comfortable. They aren't faced with the threatening scenario of interacting with someone who isn't just like them. Big Church has successfully developed a world in which members never have to interact with unchurched people if they don't make an effort to do so.

Is Big Church wrong? Like so many things in life, there are good and bad things about the Big Church model. Big Church is working in the sense that it is growing and bringing in more people, which hopefully translates to more people hearing the gospel of Jesus Christ and more people growing in Christ—again hopefully. However, there are most certainly unintended consequences of the Big Church model. It feeds into our egocentrism. It isolates us from the very people we are called to go out and impact with the gospel. It makes being a part of a church body about what I get out of it instead of what I have to offer it.

Something for the Kids

A major part of the strategy for church growth gurus is making certain there are high-quality programs for children and youth. The strategy is if the kids are excited about what's going on, the parents will be more inclined to become a part of the church. Parents are looking for something good for their kids, and they are going to attend wherever they find it. But what constitutes something good? What does a high-quality program look like? Usually a high-quality program has an area dedicated to children and youth. The children's area must have bright colors and plenty of iPads so there's no question as to whether the program is up-to-date. There must be great music with a lot of fun activities, and if you have an indoor playground, especially one disguised as a treehouse with some giant mushrooms, dinosaurs, or colorful, oversized insects … It just doesn't get any higher quality than that.

For the youth, there must be a large room with all sorts of couches and slightly subdued lighting. I'm not certain where the edict came from that the youth couch room is mandatory, but it seems to be a fairly standard operating procedure in all of the churches "doing things right." There also needs to be cutting edge Christian music being piped into the couch room—an area over to the side with some stage lighting is added only if the church is really trying to nail it.

What about content? It doesn't really seem that content is assessed by church visitors. Perhaps they assume the content will be sound, that their children's spiritual undergirding will be fostered by whatever is being doled out on those iPads. In the end, it boils down to families visiting churches and polling their children on where they want to go back, which is based on where the kids had fun. Is it the fault of the churches employing the strategies? Yes and no, perhaps. It's not the churches' faults that families are basing the decision as to where they are going to become a part of God's work and worship on whether their five-year-old had fun in the Kid Zone. But it is the churches' faults that such expectation and self-centered demandingness is being propagated and approved of.

What if we took all of the effort and energy we pour into making hip and exciting areas for ourselves and our kids and instead put it into making an area in our church to house the homeless? What if we used our church cafeterias or gymnasiums to feed and shelter those who are hungry and cold? We can come up with all sorts of excuses about zoning or safety or whatever else we can think of, but what's at the heart of those arguments? Isn't it really about our own comfort? Isn't it about what is easiest and best for us? Think about the impact we could make on our children and the world if we set the precedent that we were going to put those people, "the least of these," first. If we really want our children to know the love of Jesus Christ and to live it out, there is no better object lesson than to be active and intentional in loving the outcasts and downtrodden in society. That's what Jesus did. Doing something like that would surely result in church growth; it just might not be the kind of growth we are really wanting.

The Importance of Church Numbers

In today's church culture, church growth is extremely important. It is a commonly held idea that if we aren't advancing spiritually in our faith as individual believers, we are becoming stagnant and even withering. We should be growing and producing spiritual fruit. In the age of information and science, we like to quantify things; we have a need to put a number on everything. Whether we like it or not, it is difficult to quantify spiritual growth. What are the metrics we would use? Is it souls who have come to Christ? Is it churches planted? Is it percentage of annual income above 10 percent? How do we quantify it?

This same desire to quantify things is directed toward the church. We want to see that there is fruit as a result of what we are doing. If we are giving our money faithfully, we want to see some results. What metric do we use to assess the results? How can we know the people we are paying to do the work of the church are getting the work done? The easy answer is by looking at the number of people who are attending. If the number is high, the professional Christians are doing their jobs. If the numbers are not high, then we need to address someone's performance, that is to say the performance of those who are being paid. Because this sort of thinking plays a major role in the evaluation of pastors and church personnel, there is a big focus on growing the numbers but not necessarily on growing, or perhaps the better word would be cultivating, the church.

It would probably upset us to know God does not keep a count of things the way we do. He doesn't look at the number of plants growing in our garden; He looks at the fruit being produced. He looks at the end product. How do all of the things we are doing work out in the end to His glory—that's what He's looking at.

On January 6, 1850, a fifteen-year-old Englishman was making his way to church through a heavy snowstorm; however, he was driven instead into the Primitive Methodist Church. As it turned out, the preacher did not make it due to the storm, and there were a few congregants there who sang together. After the singing, a man from the small group, a shoemaker by trade, went up to the pulpit to preach. He spent about ten minutes speaking on Isaiah 45:22, "Look to Me, and be saved, all you ends of the earth! For I *am* God, and *there is* no other" (NKJV). After this short sermon, the man called out to the fifteen-year-old boy and said, "Young man, look to Jesus Christ. Look! Look! Look! You have nothing to do but to look and live." At that moment, Charles Haddon Spurgeon realized his need for Jesus Christ and came to salvation. In a little church on Artillery Street in Colchester, England, the boy who would become the man known as the Prince of Preachers came to faith.[31]

Spurgeon went on to become one of the greatest preachers and Christian authors in history, having seen the conversion of tens of thousands of souls and having had an influence through his writings in the lives of millions. The fruit of the little group of believers there in the Primitive Methodist Church is innumerable. If we looked in on that little group of believers with the thin, old shoemaker and his short exposition on Isaiah 45:22, would we have thought of them as being successful? Would we say they were doing things the right way? How does our assessment compare to what God saw and did? Unlike Big Church, the Primitive Methodist Church in Colchester, England, could only claim one widely known convert, but look at the impact he made on the world for Jesus Christ. Maybe we should change our approach to numbers in the church.

CHAPTER 9
IT'S NOT ABOUT WHAT YOU GET OUT OF MARRIAGE

I f there is one relationship that really exposes us for what we truly are, it must surely be marriage. In the setting of marriage, we cannot run and hide. Our excuses are exposed as what they are—excuses. Our self-centeredness and egocentricities come out. The little things we initially find cute or only slightly irritating can slowly build up in our minds until what we really think bursts forth in a torrent. Take for instance the proper use of a tube of toothpaste. A sane person can only put up with someone squeezing the toothpaste in the middle of the tube for so long before he snaps; the thing has instructions on how to use it, and they say start at the bottom and squeeze! It's kind of like that. It just eventually erupts, and the real you will come out, even if you use separate tubes.

Mutual self-sacrifice is mandatory if a marriage is to survive and thrive. Sacrifice is an imperative in marriage. Whether it's toothpaste, where to live, what sort of car to drive, or which family to visit on whatever holiday, a marriage without self-sacrifice on the part of both the husband and the wife is in dire shape. There is a reason God uses marriage metaphorically to represent the relationship between Christ and the church. Christ died for the church, and the church must die to self for Christ. The same is true in the setting of marriage.

Marriage is an interesting topic in our churches today. We say we support the sanctity of marriage. Led largely by Christian groups, votes have been cast across the country to define marriage as being a union of one man and one woman, as is consistent with the Bible. We picket and protest, petition and preach to save marriage. But are we really interested in defending marriage, or are we defending something else?

The Failure of Marriage

Discussing marriage can be a difficult endeavor. While a lot of people are anxious to define marriage as a relationship between one man and one woman, everyone wants to leave it there. To go beyond the somewhat superficial discussion involving homosexuality to a meaningful discussion on what marriage is to be between a husband and wife is something we are not so excited about. The topic of homosexual marriage has allowed us to divert our attention away from a much bigger problem in the church—the failure of traditional marriage.

When we talk about the failure of traditional marriage, are we talking about divorce? Yes and no. Certainly the issue of divorce is an end product of the failure of marriage. However, there are plenty of marriages that fail miserably without ending in divorce. Have you ever known a couple who made you think to yourself, *Wow, they should just get a divorce and stop pretending*? I have, and that's a terrible attitude on my part, and a terrible statement about the condition of their marriage.

The topic of divorce is a sore subject in the church. Why? There are a lot of people who are divorced, and a lot of them are in the church. Estimates of the divorce rate in our country consistently show that for every two marriages occurring in a given year, there is about one divorce that also occurs. This is how people come up with the figure that "50 percent of all marriages end in divorce."[32] That's not exactly correct, but the point is, there is a lot of divorce going on in our nation. The Barna group has conducted research on the topic of marriage, and they have found about one out of every three marriages among evangelical Christians ends in divorce.[33] That's 33 percent, which is less than the general population, but it is still far off of the mark. It's definitely not a victory for Christian marriage by any stretch of the imagination.

When we talk about divorce, it becomes personal. It's a terrible subject we would much rather dance around or totally ignore. Why? Statistically speaking, divorce has affected us all in some way or other. It has caused us all a lot of pain. We would rather not face the pain again but would instead rather pretend it didn't happen. Is that a biblical approach to the issue?

When I was a kid, I looked up to my dad. I held him in such a high regard. I wanted to be just like my dad when I grew up, in much the same way my son wants to be like me. He was my hero. However, my dad was unfaithful to my mom for years. I remember lying in my bed one night when I was around eight-years-old and listening to my parents fight over my dad's unfaithfulness; let's call it what it was, his adultery. My mom was trying to make things work, within the ability she had, but he kept being unfaithful. Ultimately, he left when I was eleven-years-old, and they were divorced on June 2, 1987. I still remember what I had for lunch that day. It was a terrible trauma for my sister and me but also for my mom.

After my parents' divorce, my mom worked hard to maintain some semblance of normalcy in our lives. Our financial situation was always tenuous, but she worked overtime and extra jobs to keep us afloat. We were always at church too, as a means of giving us support and an encouraging social environment. One day, an older lady in our church approached my mom to talk to her. This particular lady was held in high regard in our church, as one of the pillars of our little church almost. She made short order of telling my mom that my parents' divorce was my mom's fault and that she had set a terrible example for my sister and me. Somehow that person thought her words were representative of what God would say. My mom was devastated. She was deeply wounded by the callous and misguided words the woman had spoken to her. Any healing that could have been taking place from the divorce itself, as well as her own self-imposed guilt over it all, was torn away, and the wound was left gaping and hemorrhaging, right there in the little church where she had played an active part for her entire life. As a result, my mom stopped going to church. She couldn't face the shame and pain from the hateful and unfair accusations she had received. I'm not sure what the woman had hoped would come from approaching the topic of my mom's divorce in such a manner, but I'm fairly certain it missed the mark.

In our current American church environment, the pendulum seems to have swung completely in the opposite direction when it comes to divorce. Now, out of a fear of offending or hurting someone's feelings, we tend to ignore the topic altogether. In keeping with our society, a laissez faire mentality toward divorce is becoming more and more prevalent. Is this the way we should view divorce? How does Jesus view divorce? What has caused so many marriage failures?

If we look at the Samaritan woman at the well in John 4, Jesus didn't directly address the issue of her having had multiple husbands or that she was living with someone else. Instead, Jesus addressed her need for salvation. Twice in the book of Matthew, Jesus addressed divorce. In both Matthew 5:32 and 19:9, Jesus said, "But I tell you that anyone who divorces his wife, except for sexual immorality, makes her the victim of adultery, and anyone who marries a divorced woman commits adultery" (Matthew 5:32 NIV). This was obviously important to the Lord because He said it twice in one gospel. He said the same thing in Mark 10:11 and Luke 16:18. It is clear from His own words the Lord wants marriage to be a lifelong commitment. Yet when given the chance to address the issue with someone who had experience with it, He chose to look beyond the surface issue of divorce and instead look at the heart of the problem.

In addition to divorce, there are plenty of failed marriages where the couple continues to stay together, whether for the sake of the kids or out of a moral obligation. Are those relationships really God-honoring? If you remain legally married but you aren't committed to the marriage in your heart, is the point not being missed? Is it not similar to the issue of adultery being an issue of the heart, which Jesus discussed in Matthew 5:28 when He said, "But I tell you that anyone who looks at a woman lustfully has already committed adultery with her in his heart" (NIV)?

Our Problem with Commitment

What are the reasons people end up getting a divorce? There are things like adultery and abuse, for sure. There are a number of other things commonly mentioned for reasons why couples get divorced today, such as: "We just grew apart"; "We were in different places"; "I just don't love her anymore"; or the ultra-vague "It just didn't work out," or "It just wasn't working for me." The truth is, we don't even feel compelled to have a legitimate reason to get a divorce anymore. That's the point we as a society have reached, and it is reflected in the commonality of divorce in our country. But what's the heart of the problem?

When a couple is married, they vow to be committed to their spouse for "as long as [they] both shall live." That's easy to say on a day when everyone's happy, encouraging, great looking, and full of delicious cake. It's a different story down the road when the bills are due and there's no money, the baby is sick, cancer has struck, or my hairline has run to the back of my head. What is lacking? Is it that there wasn't some degree of love at the beginning? Is it simply that two people "grew apart"? It seems more likely we, as a culture, have a major problem with commitment.

If we look at our society today, what real evidence do we have that commitment is important? Sadly, society takes a lot of cues from the world of professional sports. In the not-too-distant past, if a player were drafted to play third base for the Phillies, he would be expected to end his career there. The concept of free agency changed that expectation. Quickly, players began to seek out the opportunity that would provide them with the biggest financial reward. They were no longer committed to the team that gave them their opportunity in the first place. Coaches are the same way, especially college football coaches. How often have you heard college coaches talk about great plans to invest in the players, build a championship program, and leave a legacy, only to see them donning a different school's colors two years later when a higher salary is waved under their noses?

The lack of commitment in our society can also be seen in our own tendency toward changing jobs. According to the Bureau of Labor Statistics, the average American changes jobs 11.3 times during his life.[34] What's more, as opposed to pro athletes or coaches, the majority of our job changes actually represent entire career changes, such as from being an engineer to being a business owner or otherwise. We are lacking the commitment or dedication to stay with a given endeavor over the long haul. When people are asked why they change jobs or careers, they give answers like: "I wanted to try something new"; "I wanted something more exciting"; "I was tired of the same old thing"; or "I just didn't want to do it anymore." Strikingly, the same sorts of reasons come up when people are asked what led them to an adulterous affair or to get a divorce. In the end, they had some need they wanted to have met, and it wasn't being met in their current relationship. They weren't committed to find it in their marriage relationship, so they looked elsewhere.

What do we see in regard to commitment in the Bible? Who are those people who remained committed, or faithful, and what was the outcome? The Bible is full of people who displayed unwavering commitment. An example who comes to mind is Noah. Think about that guy for a minute. In Genesis 6 God told him to build a giant boat, out in his front yard—an enormous boat the likes of which had never been seen. Imagine that. Noah wasn't a professional boat builder. He didn't live anywhere near a big body of water. No one had ever even seen rain, so Noah was going to build this giant boat in his yard, miles from the nearest suitable body of water. But Noah knew God wanted him to build the giant boat, and he agreed to do it. He and his family set to work on the ark. How committed was he to the project? While it is uncertain how long it took to build the ark, it was likely around one hundred years based on the timing in Genesis.

For about one hundred years Noah and his family were busy constructing this giant boat on dry ground, with no way to move it to water. What must the people around him have thought? Surely they thought he was insane! Undoubtedly they would've mocked him about the whole situation. In the midst of certain maltreatment, Noah was committed to the task he had been given, and in the end it was well worth it. Could Noah have used all of the wood to build a mansion and live in opulent comfort? Yes, and it would have likely seemed like a great idea at the time. But in the end it would've been deadly. The same is true of our commitment to our marriages.

Persevering unto Love

While a lack of commitment is a glaring problem in our society today, does it represent the root of the problem? It's easy to be committed when things are going well. It's different when hard circumstances arise. Commitment is not measured by our ability to continue during the easy times; commitment is measured by our ability to persevere during the difficult times. Perseverance is imperative to our ability to be faithful to our commitment. We don't like to think about perseverance because the word alone sounds hard, never mind the circumstance requiring our perseverance. It takes something we really shy away from—sacrifice. We don't like to make the sacrifices necessary to persevere. Those sacrifices take a million different forms, but in the end, they all point toward denying ourselves, which goes against our nature and our culture.

Our cultural mind-set is that marriage is the natural outgrowth that occurs when two people love each other. We think love comes first and gives us the wherewithal to persevere when hard times come. That may be true in part, but the Bible says something different in 2 Peter. There, Peter was writing to an unidentified group of believers about growing in their faith. In regard to growth, he wrote,

> For this very reason, make every effort to add to your faith
> goodness; and to goodness, knowledge; and to knowledge, self-
> control; and to self-control, perseverance; and to perseverance,
> godliness; and to godliness, mutual affection; and to mutual
> affection, love. (2 Peter 1:5–7 NIV)

According to Peter, love is the end product. Perseverance comes before love in this sequence. The word for love there is *agape*, indicating an unconditional, selfless love that is the type of love we are to have in our marriages. Based on Peter's words, we must persevere if we want to truly love, as love is built on perseverance.

The issues we see in marriage can be traced to a couple of things. The first issue we face in marriage is we do not want to make any real, meaningful sacrifices. We don't want to deny ourselves; that's our nature. We want it to be about us. We can say we want to make sacrifices on the front end, but that's not what the statistics show us. It's easy for us to blame someone else when the marriages fail too. How often do we hear, "He doesn't love me anymore" or "I didn't walk away; she did"? This sort of thinking points toward a second issue, which is we don't really understand what marriage is meant to be.

Biblical Roles in Marriage

In Ephesians 5 Paul deals with living out aspects of the Christian life, as individuals, as the church, and as husband and wife. He focused his discussion on the marriage relationship in Ephesians 5:22–33. This was further broken down as Paul wrote to wives in verses 22–24 and husbands in verses 25–29.

While having done a great service to improve the standing and treatment of women in our society, all of the effects of the women's liberation movement have not necessarily been good. Nowhere in the church is this more noticeable than as it pertains to the idea of the submissive wife. If you want to start a riot, say without qualification women should be submissive to their husbands. It stirs up all sorts of ill feelings. Why? It's a biblical precept we find in the writings of both Paul and Peter. Why is there such a backlash against it? Ultimately it boils down to a lack of understanding of the biblical model. To help alleviate this issue, let's flip the order around with regard to the discussion. Let's start with a discussion of what is mandated for the husband. Once we have the husband's task ironed out, maybe then we can address the actions of the wife.

In Ephesians 5, Paul writes the following to husbands:

> Husbands, love your wives, just as Christ loved the church and
> gave himself up for her to make her holy, cleansing her by the
> washing with water through the word, and to present her to

himself as a radiant church, without stain or wrinkle or any other blemish, but holy and blameless. In this same way, husbands ought to love their wives as their own bodies. He who loves his wife loves himself. After all, no one ever hated their own body, but they feed and care for their body, just as Christ does the church. (Ephesians 5:25–29 NIV)

Take a second to really process Paul's instruction. As a husband, I am to love my wife to the fullness that Christ loved the church. Christ gave up the glory of heaven to come to earth; to live a perfect life; to be treated horrifically and be crucified for the sins of everyone, including those who persecuted Him; and finally to be separated from God and die. He sacrificed everything He had for a singular purpose. Why would He do that? He did if for the church, to rescue and redeem the church to God's glory. He did it willingly. He did not count the cost but rather undertook the humiliation, pain, loneliness, and death for the sake of the church. That is what I am commanded to do as a husband.

Loving my wife as Christ loved the church is, as far as I am concerned, the most difficult commandment in the Bible. If I am honest, I don't think of myself as having that sort of ability. I would like to think I do, but if I am truthful, I cannot, at least not within my own strength. The ability to love someone to such an extent requires the active working of God within a person. The Holy Spirit works in me to bring me to the place where I can love my wife in the way I am commanded.

The husband is not only to love his wife as Christ loved the church, but he is also to work to lift her up, to glorify her. The husband is tasked to ensure the wife is to grow in faith and holiness. While spiritual growth is ultimately the task of the Holy Spirit, husbands can certainly do things to hinder the spiritual growth of their wives.

If a husband loves his wife as Christ loved the church, he is going to take care of her. He is going to supply her needs and protect her. He is going to build her up and encourage her. If a husband loves his wife in such a way, he is not going to be domineering, self-centered, unkind, crass, flippant, or unfaithful. He is going to be seeking the best for her and for her relationship with God. In short, a wife who is loved by her husband as Christ loved the church is going to be in the best possible relationship. In such a relationship, one that is spiritually, physically, and emotionally nourishing, the wife can grow and will become more like Christ. She will be fulfilled. With this sort of love, this sort of relationship, in mind, now we can turn our attention toward what Paul wrote to wives.

In Ephesians 5:22–24 Paul wrote,

Wives, submit yourselves to your own husbands as you do to the Lord. For the husband is the head of the wife as Christ is the head of the church, his body, of which he is the Savior. Now as

the church submits to Christ, so also wives should submit to their
husbands in everything.

The idea of submission is a difficult pill to swallow in our culture. We don't like to think of surrendering our own desires to someone else. Why is that? Is it not because we are afraid we will be taken advantage of? Aren't we afraid someone else—the person to whom we are supposed to submit—is going to then get a better deal out of the arrangement? Of course we are! That's how submission works in the world apart from God. But the relationship Paul is describing is something completely different. It was novel when he wrote it, and unfortunately it remains novel today, almost two thousand years later.

In the marital relationship described in Ephesians 5, the act of submitting does not really entail a sacrifice on the part of the submitting wife. She is surrendering to a husband whose sole aim in the relationship is to love her and seek the absolute best outcome for her, God's best outcome for her. In fact, the Ephesians 5 husband wants better things for his wife than she wants for herself. He will subjugate his own self-interest to the glory of the wife, which is what Christ has done for the church. In this regard, the act of submitting on the part of the wife is one of trust that her husband does have her best interests at heart and that it is his goal to love her as Christ loved the church.

The immediate rebuttal to this sort of discourse is quite often something along the lines of, "But what about husbands who don't love their wives like that ...?" As it turns out, Peter spoke to this point in 1 Peter 3:1 when he wrote, "Wives, in the same way submit yourselves to your own husbands so that, if any of them do not believe the word, they may be won over without words by the behavior of their wives" (NIV). In that particular section, he was writing to wives married to unbelieving husbands, but the principle is the same for wives whose husbands profess to be believers.

Choosing to Ignore the Warnings

This is in no way intended to reflect flippancy with the issue of wives who are in a bad marriage situation, but when the husband doesn't love his wife as Christ loved the church, that's a problem that was present at the beginning of the relationship, long before any vows were said. The issues leading to problems five or ten years down the line were present at the outset. Unfortunately, when we are dating people, our infatuation with them often drowns out our ability to be objective; that is, we don't have the ability to make good decisions because, as we saw in a previous chapter, our emotions alter our perception. We see all of the good things in the person and fail to see those things that warn of difficulties down the road.

I have specifically attempted to stay away from 1 Corinthians 13 during this discussion of marriage, but in verse 7 of that chapter Paul writes, "love hopes all things." This is true for *agape* love, but it is also largely true for *eros* love, which is really what we are dealing with in the dating situation. When we are dating, we become infatuated and emotionally charged. We are hopeful about the future, and our hope colors our fundamental ability to make objective assessments. When we lose our ability to make objective assessments of the situation, we put our marriages in jeopardy before they even begin.

We have all known someone, whether a friend, a family member, or even ourselves, who has been in an ill-advised relationship that was heading for disaster before it even got off the ground. Have you ever tried to say something to someone involved in that sort of relationship? They can't, or more to the point won't, hear you. Their perspective is totally different from yours. They don't see what you are talking about, and unfortunately they usually think you are against them. That's what infatuation does for us. This is how we end up with a 33 percent divorce rate among evangelicals. People don't go into marriages thinking they are going to end up a divorce statistic. But the fundamental problems leading to the erosion of the marriage are there in the beginning: the lack of trust, communication, honesty, commitment, respect, mutual sacrifice, and real love.

There are also those relationships we see where people have been dating for years and no real commitment has been made. While the lack of a defined commitment would usually be viewed as a major red flag to anyone else, the people in those sorts of relationships fail to recognize it. They keep waiting and hoping at some point the person they are with is going to suddenly realize they should get married and then they can live happily ever after. Maybe it's driven by the fact they have spent a large amount of time in the relationship and don't want to lose their time and emotional investment. Maybe it's because there is real love there, at least on the part of the one waiting and hoping marriage is just around the corner if they wait long enough.

These sorts of protracted dating relationships seem to end up not infrequently in the couple living together, as a concession on the part of the noncommittal party. It's sort of an "ease into the marriage" approach for some people, and one party feels like they have a commitment while the other doesn't really have to commit. Apart from the whole issue of maintaining sexual purity, cohabitation sounds like a grand ol' idea. But is it?

If we look again at the work of our friends in the Barna Group, they have studied the results of cohabitation. As you might have guessed, the rate of couples living together is increasing. For couples who live together before marriage, the ones who are "really getting to know each other," or "having a trial period to see if it's going to work out in the long haul," the likelihood of divorce increases.[35] In fact, couples who cohabit have a 46 percent greater risk of divorce than couples who do not live together before marriage.[36] Based on the available research, the whole idea of giving marriage a trial run before actually getting married hasn't really panned out. Why?

Marriage is a crucible. There is no relationship in the world that can imitate it.

The situations arising in a committed marriage cannot be replicated by living together. It's where we are tried by fire and refined into something greater. Traditionally, the wedding vows include a statement that the bride and groom will love and cherish … for better or for worse. In reality, the vow of loving and cherishing should not be difficult in the setting of "better." It's in the setting of "worse" where a husband or wife reveals his or her heart.

If you are serious about your marriage and want the best for it, the marriage relationship can really beat you up. In it, you will see your shortcomings and flaws more readily than you might in other relationships. The person to whom you are married should, theoretically, know you as well as or better than anyone, and that person's knowledge of you should only increase over time. That means the person to whom you are married will know the darkest parts of you, the things you think you hide from everybody. Those things come out in the setting of marriage. When the mortgage is due and you don't have the money; when your child is diagnosed with a life-threatening illness; when your own insecurities rear their heads; when you struggle with pornography—whatever the case—your spouse will be there and will see those character traits you wish would stay hidden.

In the end, when it comes to assessing our own dating and romantic relationships, we are prone to ignore the warning signs because they don't make us feel good; they give us some things we crave. We enjoy the pleasure infatuation brings, the attention we get from the person we are dating, and the often-misguided promise of a carefree future. Ultimately, doesn't it boil down to what we see as doing the most for us?

In Mark 10:7–8, Jesus quoted Genesis 2:24 when He said, "'For this reason a man will leave his father and mother and be united to his wife, and the two will become one flesh.' So they are no longer two, but one flesh" (NIV). In the marriage relationship, we are to mutually surrender ourselves to become one entity, inseparable. This relationship ultimately entails relinquishing our rights to be ourselves—one of the various rights we have given up to Jesus' lordship anyway. The process, the nonsexual phenomenon of becoming one, is what defines marriage. It's the self-sacrifice, the dying to self, that makes marriage what it is. If we aren't willing to surrender ourselves to that, are we really willing to be married, even if we are in a marriage relationship? If we aren't truly willing to surrender to the marriage relationship, what is the cause? Are we afraid of losing something we hold dearer than our spouse?

CHAPTER *10*
IT'S NOT ABOUT YOUR PROSPERITY

If you turn on the television or go to a local bookstore, it won't take long to find someone selling you a story that God wants you to be rich and without any sort of financial encumbrance. While God doesn't want us to be encumbered by money—that is, He doesn't want us to be enslaved to it—it is quite difficult to make a legitimate case that God wants us to have financial riches.

In our current culture, we have convinced ourselves we can go about our daily lives, blending into the world, without a legitimate self-sacrifice. It's commonplace to hear people talk about their calling. The majority of people in the American church seem to be convinced their calling is to blend into the culture, live a life of comfort, and be good citizens. It's their calling to live a life just like all of the nonbelievers to prove that believing in Jesus and having fun are not mutually exclusive. If you ask them why they aren't actively feeding the homeless, from their own pantries with their own hands, "it's not [their] calling." Why aren't they adopting orphans? They might respond with, "Our family is complete, and it's not our calling." Or perhaps it's, "We've seen too many horror stories about adoptions that have turned out poorly." How about going to India to provide care for those who are hurting? "Well, I've used all of my vacation on that trip to Disney, and going overseas is really not my calling." Well, at least that is if it isn't going overseas for an exotic vacation … Does any of this sound remotely familiar? Have you run into anyone like this?

The Comfortable Guy in the Mirror

There's a guy exactly like this who lives in my mirror. He thinks he is sincere. He's convinced he even has a biblical reason to think he should keep right in the center of his comfort zone. After all, we know from Ephesians 4 that God "gave some *to be* apostles, some prophets, some evangelists, and some pastors and teachers" (Ephesians 4:11 NKJV). This means some people aren't called to be those things, right? Also, in John 10:10, Jesus said, "I have come that they may have life, and that they may have *it* more abundantly" (NKJV). "What does Christ mean if he doesn't mean I'm supposed to have a life of opulence? Isn't that an abundant life?" asks the guy in my mirror.

There are certain people in Christian culture who have made it their goal to inform others God only wants what is good for you, moreover not only what is good, but what is *best* for you. That's all well and good to contemplate. But what does it actually mean? What is truly best for me? If you listen to those people who are pushing what has become known as the prosperity gospel, you will soon learn God wants you to be free of financial cares, which when translated in the language of prosperity means rich. They ignore the very words of Jesus in Luke 6:24 when He said, "Woe to you who are rich" (NKJV). They will tell you God wants you to experience all of the wonderful, material things the world has to offer. They will tell you that if you have enough faith in the Lord, you will be without illness or pain. In short, if you are a disciple of those selling the prosperity gospel, you will believe God only wants you to experience those things in life that bring earthly pleasure. This is very appealing to our nature. We want to experience the carefree, self-indulgent pleasure being sold. So people buy into it. Is it truly biblical? Christ certainly said He came that we "might have life more abundantly," but what did He really mean? Was He thinking about me driving a BMW when He said that?

To think that the Lord was thinking of me owning an exotic vehicle when He said "life more abundantly" is frankly ridiculous. If anyone believes that, they are delusional. Jesus was in the midst of people who were hurting, who were enslaved to an oppressive system of religion and government. He was extending to them freedom, not physical freedom from their present predicament, but rather spiritual freedom so they might truly live. Christ made it clear His kingdom was not physical but rather is metaphysical or spiritual. He did not come to be the conquering earthly King the Jews were expecting. Why would we then take the same Christ and think He would suddenly be talking about a BMW when He spoke of abundant life? Marrying the two is completely incoherent. So too, why would we think that if He truly has called us, He would call us to a life of wealth and luxury? Such a call, were it to exist, is convenient for us. We don't have to do anything differently. We don't have to make any real sacrifices. We can give our 10 percent, or even 15 percent because we really are living for God, at church and feel great about it as we drive away in leather-lined comfort. But where is the sacrifice? What is the proof we have sacrificed anything for the Lord?

I have met adherents of the prosperity gospel who like to bring up the words of Jesus in Mark 10:29–30. For completeness, here's what Jesus said in Mark 10:29–31:

> So Jesus answered and said, "Assuredly, I say to you, there is no
> one who has left house or brothers or sisters or father or mother
> or wife or children or lands, for My sake and the gospel's, who

shall not receive a hundredfold now in this time—houses and brothers and sisters and mothers and children and lands, with persecutions—and in the age to come, eternal life. But many *who are* first will be last, and the last first. (NKJV)

Interestingly enough, the prosperity proponents seem to always leave out the "with persecutions" part of verse 30 and don't mind remembering verse 31 at all. In the prosperity gospel, there is no room for persecution. There is no room for trial, tribulation, or pain. There is the misguided yet perceived abundance of the hundredfold increase in verse 30 but no sign of the promised persecution. Parsing the passage this way works out great for the proponents of prosperity.

If we are to be Christians, we must be like Christ. Jesus Christ lived a life that demonstrated sacrifice, and to follow Him means to accept, even embrace, a life of sacrifice. We are called to such a life. To live without sacrifice—something that is real, tangible sacrifice—is to live an unchristian life. When we love God and are filled with the Holy Spirit, we will be compelled to actively love others as Christ did. Such a love drives us to sacrifice for the sake of God and others. If we are not making those sacrifices, ones that we feel in some way or other, in a way that makes us uncomfortable, it is hard to make the case we are living like Christ.

Dietrich Bonhoeffer was well-versed in sacrifice. As a theologian, he was one of the greatest of the twentieth century. In *The Cost of Discipleship*, Bonhoeffer was very direct about addressing our natural inclination to remain in our comfort. He argued that the call to discipleship requires a very real, tangible risk to the would-be disciple. It is in the call to follow that the disciple is given the opportunity to believe. When Peter left his nets to follow Christ, he left every bit of security he had. This was, in that moment, a very real sacrifice. Further, as Bonhoeffer pointed out, "Peter had to leave the ship and risk his life on the sea, in order to learn both his own weakness and the almighty power of his Lord."[37] In that moment, Peter had no option. He didn't have the faith to step out, but he knew if Christ commanded him, he had no option to remain in the boat. So, Peter said, "Lord, if it is You, command me to come to You on the water," and the Lord said, "Come" (Matthew 14:28–29 NKJV). In that instant, it was a command from the Lord, and Peter was obliged to obey it. He knew he didn't have the faith to take the step. Bonhoeffer wrote, "If men imagine that they can follow Jesus without taking this step, they are deluding themselves like fanatics."[38] Later in *The Cost of Discipleship*, Bonhoeffer wrote the following:

> If our Christianity has ceased to be serious about discipleship,
> if we have watered down the gospel into emotional uplift which
> makes no costly demands and which fails to distinguish between
> natural and Christian existence, then we cannot help regarding
> the cross as an ordinary everyday calamity, as one of the trials and

tribulations of life. We have then forgotten that the cross means rejection and shame as well as suffering.[39]

The striking thing is we have a church culture wherein people want to maintain the *status quo*. Those people are convinced they are called to keep doing what they are doing. They are certain God wants them to go to work, earn a retirement, go on vacations to promote the health of their families and maintain morale, and get the car they've always wanted. They are convinced if they show up on Sunday morning and give 10 percent of their salary, then they are in good shape. They believe they have been called to this task by God—of that they have no doubt. But if we stop for a moment and think about it, what examples of this sort of call do we find in the Bible? Can you think of one place in the Bible where anyone was called by Christ to remain in his current state? Was there anyone in there to whom the Lord said, "Keep doing what you are doing. You are not responsible to minister to the needy. You are not responsible to go and make disciples. You are only responsible to make money and give a little bit of it to the cause"? I don't find anything of the sort in the Bible I read. I can readily find disciples who were beheaded, crucified, stoned, imprisoned, and beaten. I don't find those guys who got the call to live the life of convenience and luxury. Faith in Jesus Christ is not a matter of convenience.

Let's be honest about it. We have no desire to suffer. We do not want to be persecuted. We want to be comfortable. This is nothing new in the church. The disciples were the same. When the Lord predicted His suffering and crucifixion, it was Peter who attempted to rebuff Christ. In that instant, Peter revealed his own desire to be free of suffering. He did not want a crucified Lord, and Christ called his desires out as what they were—from Satan. Our own insistence that we are not called to suffer or sacrifice is a manifestation of the same spirit, one not seeking to serve the purposes of God.

Bonhoeffer again offers godly insight into this important point, as he wrote the following:

> If Jesus said to someone: "Leave all else behind and follow me; resign your profession, quit your family, your people, and the home of your fathers," then he knew that to this call there was only one answer—the answer of single-minded obedience, and that it is only to this obedience that the promise of fellowship with Jesus is given. But we should probably argue thus: "Of course we are meant to take the call of Jesus with 'absolute seriousness,' but after all the true way of obedience would be to continue all the more in our present occupations, to stay with our families, and serve him there in a spirit of true inward detachment."[40]

Bonhoeffer goes on to describe a number of ways we may try "to evade the obligation of single-minded, literal obedience."[41]

What is it that compels us to evade literal obedience? Why do we disregard the true call of Christ for some nonbiblical, have it your way sort of belief system? Isn't that really what it is? Isn't it really a nonbiblical belief system we carry around under the guise of being Christian? It certainly isn't in keeping with the teachings or life of Christ, and therefore can we call it a Christian life? In the end, have we not disregarded Christ and put Him aside? This is reminiscent of Paul's writing in Romans 1, when he wrote, "Professing to be wise, they became fools, and changed the glory of the incorruptible God into an image made like corruptible man" (Romans 1:28–29a NKJV). We have allowed our flesh to corrupt the truth. When I bend the gospel and the teachings of Jesus Christ into something that caters to my own desires and natural sensibilities, I have taken the Rock of Ages and tried to chisel Him into something convenient, something He is not.

CHAPTER 11
IT'S NOT ABOUT PRAYING FOR YOUR WILL

When you pray, "God bless America," what is it you are really praying for? To be more to the point, what is it we think the word *blessed* means? While the word, as defined, carries the meaning of *contentment, happiness, divine favor, or being sacred*, in our present culture, it seems to have come to be viewed as monetarily or defensively secure. When we pray that God would bless America, are we not really intending to pray that God would keep America from harm? In our hearts are we not really asking God to make sure our financial markets are secure and the values of our homes are maintained? Is it really that we are concerned about America, or is it we are concerned about our lifestyle in America?

Is praying for our nation wrong? No. In fact, we are instructed to pray for our leaders (1 Timothy 2:1–3). But what is at the heart of our prayers? What motivates us to pray the way we do? Certainly we should pray that God would give wisdom to our leaders. We should pray that our nation would be one led by God. However, we must realize there are times when God's will is *not* to bless a given nation. This is evident throughout the Old Testament when God gave Israel over to the hands of other nations. It was God's desire to bring Israel back to Himself. God wanted Israel to be blessed by a relationship with Him. For that to occur, He had to allow them to suffer greatly. Had God continued to prosper them, they would've continued to stray from Him. To be away from God, no matter how prosperous, is to not be blessed. So, ultimately God blessed Israel by allowing them to come under persecution and hardship.

The Blessing of Persecution

Can we in the American church really wrap our minds around how persecution and hardship could be a blessing from God, how it can be God's best for us? Someone laughs at our belief in God and we think we are being persecuted. They make fun of our Jesus shirt and we claim we are being persecuted. We don't want persecution. We don't want our prosperity to be compromised for the sake of the gospel. We would just as soon be left alone with our comfort and our beliefs, and everyone else can believe whatever they want to believe and quite literally, go to hell.

Persecution—true persecution—is viewed by other believers in other places as being a necessity. In *The Cost of Discipleship*, Dietrich Bonhoeffer wrote, "Suffering, then, is the badge of true discipleship."[42] He went on to refer to a memorandum drawn up before the Augsburg Confession that defined "the church as the community of those 'who are persecuted and martyred for the gospel's sake.'"[43] While the Western church tends to think of persecution as completely evil and of no good for us, other believers see it as a means by which their faith and relationship with the Lord are confirmed and strengthened. Those believers rest in the words of Jesus in John 15:18–19 when He said, "If the world hates you, know that it has hated Me before it hated you. If you were of the world, the world would love you as its own; but because you are not of the world, but I chose you out of the world, therefore the world hates you" (ESV). If those believers are hated, they know they are following Christ. Do we want our faith to be so real we are hated for the sake of Jesus Christ?

Brother Yun is a Chinese house-church pastor and author who wrote the following as it pertained to the church in China:

> Without opposition we will not be as effective as God wants us to be. Without persecution in China there would not have been revival, and without a crucifixion there would not have been a resurrection.[44]

Similarly, in his book *Tortured for Christ*, Richard Wurmbrand wrote the following regarding the persecution of Christians:

> It must be understood that there are no nominal, halfhearted, lukewarm Christians in Russia or China. The price Christians pay is far too great. The next point to remember is that persecution has always produced a better Christian—a witnessing Christian, a soul-winning Christian. Communist persecution has backfired and produced serious, dedicated Christians such as are rarely seen in free lands. These people cannot understand how anyone can be a Christian and not want to win every soul they meet.[45]

In his powerful and convicting book, *The Insanity of God*, Nik Ripken writes about persecuted believers in closed countries, places where being a disciple of Jesus Christ is a life-threatening proposition. He recounts stories of believers in various countries from Russia to China to the Middle East, and the faith of those believers, those *persecuted believers*, is astonishing. Later in the book, he describes an interaction with Chinese house-church believers when he asked them how they could withstand a totalitarian oppressor. In their response, the Chinese house-church members described a typical scenario between house-church believers and the security police who harass them to stop meeting. Through the course of those interactions, the police will threaten to take away their homes, and the believers' response is that the houses belong to Jesus. After a few rounds, the security police will become increasingly threatening. The usual dialogue, as described by those Chinese believers, is as follows:

> "If you keep this up, we will beat you!" the persecutors will tell them.
> "Then we will be free to trust Jesus for healing," the believers will respond.
> "And then we will put you in prison!" the police will threaten.
> By now, the believers' response is almost predictable: "Then we will be free to preach the good news of Jesus to the captives, to set them free. We will be free to plant churches in prison."
> "If you try to do that, we will kill you!" the frustrated authorities will vow.
> And, with utter consistency, the house-church believers will reply,
> "Then we will be free to go to heaven and be with Jesus forever."[46]

In America, we do not desire persecution. We do not want conflict over our faith. Even though religious persecution led to the founding principles of our nation in the first place, that seems to be lost from our consciousness. It was persecution that solidified the faith of those believers who set sail for a new land. Without their persecution, what would our country be today? But we do not want persecution. We pray against real persecution on one hand and try to magnify hurt feelings as persecution on the other, perhaps in an attempt to legitimize ourselves. However, according to Paul in Romans, we should not fear persecution and troubles but rather realize what those things work out in us. We should "rejoice in our sufferings, knowing that suffering produces endurance, and endurance produces character, and character produces hope" (Romans 5:3–4 ESV). Without sufferings, tribulations, persecutions, and difficulty, there is no reason for perseverance. The Holy Spirit wants to work these things out to make us more like Jesus. If we don't want those things worked out in us, can we say we really want to be like Jesus?

When you pray, "God bless my family," what is it you really want? Is it that you want your family to be sanctified in the sight of God? Is it that you want your family to be dedicated to the task to which God has called you, no matter the circumstances or outcome? Or is it that you want your family to be prosperous, to be acclaimed, or maybe even to be envied?

As a parent, I want my children to do well in life. I want them to use their God-given talents to the fullest of their abilities. I think it is best for them to do so. I think they are being faithful stewards of those talents and gifts when they use them to their fullest, for God's glory. But into that, if I am honest and not careful, personal gain can also creep. Surely, if my daughter is an all-star soccer player, it reflects on my wife and me. If my son is brilliant, charismatic, and well-mannered, it must certainly be because of the great parenting he has received. When we take the credit, or the glory, for God's work, and it really is all God's working in our children whether through us or someone else, that is sin. That's stealing the glory of God.

There is secondary, personal gain in the success of our children—they can bring glory, or dishonor, to us. We have all seen the parent—we'll say a dad, though that is not always the case—at a youth sporting event who is screaming at anyone he can, whether his child, the other children, other parents, the coach, the referee, or the water boy. Anyone around within earshot is getting the brunt of this guy's disappointment with all he can muster. For that parent, it's clearly not about the child enjoying the sport and learning all of the great lessons like teamwork, dedication, and sportsmanship that come with organized sports. It is readily apparent in his case it's all about him. He doesn't want to look bad. He doesn't want people to think he is less of a man because his child isn't the all-star athlete he wanted or needed to be. If his child fails to be everything the dad insists in a given athletic endeavor, then everyone will know it is the dad's fault. This is the sort of twisted thinking playing out in those sorts of relationships and scenarios in sporting venues across our nation week in and week out.

Just like we have an aversion to persecution in our nation, we have an aversion to persecution of our families. As a husband and father, I don't want my family to suffer. I don't want them to face trials, and that's wrong of me. My sinful nature is to say it is best for my family to never face trials, tribulations, or persecution. But as we just saw a few paragraphs back, that is clearly not a biblical concept. To add to the point, in James 1:2–4, we are admonished to "Consider it pure joy, my brothers, whenever you face trials of many kinds, because you know that the testing of your faith develops perseverance. Perseverance must finish its work so that you may be mature and complete, not lacking anything" (NKJV). So if I want my family to be "mature and complete" in the Lord, then I must want them to face trials. According to 2 Timothy 3:12, if I want my family to live godly in Christ Jesus, they "will be persecuted" (ESV). Notice there is no question as to if persecution will happen. There is no "may be persecuted." It is a guaranteed thing—we *will* be persecuted. This is a difficult idea to embrace, but the Bible is clear on the fact that if we are following after Christ, the world will persecute us, just as it did Him.

Nik Ripken met an amazingly faithful believer in a Muslim country, where the man's faith was a very real life-threatening situation. The man had given up nearly everything, except his family. He had been beaten nearly to death for his faith in Christ. Through the course of the interview, it was obvious this man is completely committed to Jesus Christ. Then, when asked about the involvement of his wife and children, whom he had led to the Lord, in his ministry, he became nearly enraged and demanded, "How can God ask it? Tell me! How could God ask that of my wife and children?" Even for a man of amazing faith, he did not want his family to suffer the same as he had. Then, in a question we all must answer, Nik Ripken asked the man,

> Is Jesus worth it? Is He worth your life? Is He worth the lives of your wife and children?[47]

The persecuted Christian is not focused on the temporal but rather on the eternal. The Christian in the midst of tribulation is able to look beyond the present situation to see God and His glory. It is from such a place Paul, while in a prison in Rome awaiting a possible death sentence, was able to write in Philippians.

> Not that I speak from want, for I have learned to be content in whatever circumstances I am. I know how to get along with humble means, and I also know how to live in prosperity; in any and every circumstance I have learned the secret of being filled and going hungry, both of having abundance and suffering need. (Philippians 4:11–12 NASB)

Paul was able to look beyond his present circumstances to the eternal hope of glory, and he was at peace and content. Is that our mind-set? When we are in the midst of the tumult of life's trials, are we looking to God's glory and resting in His "peace that passes all understanding"? Or are we praying God would end those temporary troubles so we can return to our regularly scheduled lives?

It was in the midst of Paul's sitting in a dark, dank prison cell, immediately following in Philippians 4:13, he wrote one of the most frequently quoted verses in the New Testament: "I can do all things through Christ who gives me strength" (NKJV). How many of us have drawn strength and encouragement from those words? What an amazing impact these words from Paul have had on the church down through the centuries! But would Paul have been in the place to hear the Spirit and write those words if he had not been in the Roman prison cell, if he was not the furthest place from Easy Street?

If we look at Matthew 6:6–13, which includes the Lord's Prayer in verses 9–13, we can learn a lot about what our attitude and approach to prayer should be. In verse 6 Jesus instructs the disciples to pray secretly, as opposed to those who pray openly in public places, seeking to gain the admiration of others for their religious dedication. He also admonishes the disciples in verse 7 to refrain from "vain repetitions" when they are praying. This is to say that just because we may pray using a lot of words does not mean we have said anything meaningful. Jesus' advice is to pray meaningfully without using excess verbiage in the hopes of impressing someone.

Think about it for a moment. Why would we try to use a lot of words to speak to God? Do we think we are going to somehow step up our intellectual or spiritual credibility with God? Does God ever say, "Oh wow, he used two verses from Psalms, one from Philippians, and the word propitiation! I really need to listen to what he's asking …"? When we look at things in that sort of manner, it reveals verbose approaches to prayer as what they really are—silly. Nevertheless, we do it all the time. We want to get our prayers "just right," as if there is some sort of reward, or as if God is going to be more inclined to hear us. Is there a way to make sure our prayers are answered in accordance with what we pray? There definitely is, but it isn't what we think.

Prayer Perspective

The Lord's Prayer is Jesus Christ's instruction on how we should pray, so let's take a closer look into it. This isn't intended to be an exhaustive, in-depth look at the prayer. There have been books written solely for that purpose. Instead, this look is to help us see what we should be doing, and how we don't do it because we are focused on something else—ourselves.

Jesus began by addressing God. He prayed, "Our Father in heaven, hallowed be your name" (Matthew 6:9 NIV). It seems straightforward enough that we should first address God, but there is more to it. We need to recognize God is our Father. He is the one who provides for us, certainly. But He is our Father in heaven. This statement puts us in the right position relative to God, that being beneath Him. He is far above us. This is a mind-set of subordination putting us in the right spirit as we approach God in prayer.

Next, God's name is lifted up or set apart; it is hallowed. God is so great and so high above us that His name alone is worthy of praise. We see this throughout the Psalms. In Jewish culture the name of God is held in such reverence it is not written out completely. The name we derive as Yahweh, the personal name for God, comes by inference from manuscripts where it is written as YHWH. Vowels were not used in ancient Hebrew writing, and the personal name of God was never spoken—it was so holy a name. It would be similar to writing Y*hw*h. Scholars believe Yahweh is likely correct, though they have no definitive proof. Today devout Jews will often write G*d so they do not write God.

Once we have put ourselves in the right frame of reference to God, realizing where and who He really is, then our perspective is changed. When we have the perspective of who God is and who we are *not*, as was the case with the prophet Isaiah in chapter 6 of Isaiah, we realize God's awesomeness and we are changed, we are "undone." When that happens, when we are brought in line with God, the things we pray for are changed. The focus is taken off of us, our needs, our wants, what we *think* we can get from the relationship, and it is put where it should be—on

God. Once our focus shifts, we will be led to pray differently. It's from the changed perspective we then can pray in accordance with the Spirit.

In Ephesians 6:18, we are admonished to "Pray in the Spirit on all occasions with all kinds of prayers and requests" (NIV). When we are praying in accordance with what God wants, two things happen: 1. We do not pray out of self-centered motivation, seeking what we may gain, and 2. We get to see our prayers answered in a positive way. When we are praying the will of God, it will come to pass, though we may not get to see it occur. God has already planned to accomplish the things for which we are praying, He just gives us the opportunity to be involved and to grow in our faith as a result of seeing our prayers come to pass.

The Most Powerful Prayer of My Life

When I was growing up, we lived with my grandmother, whom we referred to as Granz. She was a little lady, about four feet, eleven inches tall, but she had a faith you knew could move mountains if she so desired. She and my grandfather had married before he served in World War II, and her faith sustained her when he was a prisoner of war in Germany for six months. My grandfather died when I was about eight-months-old, which left my grandmother alone in her house and was the reason we moved in with her. From the time I can remember, she was always going to our little church, and she insisted I always be there as well. When I got to college, I would come home on the weekends and I would take her to get a banana split at Sonic—she loved banana splits. She was the person in the world about whom I cared the most.

After college, I moved farther away for medical school—it was August of 1998. Shortly after starting classes, Granz had a stroke and had to be in rehab for a while. After her stroke, when I would call her on the phone, she would try to be optimistic, but invariably she would say something like, "I'm so tired. I just want to go on home." I knew she wanted to go on to be with the Lord and to see Grandpa. She mentioned it often. I would always encourage her and tell her how much I loved her, but deep down, I feared losing her; I couldn't imagine it really.

Since college, I had made it my habit to spend time in prayer after running every morning. Saturday, January 23, 1999, was a beautiful morning with a crisp blue sky. I got up early and went for a run through downtown. When I returned, I sat in the floor of my dorm room and spent time praying. As I was praying, I knew in my spirit what it was God wanted me to pray, and I started to mount my argument against it. I told God I couldn't let Granz go. I loved her. I couldn't make it without her support and encouragement. Nevertheless, God kept bringing me back to the point where I should pray that Granz would pass away. In the end, I knew it was best for Granz to go on to be with the Lord. She had run a great race, and if I really loved her and wanted what was best for her, I had to let her go. So I prayed that the Lord would take Granz on home. It was an amazingly difficult thing to pray.

The next evening, Sunday night, I was at my desk studying when I felt the need to call Granz and tell her I loved her. It was about ten thirty where she was, but I called in the hopes she would still be awake. When my mom answered, I was disappointed to learn Granz had already gone to bed. My mom, hearing the disappointment in my voice, said she would wake her up since she had just gone upstairs to bed. Shortly afterward, Granz came on the other end and asked me what was wrong. I told her, "I just wanted to tell you that I love you." She told me she loved me, and we ended the conversation.

The following day, I went off to class and didn't think any more about the events of the weekend, at least not until I returned to my dorm room. When I got back to the dorm, I saw there were a large number of messages on my answering machine. The first message told the story. Granz had suffered a massive stroke that day and was in the hospital in critical condition. I flew home immediately, and when I got to the hospital, I learned the stroke was one of such magnitude as to make the situation unsalvageable.

While my family was devastated, I was at peace. In fact, paradoxically to others, I was happy. I knew God had actively worked in my life and in Granz's life. He had given me the opportunity to be involved in the story. God had blessed me with a faith-defining experience once I had given up my own selfish desires. When I prayed for something I had for so long feared and seen as a tribulation the likes of which I could not endure, my faith and knowledge of God grew beyond measure. In that tumult, there was peace in Him, but it took me giving up my desires, and a relationship that could perhaps be viewed as an idol, to come to that place.

> This is the confidence we have in approaching God: that if we ask anything according to his will, he hears us. And if we know that he hears us—whatever we ask—we know that we have what we asked of him. (1 John 5:14–15 NIV)

Praying What God Wants

How often do Christians like to claim the promise of verse 14, with the exception of the "according to His will" part? We want *carte blanche* with our prayers, don't we? We remember John 14:14 and always make certain to pray "in Jesus' name." But we ignore the context of the promise. We ignore the fact it was really more like "in Jesus' Spirit" by which we should be praying.

> Truly, truly, I say to you, he who believes in Me, the works that I do, he will do also; and greater *works* than these he will do; because I go to the Father. Whatever you ask in My name, that

will I do, so that the Father may be glorified in the Son. If you ask
Me anything in My name, I will do *it*. (John 14:12–14 NASB)

In these three verses, Christ was speaking to the disciples regarding doing great
works. He told them they too would do great works. Jesus was telling the disciples
that if they were going to cast out a demon or heal a blind man for the purpose "that
the Father may be glorified in the Son," then if they asked for it to occur, it would.
This is a completely different context from how we apply the latter portion of verse
14. We pray for more money, a new car, less hardship in our lives, or better health,
not for the glory of God or in accordance with His will. We think as long as we tack
on "in Jesus' name I pray," we should get those things for which we have prayed.
That's not what Jesus was teaching at all. When we realize our right position relative
to the greatness of God, we are not hindered by this problem. In the Lord's Prayer,
Jesus was giving us a guideline to help us to be able to truly pray, to pray effectively.
Doing so starts with seeing God as He is and worshipping Him as He is—God—as
opposed to some sort of big slot machine in the sky.

When Jesus prayed, "Your kingdom come, Your will be done on earth as it is in
heaven," He continued to correct the direction of our focus. For us to truly pray for
God's kingdom to come on earth requires we: 1. are not infatuated by the world as
it stands, and 2. want God to rule this world, and our lives as an extension, in the
same manner He does in heaven. In this prayer we are saying we are relinquishing
this world and our position in it in favor of God's kingdom.

So much of what we do is building our own little kingdoms here on earth.
We work to earn money, to buy a house and raise a family. We go to our jobs day
in and day out investing untold time and energy to "get ahead in life." Whether
it's a pastor building a bigger church; an attorney or doctor making partner; a car
salesman selling more cars; or a businessman trying to corner the market, the goal
is the same—to have greater success, which we define by more dollars, square feet,
cars, accolades, etc. The more we have, the bigger our little kingdoms become and
the more successful we *think* we are.

Is that sort of thinking and striving in line with God's kingdom coming? Or
is such striving more in line with our own kingdoms coming? What is the eternal
significance of our little kingdoms, of our prayers? Do we *really* want God's kingdom
to come to earth so everyone will truly be equal?

It is the middle of the Lord's Prayer before any petition is ever offered. At that
point, Jesus prayed, "Give us this day our daily bread." Up to this point, He had
focused on God and His desires, what God wants—that is, to be exalted and for
His kingdom to come on earth. Jesus had established that we are obligated to have
a right relationship to God and we must be seeking God's will in our prayers. Then
He turned the focus to our needs; not our wants but our needs. In this prayer, Jesus

removes us from our station in life and reminds us of who God is and that we are dependent upon Him daily.

The term *daily bread* in Matthew 6:11 is a compound word only used twice in the New Testament, once in each of the two recordings of the Lord's Prayer (Matthew 6:9–13, Luke 11:2–4). The word carries a literal meaning of *bread sufficient for the day*. By praying in such a manner for bread sufficient for the day, Jesus was foreshadowing His command in Matthew 6:34 when He said, "Therefore do not worry about tomorrow, for tomorrow will worry about its own things. Sufficient for the day *is* its own trouble" (NKJV). Jesus prayed only for bread for the day. He was not concerned with bread for tomorrow, and neither was He concerned with an abundance of bread, only what was necessary for the day.

Jesus was teaching the disciples that their prayers, and likewise our prayers, should be only for those things we need for the day. Is that how we pray? How often are we praying, or attempting to pray, in advance? If we are commanded by the Lord not to worry about tomorrow, and if we are to be praying in the Spirit, the means by which our prayers are received, then how can we be truly praying if we are praying about future things?

Jesus' prayer for daily bread is reminiscent of the words of Agur in Proverbs, which say,

> Remove falsehood and lies far from me;
> Give me neither poverty nor riches—
> Feed me with the food allotted to me;
> Lest I be full and deny *You,*
> And say, "Who *is* the Lord?"
> Or lest I be poor and steal,
> And profane the name of my God. (Proverbs 30:8–9 NKJV)

These two verses are a prayer by Agur. In his prayer, Agur prayed for an honest heart. He admitted he harbored lies and deceit and prayed for God to remove them. Then his prayer reveals a great deal of wisdom. Instead of praying for great riches, he prayed he would not be in poverty or be rich; he desired to have what was sufficient for the day. If given the opportunity, would we pray that we not be rich? Next Agur's prayer regarding food was that he would only receive the amount he needed for the day. He was only seeking sufficiency, not abundance. How often have I prayed only for sufficiency? What is our culture's approach toward sufficiency versus abundance?

The prayer of Agur gives us insight into why Jesus would pray only for bread sufficient for the day. Why did Agur pray that he would only receive sufficient food and not riches? By Agur's own words he said he prayed in such a manner, "Lest I be full and deny You, and say 'Who is the Lord?'" He was wise enough to realize that in abundance it is our nature to forget God, to turn from Him and deny His existence. Atheists contend atheism is more prevalent in affluent nations because of a greater degree of education; however, the words of Agur point toward a different reason.

Agur also knew if he was impoverished and was without food he would be prone to "steal and profane the name of my God." Ultimately, Agur's desire was to please God, and this is reflected in his prayer. Likewise, Christ was teaching the disciples to pray in a way pleasing to God. He knew that in abundance we would turn from God. This is why Jesus said in Matthew 19:23–24, "Truly I say to you, it is hard for a rich man to enter the kingdom of heaven. Again I say to you, it is easier for a camel to go through the eye of a needle, than for a rich man to enter the kingdom of God" (NASB).

In abundance, we are prone to turn from God. As a result, Jesus taught the disciples to pray for bread sufficient for the day. To maintain a right relationship with God, we need to continually remember our dependence on Him. We need to seek Him daily for our provision. This is why Jesus taught the disciples to pray this way. So why are we so obsessed with praying for abundance, successes, and riches?

In 2000 the book *The Prayer of Jabez* was published and has since sold over nine million copies. The book was based on Jabez's prayer from 1 Chronicles, which says,

> Oh, that You would bless me indeed, and enlarge my territory,
> that Your hand would be with me, and that You would keep me
> from evil, that I may not cause pain! (1 Chronicles 4:10 NKJV)

Who was Jabez? He was a guy in the midst of the lineage of Judah who is noted to have been "more honorable than his brothers." All we know about Jabez is from two verses in 1 Chronicles 4. However, it was enough for a book to be written and sell over nine million copies. The premise of the book was if people prayed the prayer of Jabez for thirty days, they would suddenly find their lives were improved. Most readers took it to mean they would be materially blessed. Why did so many copies of the book get sold? The last part of verse 10 says, "So God granted him what he requested." This prayer, or at least the book highlighting it, promised reward from reciting the prayer of a practically unknown person from thousands of years ago. How many millions of books have been sold on the prayers of Daniel or Elijah? That's a trick question because there haven't been any such books written. Though drawn directly from a verse in the Bible, what the *The Prayer of Jabez* became is not biblical. It goes against the teachings of Christ and effectively represents a "vainly repeated," magical incantation to reap material rewards.

After praying for bread sufficient for the day, Jesus moved on to praying for forgiveness of our sins. Obviously Jesus did not need to pray this. He wasn't praying this for His own sake but rather for the sake of the disciples. In this manner, He prayed, "Forgive us our debts as we forgive our debtors." I must admit I am fonder of Luke's wording in 11:4 because he wrote, "Forgive us our sins as we forgive those who sin against us" (NKJV). Either way, the point is we need to ask for forgiveness of our sins, and this should be taken to mean on a daily basis. Because this was the model prayer and because Jesus had previously set the expectation that we are to pray daily, thus the need for daily bread, the same is the case for praying for forgiveness of our sins. In truth, I need to pray for forgiveness much more than daily, and I do.

The request for God to forgive our sins is bound to a requisite stipulation. We must forgive others. Jesus taught to this point multiple times. Not only did He mention it in the prayer itself, but immediately after He finished praying, Jesus told the disciples the following:

> For if you forgive others for their transgressions, your heavenly Father will also forgive you. But if you do not forgive others, then your Father will not forgive your transgressions. (Matthew 6:14–15 NASB)

This was the first thing Jesus spoke after praying. He wanted to emphasize that forgiveness is imperative, and unless we make it our habit, we can forget about being forgiven for our failures. In Matthew 18:21–35, Jesus told the parable of the unforgiving servant. The servant, though forgiven a great amount, was unforgiving to those who owed him money. When the master found out, he ordered the servant be given over to the torturers. Jesus then said, "My heavenly Father will also do the same to you, if each of you does not forgive his brother from your heart" (Matthew 18:35 NASB).

Jesus was serious about the need for us to forgive others. When asked how many times we were to forgive someone, Jesus answered, "Seventy times seven" (Matthew 18:22). Basically Jesus was telling the disciples we should never stop forgiving someone. After all, that's what God does for us. Along the way, it seems this need for ongoing forgiveness has been forgotten. It's easy to hold on to something someone has done against me. It makes me feel like I've got some sort of power over them, some sort of spiritual superiority. This even happens with people who haven't necessarily wronged me, but I feel the need to hold it against them, as if I am somehow some watchdog for God. Have you ever noticed people who act that way? They see those who are struggling with sin, or maybe they aren't struggling because they have simply given up, and the watchdogs feel obliged to "throw the first stone." It seems to happen a lot in our society. Why? How are we really glorifying God with those sorts of behaviors? Who is it really about, because it's not about God?

The final portion of the Lord's Prayer is for God's protection upon us, as Jesus prayed, "And do not lead us into temptation, but deliver us from the evil one" (Matthew 6:13 NKJV). In this manner, Jesus finished out the prayer with a reiteration of our dependence on God. "He is [our] refuge and [our] fortress" (Psalm 91:2 NKJV). "God is [our] strength and [our] shield" (Psalm 28:7 NKJV). Jesus leaves us with this in mind. In His model prayer, Jesus established God's rightful place as God; our subordination to God; and our complete dependence on Him for all of our needs. This is how Jesus instructed us to pray because this is how He wants us to pray. How are you praying? What are you praying for?

Section II
It's Not About Your Blessings

CHAPTER 12
BLESSED ISN'T WHAT WE WANT IT TO BE

The last chapter touched on what we usually think of when we use the word *blessed*. Our concept of the word *blessed* ordinarily has some material dimension. We think of being blessed with wealth and prosperity. If I was to have you conduct a mental exercise and asked you to close your eyes and visualize someone who is "richly blessed," what is the image that comes to mind? For most of us, the image is of someone with great material possessions, someone with a lot of money. Put simply, we translate *blessing* into financial or material gain.

One place where I have seen this philosophy of blessing played out is, of all places, on license plates. In all of the states in which I have lived and visited, and I'm sure in most of the remaining states as well, I have seen registered vanity license plates with "BLESSED" on the tag. I've also seen other tags such as "THNKFUL" or "THNKGOD." Perhaps you have seen these sorts of license plates where you live. For those who aren't the fortunate one in their state to have gotten to register "BLESSED," there are also tags emblazoned with "Blessed" that can be purchased and placed on the front of the vehicle. I've seen those tags in some Christian retail stores. Interestingly, to a vehicle, I have never seen one of those "BLESSED" vanity tags on something other than a luxury car. You never see a "BLESSED" tag on something like a 1986 Ford Tempo. In fact, those vanity plates always seem to be on a Mercedes-Benz. So right there on our highways is the tangible evidence of what our culture really believes it means to be blessed.

Don't we want blessed to mean *financially loaded*? Don't we want to have all sorts of money so we can sit back and take it easy? Wouldn't it be great to own our own island with a palatial mansion? Sure, Jesus said, "Woe to you who are rich, for you have received your consolation." (Matthew 6:24 NKJV) But He must have been talking about someone else, right? He couldn't have been talking about those of us who are citizens of the richest nation in the history of the world. He couldn't have been talking about a nation whose "poverty line" for a *single-person* household is $11,670,[48] when the world's median *household* income is $9,733,[49] which is shared between a median of approximately *5 people per household.*[50] Surely Jesus wasn't talking about us as being rich, even when we think we are poor.

The Greek word *makarios* is translated as "blessed" in the New Testament and carries a fairly straightforward definition of *blessed, happy,* or *content.* It is a contentment not based on life's lot or circumstance. The word is used fifty times in forty-nine verses in the New Testament, and not one of them carries any connotation as to material blessings. So where does this idea of material blessing or wealth come from?

In the Old Testament, the Hebrew words for bless, blessed, or blessing are used a total of 492 times. The majority of the usages (292) are translated as blessed. The Hebrew word there is *barak,* which means *to bless, to adore,* or *to cause to kneel.* In the Old Testament passages using blessed, we see those directed toward the adoration of God, such as in Psalm 113:2, when the psalmist wrote, "Blessed be the name of the LORD. From this time forth and forevermore!" (NKJV). We also find those wherein God blessed chosen people, such as in the first use of the word in Genesis 1:22, "And God blessed them, saying, 'Be fruitful and multiply, and fill the waters in the seas, and let birds multiply on the earth'" (NKJV). Finally, we find those passages where someone was blessed by another person, such as when Isaac gave his blessing to Jacob instead of Esau in Genesis 27:23. The latter two examples include a pronunciation of prosperity, which is often translated to be a blessing.

We know Jacob tricked Isaac so he would receive the blessing rightfully belonging to Esau—he stole Esau's blessing. In Malachi 4, God admonished the people of Israel for having stolen from Him in the form of not bringing their full tithes and offerings. Then in 4:10, God told the people of Israel to bring the whole tithe, the tithe they were already supposed to be bringing, and God would then pour out "such blessing that there will not be room enough to receive it." These sorts of Old Testament examples are what we have in mind when we think of the words *blessed* or *blessing*— they mean prosperity, typically in our mind in a material manner.

The idea that prosperity was indicative of having received some blessing, or divine favor, from God was prevalent in Jewish society at the time of Christ. The general belief was if a person held a high status in the community or was prosperous, it meant by extension he was living a righteous life and God had blessed him accordingly. Likewise, as we see with the blind man in John 9:2, the opposite was also believed—if someone had suffered some form of calamity or untoward life event, the person or his or her parents must have brought it upon themselves through sin. Even though the Lord dispelled that system of belief in John 9:3 when He said, "*It was* neither *that* this man sinned, nor his parents; but *it was* so that the works of God might be displayed in him" (NASB), the same belief system continues unabated today.

What if we take an opportunity to stop and look at what Jesus said about those who are blessed, though? What sort of picture did Jesus paint when He talked about blessing? Does Jesus' definition of blessing resonate with what we want blessing to mean?

As an endurance athlete who first started with running, I enjoy reading books about runners or watching movies in which running plays a significant role. When I was in about first grade, the movie *Chariots of Fire*[51] came out. I didn't know anything about the movie, but I certainly was familiar with the primary musical theme. Any time I would take off running across a playground as a kid, the theme from *Chariots of Fire* would be echoing in my head. Maybe you have had that experience—I know I'm not the only one.

A few years ago, I decided I should, as a Christian and a runner, watch *Chariots of Fire*. For those who haven't seen it, it's the story of Eric Liddell, a Scotsman borne of Scottish missionary parents in China. He was educated in England and was a gifted sprinter who went on to run in the 1924 Olympics, where he ultimately won the gold medal in the four hundred–meter race. Notably, he did not compete in the hundred-meter race, the race he was highly anticipated to win, because it was run on a Sunday, and Liddell refused to run. After the Olympics, and as the movie closed, Liddell left to serve as a missionary in China. I found Eric Liddell's story compelling, and I was interested in learning more about him. So I purchased a biography about Liddell and learned not only did he go to China to serve as a missionary, but he also died in a Japanese concentration camp in China near the end of World War II.[52] While he was in the Japanese internment camp, Eric Liddell wrote *A Manual of Christian Discipleship*, which was circulated around the camp and after being effectively lost for forty years, was published in 1985 under the title of *The Disciplines of the Christian Life*. After reading Liddell's biography, I was obliged to read *The Disciplines of the Christian Life*, which was effectively a twelve-month Bible study guide he had composed.[53] As I worked through the book, which I happened to start on New Year's Day 2012, I came to Month Four, God's Moral Law. In that chapter, Liddell dealt with the Beatitudes from Matthew 5, and he did so in two and a half pages of short, thoughtful notes. It was from these thoughts on the Beatitudes that I went on to develop a Bible study for the men's group I led. The precepts of the Bible study are, I think, helpful for the discussion on what Christ meant by being blessed.

Christ's Best Sermon

When I was growing up, my dad always told me, "If something is worth doing, it's worth doing right." I have passed along this same wisdom to my kids, though I have added a little to it. I tell them, "If something is worth doing, it's worth doing right *the first time*." It's pretty obvious to me from reading Matthew's account of the Sermon on the Mount that Jesus felt the same way. We know from Matthew 4:23 that Jesus had already been preaching and teaching, but those teachings weren't recorded. The Sermon on the Mount is the first recorded sermon Jesus preached.

In Jesus' first-recorded sermon, He wasted no time warming up. He didn't tell the crowd a few jokes to get them ready. He didn't try out a few platitudes to ease everyone into a comfort zone. He got down to business immediately, and the business He got down to was revolutionary. What Christ taught in the Sermon on the Mount went completely against the religious, social, and political cultures of the time. The sermon holds some of the Lord's most frequently quoted teachings. He did it right, the first time.

Jesus began the Sermon on the Mount with a series of statements on people who are or would be *blessed*. The striking thing, as we will see as we walk through them, was that the people Christ called *blessed* were not the type of people those in the listening multitude or if we are honest, we today would refer to as *blessed*. However, Jesus had something very different in mind as He went through those beatitudes and continued into the remainder of the Sermon on the Mount. In the span of those three chapters in Matthew, Christ walked through salvation and thereafter how to live out a faithful life.

Any time Scripture is to be studied, it is important to understand the context of a given event or passage—what was going on around what is being studied. This is the case with looking at the Beatitudes, those blessings outlined in Matthew 5:3–12 in Christ's Sermon on the Mount, and entails understanding what was happening in Matthew 4:23–25. In those verses, we see Jesus had been teaching in the synagogues, preaching the gospel, and healing all kinds of sickness and disease. He instantly became renowned throughout the region. Verse 24 of chapter 4 is telling.

> Then His fame went throughout all Syria; and they brought to Him all sick people who were afflicted with various diseases and torments, and those who were demon-possessed, epileptics, and paralytics; and He healed them. (Matthew 4:24 NKJV)

The people were not coming to Jesus for His teaching and preaching. His fame did not explode because He was speaking the truths of the gospel into their lives. It exploded because of what He could do for them in a tangible, physical way. As a means of foreshadowing, this desire for personal gain is what led the crowds to shout, "Hosanna in the highest" when Christ entered Jerusalem on Palm Sunday, and then cry out, "Crucify Him" five days later; they had decided He could no longer do anything for them.

During the Sermon on the Mount Jesus had a crowd of people from all over the region following along after Him seeking to be healed. In 5:1–2 Jesus looked out over the multitudes of people, He sat down on the hillside, and His disciples came to Him. He began to teach them. It is unclear as to whom "them" refers. Some scholars believe the Sermon on the Mount represented Christ's teaching to the disciples only. It is certain He intended for His new disciples to understand what He was teaching. However, Jesus was speaking loudly enough for the whole multitude to hear Him because when He finished with the Sermon on the Mount, Matthew wrote, "The people were astonished at His teaching" (Matthew 7:28 NKJV). If He were directing the teaching only to the disciples seated immediately around Him, it is unlikely Jesus would have spoken loudly enough to be heard by the whole multitude.

The Beatitudes are comprised of eight general statements or decrees in Matthew 5:3–10, each beginning with the word *blessed*, and one specific statement to the disciples in verse 11 that also begins with the word *blessed*. The word *beatitude* originates from a Latin word meaning "perfect happiness," and this conveys a part of the Greek word *makarios*, which we covered earlier, meaning *blessed, happy,* or *content*. In the Beatitudes, Jesus described those traits that will ultimately lead to true blessing, none of which has anything to do with earthly prosperity. Further, they are far from the trite platitudes people have made them out to be in such settings as when a loved one dies and they greet you with, "Blessed are those who mourn for they shall be comforted." This was most certainly far from the Lord's mind when He spoke to the multitude that day.

What if Christ's teachings in the Beatitudes were something different than we think? What if Christ, in a manner keeping with essentially every other thing He taught, wasn't teaching about some sort of physical blessing but rather something spiritual, something eternal? What if we looked at the Beatitudes as a comment on spiritual blessings and what they would mean? With this idea swirling around in our minds, let's move forward and think about the Beatitudes as if the Lord was teaching about something eternal, which He almost always was.

The Beatitudes were laid out in a specified, intentional order as Jesus spoke about them. Each preceding virtue sets the foundation for the one that immediately follows, and each virtue is manifest only after the one before it has. It is not necessarily prescriptive, but rather it is descriptive of the natural course of our progressive spiritual growth. In fact, the Beatitudes could be viewed as Christ's explanation of how our spiritual sanctification proceeds. When viewed from that perspective, each beatitude represents a spiritual state or attitude we grow in and through as the Holy Spirit works in us. In a sense, Jesus was saying, "When you are in this spiritual state, you are blessed because it is the place from which the Holy Spirit will be working in you to bring you to true faith. You're poor in spirit? Great! Now you know your need for a Savior." If we can entertain this idea that Jesus was talking about something spiritual, then the possibility the Beatitudes are His description of sanctification will become clearer as we move through them.

The Beatitudes (Matthew 5:3–11 NKJV)

Blessed are the poor in spirit, for theirs is the kingdom of heaven.

Blessed are those who mourn, for they shall be comforted.

Blessed are the meek, for they shall inherit the earth.

Blessed are those who hunger and thirst for righteousness, for they shall be filled.

Blessed are the merciful, for they shall obtain mercy.

Blessed are the pure in heart, for they shall see God.

Blessed are the peacemakers, for they shall be called sons of God.

Blessed are those who are persecuted for righteousness' sake, for theirs is the kingdom of heaven.

Blessed are you when they revile and persecute you, and say all kinds of evil against you falsely for My sake.

Jesus developed the Beatitudes in a progressive nature, with each trait building on the one before it. When someone is poor in spirit, he is humbled spiritually. In the place of deep, spiritual humility, a person is brought to mourning for his transgressions. When a man is humbled and mourning his sinfulness, he realizes the need for a salvation beyond himself and is brought to the point of meekness or submissiveness. This allows for faith to take hold and grow. Mercy toward others then grows out of a meek and humble heart—one having realized the mercy and grace extended to it. As humility, meekness, and mercy grow through faith, purity and cleanness of heart begin to develop, leading to an inner, spiritual peace. When these fundamental spiritual changes occur in a person, true righteousness is manifested. Like Jesus, those who are truly righteous will be sought out and persecuted. This is the progressive nature that seems to underlie the Beatitudes the Lord taught the disciples and the multitude. Paul outlined a similarly progressive growth of spiritual character in Romans.

> Not only that, but we rejoice in our sufferings, knowing that suffering produces endurance, and endurance produces character, and character produces hope, and hope does not put us to shame, because God's love has been poured into our hearts through the Holy Spirit who has been given to us. (Romans 5:3–5 ESV)

A Spiritual, Social, and Political Revolution

These Beatitudes totally up-ended everything the multitudes were expecting from Jesus. They had seen Jesus' amazing powers of healing. They were following after Him to get something from Him, something physical. He stopped and sat down, and He began to teach.

During the time of Christ, there were certain things everyone wanted, certain sought-after attributes. Then, as now, people wanted happiness, whatever they thought it was. For practically all of human existence, mankind has tried to attain happiness by acquiring power, position, praise, money, and the satiety of the senses. The vast majority of the time, these desired things are gained through the oppression of others, whether by physical or other means. Certainly in the time of Christ, this was typical. The Romans oppressed the people with brute force. The Jewish leaders oppressed the people with the law. The people oppressed each other by whatever means they could find.

Then Jesus came along. He had something people wanted. He had power like they had never seen; He healed illness and disease with a word, some spit, or a touch of His hand. They wanted to tap into His power. The amazing thing about it is Jesus then went on to tell them exactly how to tap directly into that power.

As Jesus worked through the beatitudes, He methodically destroyed the idols people set up.

> *Money*: He condemned money when He said the poor, the truly humble, will have the kingdom of heaven.
>
> *Happiness*: He overturned happiness because it is those who wail and lament who will be comforted.
>
> *Pride*: He waylaid pride when He said that the meek will inherit the earth.
>
> *Satiety of the senses*: He abandoned satiety when He revealed that those who hunger and thirst for righteousness out of their own destitution will be the ones who are filled.
>
> *Position*: He deposed position when He said those who are merciful to the undesirables are those who will be shown mercy.
>
> *Spiritual superiority*: He destroyed spiritual superiority with the revelation that it is the pure in heart, not those who are enslaved by the law, who will see God.
>
> *Power*: He slew power and domineering when He said the peacemakers shall be called the sons of God.
>
> *Praise*: He eliminated personal praise because those who are persecuted for righteousness sake will receive the kingdom of heaven.

Christ totally dismantled everyone's frame of reference. Everything upon which they had focused their energies to achieve what they thought they wanted was shown to be vanity and misguided. Christ, in the span of eighty-nine words in the original Greek in Matthew 5:3–12, not only obliterated the spiritual, social, and political systems of the time, but He also revealed the way to recreate them into what they should be—in eighty-nine words! That's incredible and masterful. Given that God created languages, it makes sense He can use it with unparalleled efficiency and precision.

CHAPTER 13
BLESSED ARE THE POOR IN SPIRIT

BLESSED ARE THE POOR IN SPIRIT, FOR THEIRS IS THE KINGDOM OF HEAVEN. (MATTHEW 5:3 NKJV)

Jesus pronounced the first beatitude in Matthew 5:3. We have already looked at the Greek word *makarios*, which is here translated as *blessed*. Before we move on to look at what Christ really meant when He spoke of "the poor in spirit" and "the kingdom of heaven," consider what it is you think those phrases mean. What context comes to mind when you think of "the poor in spirit"?

If I am honest, most of the time when I think about any of the Beatitudes, I think of hearing them in some Sunday school sort of setting. I can imagine one of my Sunday school teachers from my childhood reciting the Beatitudes with the implication that I was supposed to somehow obtain all of the virtues contained in them. How was I supposed to be poor in spirit? What does that even mean? If I try to picture in my mind someone who is poor in spirit, I think of someone who is depressed or dispirited. I can say that I have heard this beatitude spoken to people who were depressed as an attempt to somehow cheer them up, as if saying, "Well, you may be depressed, but be glad because the kingdom of heaven will be yours." In reality, this sort of misinterpretation robs Christ's words of their meaning and makes us the focus of them. What's more, it does little to truly encourage or lift up the depressed person at whom our words are aimed.

To reiterate the proper context of this beatitude, it is important to realize that in Jewish culture at the time, the Pharisees were held in the highest of regards. They were by no means "poor in spirit." They were the verbose and proud public prayers Jesus described in the parable of the Pharisee and the tax collector in Luke 18:9–14. In Jewish society at the time, the Pharisees were the ones who everyone thought "had it all together." Of all people, they were considered as having a wealth of spiritual assurance in their observance of the laws, rules, and regulations. But this was not the way Jesus viewed them. With that in mind, let's consider closely Matthew 5:3.

"Poor in spirit" is a phrase derived from two Greek words, *ptōchos*, which is translated as *poor,* and *pneuma,* which is translated as *spirit. Ptōchos* has multiple meanings that culminate into a picture of a beggar who is destitute of any meaningful thing. In our present American culture, we really have nothing that aptly fits this image—even our poor are wealthy compared to the majority of other places in the world. When we think of poor in the United States, perhaps we think of those who receive governmental subsidies or whose cars or homes are in perpetual disrepair from a lack of money to maintain them. Our American financial prosperity has, to a real degree, robbed us of the context and perspective needed to understand Christ's image of what it means to be poor in Matthew 5:3 and in Luke 5.

Between my first and second years of medical school, I spent the majority of the month of July serving on a mission team in India. Up until that trip, I had never been out of the United States. I had grown up in meager economic circumstances, and I knew what it meant to be in want, at least in US terms. But going to India changed my view of what poverty is. The first full day we were there, some of our team went to a large marketplace in Delhi. There, sights and sounds that were completely alien to me inundated us, and it was somewhat overwhelming. I had been warned by one of our team members to watch out for children who were begging, because if we gave to one of them, hordes of these children would rush in on us all. As we walked along, we came to a young girl who has, for me, come to embody in my mind's eye what abject destitution is—what real poverty is.

The little girl was about eight-years-old. She was malnourished and wore tattered and dirty clothing. Her facial features were sallow, with taut skin weathered beyond her years. Her brown eyes were sunken and were deeply and eerily hollow as she gazed up at us. In her arms, she carried what must have been her infant sister. The little girl spoke a language unknown to anyone in our group, but it was obvious from her gestures that she was imploring for us to give her money so she could take care of her sister. It was then I looked closer at the infant sister and noticed the lifelessness in the body, the rigid fingers and the eyelids frozen partially open. In that instant, I saw that this eight-year-old little girl was carrying the corpse of her baby sister. She was so destitute as to carry the corpse of her infant sister, who had clearly been dead for quite some time, in the hopes that sympathy would compel people to give her money. Since that day over fifteen years ago, that little girl has represented true poverty, true destitution, to me.

With this non-US image of poverty now available for us to reference, we can move forward in understanding what it means to be poor in spirit. The enhanced definition of the Greek word *ptōchos*, in addition to the image of the little girl on the streets of Delhi, adds to the picture Jesus was painting when He used the word *poor.* However, as with so many words, whether English, Greek, or otherwise, looking at where a given word comes from will help in understanding the word in a more meaningful way. Looking at words this way is referred to as etymology, and to keep the text in this section more streamlined, I have created an appendix at the end of the book to allow readers interested in the word origins the opportunity to look at the original Greek in a little deeper detail. The word translated as *poor* in Matthew 5:3 comes from the word translated "to crouch" and is tied to the word meaning, "to be terrified." So, here the word picture becomes much greater as it points toward someone so spiritually destitute, so lacking and powerless that he cowers, terrified of his soul's insufficiency. This image harkens back to the Old Testament.

> "For all those *things* My hand has made, and all those *things* exist," says the Lord. "But on this *one* will I look: On *him who is* poor and of a contrite spirit, and who trembles at My word." (Isaiah 66:2 NKJV)

> The sacrifices of God *are* a broken spirit, a broken and a contrite heart—these, O God, You will not despise. (Psalm 51:17 NKJV)

The picture Jesus is painting is very much in keeping with His description of the tax collector in Luke 18:13, who "would not so much as raise *his* eyes to heaven, but beat his breast, saying, 'God, be merciful to me a sinner!'" (NKJV). This is Jesus' picture of the spiritually poor, and it should be ours.

The realization of spiritual destitution is not something intrinsic to mankind. We do not have the capacity to realize our bankruptcy. As humans, we look around at our family, friends, neighbors, or coworkers and compare our spiritual aptitude to theirs. We see we are not doing too badly and think everything must be okay. It is only when we come to see the greatness and holiness of God that we realize our poverty.

Isaiah immediately realized his spiritual bankruptcy when he saw the Lord seated on His throne. Isaiah cried out, "Woe *is* me, for I am undone! Because I *am* a man of unclean lips, and I dwell in the midst of a people of unclean lips; for my eyes have seen the King, The LORD of hosts" (Isaiah 6:5 NKJV). Similarly, when Peter saw the miracle Jesus worked with the nets full of fish, he fell down and said, "Go away from me Lord, for I am a sinful man!" (Luke 5:8 NASB). In these instances, both Isaiah and Peter recognized the greatness of God, and they were left seeing their spiritual bankruptcy. This is the natural response to having an encounter with God, and it prepares us for the working of the Holy Spirit in us.

Now that we have a better picture of the poor in spirit, we can work through the remainder of the verse as it regards the kingdom of heaven. In the beatitudes, the word translated *kingdom* refers to the power and authority to rule, especially regarding the territory subject to the rule of a king. This stands in stark contrast to the cowering and contrite *poor in spirit* and was undoubtedly used by Jesus to get the attention of those listening.

When Jesus spoke of heaven in Matthew 5:3, He was referring to the place above the stars where God dwells, which is what we typically think of as heaven—not a paradise-type of image as is sometimes used in other places in the Bible. The translation of position Jesus created in this verse would have been nearly unimaginable for those listening. Here Christ took those contrite sinners from the lowest place in spiritual existence, that place of complete and utter spiritual destitution, and set them in the highest possible place, God's heaven. This teaching, the first thing Jesus spoke in the Sermon on the Mount, was completely different from everything those listening had heard before. From the first sentence, the Lord completely nullified what the people thought they knew; namely, if they kept all of the laws, rules and regulations—if they lived a Pharisaical life—then they would be rewarded.

In Christ's teaching here, it is important to recognize He did not speak of the worthiness of the poor in spirit. He did not describe any efforts on their behalf. He simply stated that the kingdom of heaven would belong to the poor in spirit. Christ was not addressing how one who is poor in spirit would obtain the kingdom of heaven. Rather, He was really stating that to obtain the kingdom of heaven, one must realize his own spiritual bankruptcy, that none of us has any spiritual currency to bring to the table. Christ was setting the stage for the pathway to salvation, which here begins with the realization of spiritual destitution.

CHAPTER 14
BLESSED ARE THOSE WHO MOURN

BLESSED ARE THOSE WHO MOURN, FOR THEY SHALL BE COMFORTED.
(MATTHEW 5:4 NKJV)

In Jesus' day, there were professional mourners. If someone in your family died, you could hire a group of people who would come to your house and wail and mourn for the loss of the loved one. I'm not sure why this service was available. As with so many things in our culture, it probably started out with some rational reason, like you needed to get the body taken care of in a timely manner and couldn't spend all day in mourning so you hired someone to do the mourning to make you look like you cared about the loss of your loved one. Eventually, it developed into just a group of people who were hired for the mourning duties. These people were mentioned in Mark 5:38 when Jesus saw all of the mourners at the house of Jairus wailing over his daughter's death. We know they were hired mourners because when Jesus told them the little girl was sleeping, they ridiculed Him; had they been true mourners, it is unlikely they would have ridiculed Jesus. In fact, given the master of the house had gone to request Jesus, as a miracle worker of growing fame, come to the house, those truly in mourning would have welcomed Jesus' assessment.

How many times have you been to a funeral or witnessed someone who has sustained a life-altering situation and then heard a well-intentioned person recite Matthew 5:4 to those who are mourning? I must admit that prior to actually studying the Beatitudes in detail, in the hopes of speaking encouragement into someone's life, I have been guilty of such an act. As it turns out, I was completely misguided. Jesus had no intention of cheering us up at a funeral when He spoke the words recorded in Matthew 5:4.

The word translated as *mourn* in Matthew 5:4 means to *mourn* or to *lament*. In our current culture, using *lament* here may give a better idea of what is intended in the verse, as it carries a greater sense of grief and sorrow than is typically conveyed with the word *mourn*. The question then is what is being lamented? Certainly when we think of mourning, we think of death. The image comes to mind of a silently mourning widow dressed in black with a sullen face hidden behind a black veil. Lamenting is something different, however, as it usually carries with it the image of crying out or wailing over the event being lamented. This is what Jesus was describing when He said the word translated *mourn*. In this beatitude He was not talking about death, at least not physical death.

While the Sermon on the Mount and the Beatitudes did overturn practically every relationship in Jewish society (spiritual, personal, and political), the heart of the message was directed toward the spiritual. The lamentation in this beatitude is due to sin. Regarding this passage, St. Chrysostom, the Archbishop of Constantinople wrote,

> And here too again He designated not simply all that mourn, but all that do so for sins: since surely that other kind of mourning is forbidden, and that earnestly, which relates to anything of this life. This Paul also clearly declared, when he said, "The sorrow of the world worketh death, but godly sorrow worketh repentance unto salvation, not to be repented of." (2 Cor 7:10)[54]

This "godly sorrow that works repentance unto salvation" was exactly what Christ was speaking of as He continued His description of the progressive spiritual condition leading to salvation.

The word translated as *comforted* in Matthew 5:4 comes from a compound word carrying a number of definitions including *to comfort, console, encourage,* and *teach.* This word is built from words that paint a picture of people who are calling us, by name, to come alongside them. The words create an image of an intimate, personal relationship. With whom is the relationship? Remembering this beatitude deals with being comforted as a result of mourning over sinfulness, there is only one who can comfort us in such a situation. Those who mourn will be called by name and encouraged, not by man but by God. This is God "coming alongside" us to encourage us in our brokenness. This is not the image of an, "Oh, I'm sorry you are overcome with lamentation and grief. Have a great day!" sort of encouragement. This is something much greater. Here we find God coming alongside those who are wailing, lamenting, and grieving over their own sinfulness. He calls them by name and actively comforts them. That's the picture Jesus is painting in Matthew 5:4, and it is truly a comforting thought.

If I am honest, it has been my tendency previously to think of this beatitude as God comforting me because of some intrinsic worth of my own. Somehow, I think of myself as being worthy of being comforted by God. I have made it about me, as one deserving of God's comforting. However, there is no evidence of such a thing here in this beatitude at all. Those who are comforted have not done anything to earn God's favor. In fact, if we take the image of the poor in spirit and couple it with those who mourn, we find someone who is cowering and terrified, wailing and lamenting his sin and spiritual bankruptcy. Where is the one deserving of anything in that picture?

The depiction Jesus created is hardly the saintly image we would normally think of when we think of God wanting to comfort or console someone. Perhaps we tend to think of the widow in her mourning because it is an easier image to handle. We can see her prim and proper sitting by the graveside with her veil and dress neatly arranged. But that was not at all the image Jesus painted. Jesus was painting the image of the spiritually destitute sinner en route to eternal damnation right up until God comes alongside him to change it. To come to faith in Christ, we must first realize we have nothing of any worth to offer Him. Our best is spiritual bankruptcy. Once we realize that, which is a realization given through the Holy Spirit, the result of our understanding is frank lamentation. The place of spiritual brokenness is then preparatory for the eventual acceptance of God's grace, which culminates in faith and salvation.

CHAPTER 15
BLESSED ARE THE MEEK

BLESSED ARE THE MEEK, FOR THEY SHALL INHERIT THE EARTH.
(MATTHEW 5:5 NKJV)

Meekness is not a characteristic we usually think of as being very positive in our culture, including within the church. I suspect this stems largely from a lack of understanding of what meekness really is. Usually we think of people who are meek as being quiet, unassuming, and frankly weak. But that is not true.

In the late 1990s, I had the opportunity to hear Dr. Adrian Rogers preach. I can say, without a doubt, he was the most dynamic and captivating teacher I've ever heard. Every time I visited his church or heard him on the radio, I felt as though he was the voice of God—I always got something great from the experience. I remember once hearing one of his sermons, which I subsequently heard again on a syndicated radio program called Love Worth Finding, where Dr. Rogers talked about meekness. I do not know if he is the author of the quote, but he was the first one I ever heard say, "Meekness isn't weakness, it's strength under control." Ever since hearing that sermon, any time I think of the word *meek*, I can hear his voice echoing in my head, "It's strength under control."

We don't think of Christ, the Son of God, as being weak and powerless. But in Matthew 21:5, Jesus references Zechariah 9:9 and says of Himself, "Behold your King is coming to you, *meek*, and sitting on a donkey" (NKJV, emphasis added). So we know Christ was meek; He described Himself as such. He had all of the power of the universe, but He chose not to use it. This was "strength under control." The same is true of those who are meek, the ones about whom Jesus was speaking in this beatitude. Those meek are they who have elected to place themselves into submission. They have determined to put themselves under the control or authority of another.

In Matthew 5:5, as Jesus was speaking of the meek, He was making a direct reference to Psalm 37:11, which says, "But the meek shall inherit the earth, and shall delight themselves in the abundance of peace" (NKJV). Shortly afterward in Psalm 37:22 we see the promise that those who are blessed by the Lord shall inherit the earth. Psalm 37 encourages the righteous to rest in God and promises that God will uphold them. It is a wonderful psalm and worthwhile for the discussion of the beatitudes. Take a few minutes to read it here and consider this great psalm.

Psalm 37 (NKJV)

Do not fret because of evildoers,
> Nor be envious of the workers of iniquity.
> For they shall soon be cut down like the grass,
> And wither as the green herb.
Trust in the Lord, and do good;
> Dwell in the land, and feed on His faithfulness.
> Delight yourself also in the Lord,
> And He shall give you the desires of your heart.
Commit your way to the Lord,
> Trust also in Him,
> And He shall bring it to pass.
> He shall bring forth your righteousness as the light,
> And your justice as the noonday.
Rest in the Lord, and wait patiently for Him;
> Do not fret because of him who prospers in his way,
> Because of the man who brings wicked schemes to pass.
> Cease from anger, and forsake wrath;
> Do not fret—it only causes harm.
For evildoers shall be cut off;
> But those who wait on the Lord,
> They shall inherit the earth.
> For yet a little while and the wicked shall be no more;
> Indeed, you will look carefully for his place,
> But it shall be no more.
> But the meek shall inherit the earth,
> And shall delight themselves in the abundance of peace.
The wicked plots against the just,
> And gnashes at him with his teeth.
> The Lord laughs at him,
> For He sees that his day is coming.
> The wicked have drawn the sword
> And have bent their bow,

To cast down the poor and needy,
To slay those who are of upright conduct.
Their sword shall enter their own heart,
And their bows shall be broken.
A little that a righteous man has
Is better than the riches of many wicked.
For the arms of the wicked shall be broken,
But the Lord upholds the righteous.
The Lord knows the days of the upright,
And their inheritance shall be forever.
They shall not be ashamed in the evil time,
And in the days of famine they shall be satisfied.
But the wicked shall perish;
And the enemies of the Lord,
Like the splendor of the meadows, shall vanish.
Into smoke they shall vanish away.
The wicked borrows and does not repay,
But the righteous shows mercy and gives.
For those blessed by Him shall inherit the earth,
But those cursed by Him shall be cut off.
The steps of a good man are ordered by the Lord,
And He delights in his way.
Though he fall, he shall not be utterly cast down;
For the Lord upholds him with His hand.
I have been young, and now am old;
Yet I have not seen the righteous forsaken,
Nor his descendants begging bread.
He is ever merciful, and lends;
And his descendants are blessed.
Depart from evil, and do good;
And dwell forevermore.
For the Lord loves justice,
And does not forsake His saints;
They are preserved forever,
But the descendants of the wicked shall be cut off.
The righteous shall inherit the land,
And dwell in it forever.
The mouth of the righteous speaks wisdom,
And his tongue talks of justice.
The law of his God is in his heart;
None of his steps shall slide.

The wicked watches the righteous,
> And seeks to slay him.
> The Lord will not leave him in his hand,
> Nor condemn him when he is judged.
Wait on the Lord,
> And keep His way,
> And He shall exalt you to inherit the land;
> When the wicked are cut off, you shall see it.
> I have seen the wicked in great power,
> And spreading himself like a native green tree.
> Yet he passed away, and behold, he was no more;
> Indeed I sought him, but he could not be found.
> Mark the blameless man, and observe the upright;
> For the future of that man is peace.
> But the transgressors shall be destroyed together;
> The future of the wicked shall be cut off.
But the salvation of the righteous is from the Lord;
> He is their strength in the time of trouble.
> And the Lord shall help them and deliver them;
> He shall deliver them from the wicked,
> And save them,
> Because they trust in Him.

Psalm 37 was instructive to the righteous, especially as it regards meekness. Because meekness implies a submissive character, here the righteous are to be submissive to the prosperity of the wicked. The righteous are to wait for the Lord to reconcile the situation. The scenario presented in Psalm 37 is one that requires the utmost in meekness, and this is undoubtedly what Christ had in mind when He spoke the beatitude.

If I am honest, the thought of being completely submissive in a situation where there are evildoers who would do harm to my family and me is not something I find appealing. In fact, it's a scenario I have a very hard time imagining as far as my being meek. Meekness is not a part of who we are as Americans. It's not really a part of our cultural makeup. But that is not what Christ wants for His church. He wants us to be like the righteous in Psalm 37. To be so, we must disregard our rights to fairness—you know, the rights we no longer have anyway under Christ's Lordship, which we discussed in section I of this book. We have to trust in the Lord to take care of the situation. We have to not concern ourselves with the outcome. It is tough to consider, but this is the kind of meekness we are called to in both Psalm 37 and Matthew 5:5. Keep this meekness in mind as we move forward and look deeper into what the Lord was saying in this beatitude.

The word translated *meek* in Matthew 5:5 simply means *meekness* or *gentleness of spirit*. A notable thing about the word is what it is lacking; it lacks self-assertiveness, self-interest, or self-aggrandizement. The original Greek word is used in only two other places in the New Testament. One was the reference in Matthew 21:5 to Zechariah's prophecy of the Messiah's entry into Jerusalem, which we read earlier. The other is found in 1 Peter 3:4, where Peter speaks of "the incorruptible beauty of a *meek* and quiet spirit, which is very precious in the sight of God" (NKJV). Based on Christ's teachings, the words of David in Psalm 37, and those of Peter, it's pretty clear God values meekness greatly, even if our society does not.

The uses of the word *meek* in Matthew 21:5 and 1 Peter provide more insight into what the Lord had in mind when He spoke the beatitude in Matthew 5:5. In both situations, the meekness presented is a character trait. It is not an action to be undertaken but rather a virtue. In this regard, it is not something we can conjure up in and of ourselves. One may attempt to be meek and might appear to be meek for some period of time; however, in the long term, the attempt will fail without the working of the Holy Spirit to manifest meekness in the heart of the believer. Our sin nature looks at the promise of inheriting the earth if we are meek, and we seek to create meekness in ourselves, missing the point and making it about something we have done. Instead of it being about the power and glory of God working in us to make us meek, we make it about ourselves in the hope we will be rewarded. But that is not what Christ wants for us. He wants us to know the power of God that changes our evil hearts into something blessed. He wants His righteousness to transform us into His image, which then will result in meekness.

The verb translated as *inherit* means *to receive an allotted portion as via inheritance*. This word is derived from the word for an heir. When used in a Messianic manner, this is a person who receives his allotted possession by right of sonship. So when Christ was speaking about the meek inheriting the earth, He was describing an inheritance directed toward those who have been made heirs through sonship, which we know comes through faith in Him. This again points toward the Beatitudes as a description of the progression to faith. In essence it is the gospel according to Christ.

From a human perspective, the attainment of land, governance, or dominion is achieved through force or power. The same was true in the time of Jesus. The Romans controlled vast parts of the civilized world, including all of Israel. They did not obtain their empire through meekness. They obtained it by brute force, which is the nature of mankind. It is the nature we wrestle with as we seek to be more like Christ. It is anything but meek. Yet here Christ has clearly said that those who are meek will be given the earth—they will not have to take it. It will be handed to them. That was revolutionary then, and it remains the same today. If we rest in the faithfulness of God, He will give us the earth. Is it the present earth? The one mankind has been pillaging for millennia? Would God give us such an earth? No. Jesus is talking about the new earth to come.

One issue we face with our understanding of the Beatitudes is the timeline of the promised blessings. We think in the immediate and temporal realm. We want to inherit the earth now. We want the kingdom of heaven to be ours now. But Jesus looks at the eternal. He sees beyond our temporal situation and looks into forever. The blessings Christ promises are not necessarily to occur in this life. While we do receive spiritual blessings once we come to faith in Christ and are endowed by the Holy Spirit, the ultimate blessings will occur in heaven, which was what the Lord was speaking more specifically about in the beatitudes. This is clear from Luke's shorter recording of the Beatitudes where in 6:23 Christ says, "Be glad in that day and leap *for joy,* for behold, your reward is great in heaven. For in the same way their fathers used to treat the prophets" (NASB). Jesus was admonishing those listening that their reward was in heaven, not during this life. How often do we try to make the Beatitudes about material blessing in this life? That was never Jesus' intent.

CHAPTER 16
BLESSED ARE THOSE THAT HUNGER AND THIRST

BLESSED ARE THOSE THAT HUNGER AND THIRST FOR RIGHTEOUSNESS,
FOR THEY SHALL BE FILLED. (MATTHEW 5:6 NKJV)

In our culture, most of us have no real understanding of what it means to be truly hungry. We feel a hunger pang and say things like, "Man, I'm starving," without thinking about what we are actually saying. I have never had to beg for food on the street. I have never dug food out of a garbage dump to try to survive. To do so, I would have to be excruciatingly hungry, and sadly there are people around the world who are forced to scavenge for food in dumps and landfills every day. That is a completely different kind of hunger than what I'm experiencing when my body notifies me that I'm a few minutes late for lunch.

A few months ago, my wife and I were looking at the possibility of leaving my current position and moving twelve hundred miles away to where we had lived before we came to where we are now. There were a large number of pros and cons to staying and going. There was no clear answer. I had been praying over the situation, and enlisted a number of my close spiritual confidants to pray as well. I was getting no direction from God on what "the right decision" was. I had the very real sense that neither staying nor going would be the wrong decision. I was certain the whole process was a growth opportunity for me, but it didn't change the fact I wanted to make the right decision.

After months of considering things, weighing the options, and praying, I decided I should fast and pray. To be honest, I had never really intentionally fasted like this. I have been a devout believer in Jesus Christ for over thirty years, but I had never fasted. That's me. I'm that guy. Maybe you can relate. Anyway, I decided to go away to a nearby state park for a couple of days to fast and seek the Lord's guidance. I ended up breaking the fast at forty hours. But I didn't do it for the reason you might think.

I mentioned previously I'm an endurance athlete. I enjoy triathlons, in addition to running and cycling. I think it is fun to push myself beyond the limits I think I have. So, as I was fasting, my focus began to shift slowly from fasting to focus on God and His will to wondering how long I could go. How long could I fast? As my fast progressed, I was certain I could go for days. The spiritual retreat to commune with God and deny myself began to become something it was never intended to be. The focus shifted from God to my ability to go without food, to endure the demands of my body. For that reason, I stopped the fasting, which in a real and counterintuitive sense, was denying myself. This is an example of how we take something pure and God-centered and defile it, and make it something about ourselves—we will address this a little more in the final section of the book. Defiling something good is easy to do if we are not extremely careful. Even during my fast, I didn't come to be truly hungry. Nevertheless, God is faithful, and my fasting experience was greatly beneficial. God did not hand me an answer then, but He prepared me for when the answer came later.

Because of our lack of acquaintance with true hunger or thirst, we need to work to understand what Christ was really saying. The word translated as *hunger* in Matthew 5:6 means *to suffer need* or *be hungry*. It also means *to crave ardently* or *to seek with eager desire*. The word carries a sense of deep, painful, punishing longing, which is far greater than what we typically think of when we think of hunger. Such a longing is something much greater than can be quickly satisfied. It is the kind of painful longing that will cause one to do whatever is necessary to stop it. If I may borrow an image from Shakespeare, this deep, painful longing is the sort of experience that drove Juliet to take her own life. It is of an intensity we cannot imagine, at least as it refers to a hunger for food. This is the kind of hunger being spoken of by Jesus in this beatitude.

The word translated as *thirst* carries some of the same images as the word for hunger. It means *to suffer thirst* or *suffer from thirst*. The suffering in this word is an indispensable part of the meaning. The thirst described here is so great as to be painful—those who are thirsty eagerly long for refreshment. As with the picture for hunger, there is the sense of a longing so great as to cause painful suffering. This isn't an "I-sure-could-go-for-some-nice-cold-lemonade" sort of longing. This is a "French Foreign Legion, crawling-across-the-Sahara-on-your-belly-with-parched-and-bleeding-lips, overwhelmed-by-dehydration, praying-to-God-that-the-oasis-in-the-distance-isn't-a-mirage" kind of longing. Have you ever felt that sort of deep longing? If I am honest with myself, I can't say I have. Yet, this is the deep, aching desire Christ is describing in this beatitude.

The word translated as *righteousness* has a number of meanings but encompasses the qualities of virtue, integrity, rightness, and correctness of thinking, feeling, and acting. It is condensed into righteousness, but it is multifaceted, including not only rightness with God but also rightness in acting toward our fellow man and in our dealings with ourselves. This is a righteousness that is complete and true, as opposed to what is feigned and observed, which would be the case with the Pharisees of Jesus' day.

The final word in the Matthew 5:6 beatitude means *to fill* or *satisfy the desire of one.* The word translated as *filled* carries so much more than what we usually consider. This word was commonly used to describe the feeding of animals—that is, to fatten animals with food. The root word is *the place where grass grows and animals graze.* When you read that, what comes to mind? I immediately think of a pasture. Typically when we think of "pasture" in a biblical context, we are often led to remember Psalm 23. The imagery is one not only of satiety but also of comfort and rest. Jesus was describing a place of fulfillment, comfort, and rest for those with a deep hunger and thirst for righteousness.

In the end, the heart of this beatitude is that those who have a deep, aching, painful hunger and thirst for a right relationship with God will be filled, that is completely and utterly satisfied. Who is doing the filling? Certainly we do not fill ourselves. How are we filled then? In Ezekiel 36:27, the Lord says, "I will put My Spirit within you and cause you to walk in My statutes, and you will be careful to observe My ordinances" (NASB). When we come to faith in Christ, we are filled with the Holy Spirit who indwells us and causes us to walk in righteousness. God literally fills us with the righteousness for which we hunger and thirst. This is not something we do but something He does in us—the living God coming to dwell in us. This is salvation!

Out of the Spirit's indwelling of us, as we "walk by the Spirit" (Galatians 5:25 NASB), we will begin to bear the fruit of the Spirit, including "love, joy, peace, patience, kindness, goodness, faithfulness, gentleness, self-control" (Galatians 5:22–23 NASB), something Jesus touches on in the subsequent beatitude.

CHAPTER 17
BLESSED ARE THE MERCIFUL

BLESSED ARE THE MERCIFUL, FOR THEY SHALL OBTAIN MERCY.
(MATTHEW 5:7 NKJV)

When we have come to faith in Christ, we are filled with the Holy Spirit, who immediately sets about to make us more like Christ. As mentioned at the end of the last chapter, when we grow to be more Christlike, we manifest the fruits of the Spirit. Jesus touched on this growth here in Matthew 5:7.

What does it mean to be merciful? Sure, the simple answer is to show mercy to someone. But there is something important there. The person must be in a position as to require mercy to be extended. If I steal something from you, you have the opportunity to extend mercy to me by not prosecuting me for the crime. You are withholding a punishment I deserve. If I have done you no wrong, you cannot extend mercy to me in this regard. Likewise, if I am financially destitute, you may show me mercy by giving me food, clothing, or some other material good. However, if I have no need for such things, you cannot extend such mercies to me. I cannot extend physical mercy on those who do not need it. I cannot extend emotional mercy to those who do not need it. I cannot extend spiritual mercy to those who do not need it. This is an important concept with regard to what mercy really means and will be covered in greater detail in the final section of the book. For now, we must recognize that mercy is given to those who are in a position to receive it. I have received mercy because I needed it, not because I deserved it.

The origins of the word translated as *merciful* address this requirement of a position to receive mercy. Ultimately, the word for mercy embodies kindness or goodwill toward the miserable and the afflicted, joined with a desire to help them. So, what Jesus was really describing in the word *merciful* is the bestowing of kindness, goodwill, and ultimately love to *the miserable, the afflicted, and those everyone else has deemed as undesirable or worthless*; these are the very "least of these" the Lord spoke of in Matthew 25:40. Is this the sort of mercy we want to bestow? Would we not rather bestow mercy on those we love, those from whom we might get something in return?

The mercifulness the Lord was describing, which can also be called kindness, is a fruit of the Spirit, as we discussed in the previous chapter. This is not something innate in our character but rather grows out of God's active working in us to make us more like Jesus. He works in us to bring about mercy, which then translates into our being merciful to "the least of these," as well as others. In Ephesians 2:10 Paul says, "For we are His workmanship, created in Christ Jesus for good works, which God prepared beforehand, that we should walk in them" (ESV). God has laid out good works, and we walk in them. These are not good works that we ourselves have chosen to create, but rather God determined their orchestration in advance. Our being merciful is not something we have produced but rather the Holy Spirit has produced in us. In this regard, we have no claim to any goodness in and of ourselves for those good works, no matter how much we would rather it be otherwise.

In this beatitude Jesus foreshadowed a precept He would discuss a little later in the Sermon on the Mount. In Matthew 5:46, Jesus said, "For if you love those who love you, what reward have you? Do not even the tax collectors do the same?" (NKJV). If we take this verse and replace "love" with the phrase "are merciful to," then we get a clearer insight into what the Lord was saying when He said, "Blessed are the merciful."

> For if you *are merciful to* those who are *merciful to* you, what
> reward have you? Do not the tax collectors do the same?

Being merciful in Matthew 5:7 isn't about showing mercy to those who will reciprocate mercy. It isn't about showing mercy to those from whom we will get something. It's about showing mercy to the ones who no one else thinks are worthy of mercy. It's about showing mercy to those who would spit in your face. It's about showing mercy to those who would seek to do you harm and even kill you. It's about the kind of mercy that would allow you to look down from a cross and say of those who nailed you there, "Father, forgive them, for they do not know what they do" (Luke 23:34 ESV). Do you possess that sort of mercy?

The second half of this beatitude is the promise that the merciful will receive mercy. The Greek here is probably better rendered as "will experience mercy." From whom will the merciful receive mercy? In Ephesians 2:4–5 Paul reminds us that God "is rich in mercy," and has "made us alive together with Christ" (NKJV). We have received mercy from God Himself. The paradox in this beatitude is that those who are merciful, those who have received the Holy Spirit and have therefore manifested the fruit that is mercy, have already received mercy. In a real sense, the beatitude could be, "Blessed are the merciful, for they have already received mercy."

Do you show the kind of mercy Jesus is talking about, the kind that is merciful from the cross? What keeps us from having that sort of mercifulness? Does our pride keep us from seeing ourselves and remembering the mercy we have received when we look on those who are in desperate need of mercy? Are we like the wicked servant in Matthew 18:32 who was shown great mercy only to fail to show mercy to someone else? Mercy is of utmost importance to God, as in Micah 6:8 He told Israel what it was He wanted from them.

> And what does the Lord require of you but to do justly, to love mercy, and to walk humbly with your God. (NKJV)

CHAPTER 18
BLESSED ARE THE PURE IN HEART

BLESSED ARE THE PURE IN HEART, FOR THEY SHALL SEE GOD.
(MATTHEW 5:8 NKJV)

When you think of purity, what comes to mind? When you think of something that is pure, is there a mental image you think of? Do you think of yourself as pure?

When I was young, there was a certain brand of bath soap advertised as being 99.44 percent pure. Pure what? Pure soap? What is pure soap? I'm not sure what they really meant by that advertising campaign; perhaps that's why it was abandoned. However, for those of us who are familiar with that marketing campaign, our definitions of what it means to be pure may have been corrupted. The purity of that particular soap brand was touted as being 99.44 percent, which seems pretty pure. But that is the point where we have an error in our thinking. Something is either pure or it isn't. There's no "pretty close" when it comes to purity. This is an important concept when we consider the beatitude in Matthew 5:8. When God is talking about pure, He means *pure*. He doesn't mean 99.44 percent. He doesn't mean 99.9999999 percent. He means 100 percent.

Perhaps a way to really think about what it means to be pure is by picturing a beach. When I think of beaches, I don't think of those along the Jersey shoreline that are brown, muddy, and rocky—I think of the Florida Gulf coast. I think of large swaths of fine, powder-white sand highlighted against the warm, emerald-blue waters of the Gulf of Mexico. Now, think of that beach stretching out into the distance, let's say for twenty miles. Those twenty miles of beach represent incalculable grains of sand. Purity, as we are discussing it, means the beach is composed entirely of white grains of sand. If there is even a single gray, brown, or black grain of sand in that twenty-mile stretch, the beach is impure. That's the kind of purity God talks about when He talks about purity. If that is daunting, it should be, at least if you want to attain purity by your own efforts and merit.

The word translated as *pure* in the beatitude in Matthew 5:8 is multifaceted and carries not only the meaning of purity in the physical sense, as would occur in the setting of purification by fire, but also purity with regard to religious and ethical standards. Purity in the religious or Levitical sense meant a given item would impart no uncleanness. Purity in the ethical sense, which is really where Jesus' usage was directed, meant a person was *free from sin and guilt, blameless and innocent*, and *unstained with the guilt of anything*. Ultimately, the purity in this verse carries a sense of holiness.

There is an interesting dimension to consider in the word for pure. As we just saw, part of the word carries the meaning of someone being free from sin *and* guilt. While guilt can refer to conduct involved in committing a crime, in this case it is more consistent with a sense of remorse or the responsibility of having committed a sin. Otherwise, if it is the act of sinning itself, the definition is repetitious. From this there is the implication then that when we carry a sense of guilt, even after we have confessed our sins, we are not pure. We must, as God does, forget about it, leave it behind, and move on. So often it seems we as Christians have a desire to hang onto the guilt as if it somehow enhances our piety, but doing so is not in keeping with the nature and character of purity here. It is a freedom from all that could possibly be construed as related to sin. Again, it is the sense of holiness.

When Jesus spoke about the *heart* in this beatitude, the word used not only referred to the organ at the center of the circulatory system, but it also was held to be *the center and seat of physical and spiritual life*. In this beatitude, Christ's discussion is a spiritual one, and so we can focus in more on the spiritual dimension of the word. This center and seat of spiritual life encompassed other facets of human consciousness; it included the soul, mind, intelligence, and passions. In effect, the heart was what made a person a person. Our "heart" drives our actions. Solomon gave the following advice to his son when he was writing Proverbs: "Watch over your heart with all diligence, for from it *flow* the springs of life" (Proverbs 4:23 NASB). All of the issues we face in life come out of our hearts. If our hearts are impure, we will have to deal with the impurity as it manifests in our lives.

A person who is "pure in heart" is someone whose heart and soul—everything about him or her—is without any trace of corruption, sin or even guilt for past offenses now forgiven. This purity of heart and soul is exactly what David was pleading for God to create in him in Psalm 51:10 when he said, "Create in me a clean heart, O God, and renew a steadfast spirit within me" (NASB). In his psalm, David cried out to God after he realized the gravity of all he had done with regard to Bathsheba. To enhance the discussion, let's recap David's utter moral meltdown recorded in 2 Samuel 11.

David was the king of Israel, and he had sent the army of Israel out to wage war on some surrounding peoples; apparently every spring kings would send out their armies for the sake of destroying neighboring nations—a more aggressive form of spring cleaning, perhaps. One night David was on the roof of his palace and looked out and saw a beautiful woman, Bathsheba, bathing on the roof of her house. He was overcome with lust and sent for her to come to the palace because he wanted to sleep with her, even though he knew she was the wife of Uriah the Hittite, one of the members of the army off fighting his spring cleaning wars.

Bathsheba became pregnant and David wanted to cover up the whole situation, so he attempted to have Uriah sleep with Bathsheba when he returned to Jerusalem with the army. Unfortunately for David, Uriah was an upstanding man and believed it would be wrong for him to go home to his wife when, "The ark and Israel and Judah are staying in tents, and my commander Joab and my lord's men are camped in the open country" (2 Samuel 11:11 NKJV). When David's plan did not work, he tried to get Uriah drunk and make him go home in the hopes he would sleep with Bathsheba, but Uriah again returned to his mat with the other soldiers. Uriah was an honorable and upstanding man, which contrasts sharply against the actions of David. With his schemes having failed, David ordered the commander of the army to "Put Uriah out in front where the fighting is fiercest. Then withdraw from him so he will be struck down and die" (2 Samuel 11:15 NKJV), which is exactly what happened.

Based on 2 Samuel, there is no indication that David gave much thought to what he had done until he was confronted by the prophet Nathan. As soon as David realized his sin, he was penitent. He turned to his harp and wrote what is now Psalm 51. In that psalm, David pleaded for God's mercy and asked that God would, "Wash away all [his] iniquity and cleanse [him] from [his] sin" (Psalm 51:2 NKJV). Later, in verse 10, David asked that God would *create* a clean heart in him. David saw his heart as totally corrupt and beyond recovery, so he asked God to make an entirely new heart in him. The Hebrew word translated as *clean* in Psalm 51:10 can also be translated as *pure* and carries the same dimensions as the word translated as pure in Matthew 5:8. In a real sense, in Psalm 51:10, David cried out for God to make him someone who was "pure in heart," as Jesus was describing in the Matthew 5:8 beatitude.

The word translated as *see* in Matthew 5:8 means *to look at* or *to behold*, but can also mean *to allow oneself to be seen* or *to appear*. In a real sense, we can only see God if He allows us to do so, and as such within the context of this beatitude, the idea of God allowing Himself to be seen may help in our understanding of what Christ was conveying.

In this beatitude, Christ was saying that those with a completely pure and undefiled heart would be allowed to see God. How can we, as defiled humans with corrupt hearts, obtain a pure heart? We cannot make impure hearts pure like the beach with 100 percent white sand grains. Through our own efforts, it is impossible to be pure, which is where grace comes in, and we will discuss it more in section III. God wants to create pure hearts in us, which occurs through the process Jesus has described up to this point in the Beatitudes. It happens "by the washing of regeneration and renewing by the Holy Spirit" (Titus 3:5 NASB) in our hearts so they are made 100 percent pure before God. It is through this work of the Holy Spirit that we are made more Christlike, or sanctified.

The Holy Spirit is continually at work in us to transform us into the image of the Lord (2 Corinthians 3:18). This means that even though we have been made pure in the ceremonial sense or from the perspective of the Law, meaning God sees us as pure, there are still impurities the Spirit is working out of us. God sees the end product, the purity of Christ, and it's the Holy Spirit's job to get us there.

This is to say that we are not there yet. One way to know we aren't there yet is to really look at the things we say. In Matthew 15:18, Jesus said, "the things that proceed out of the mouth come from the heart, and those defile the man" (NASB). This verse carries more depth than we might at first think. Christ here said that those things we say give us insight into what we are harboring in our hearts. Do we gossip? Do we make unkind comments about others? Do we say things in jest or flippantly? James wrote, "If anyone does not stumble in what he says, he is a perfect man" (James 3:2b ESV). So unless you are perfect, which is something I highly doubt, you say things you should not say, and this is a reflection of your heart. The second component to Matthew 15:18 is that what we say defiles us. In this regard, we may say something that really is in jest or without harboring the meaning of it in our hearts, and this action corrupts us. How imperative then is it to watch what we say! Speaking is a two-way street revealing our corruption and also corrupting us.

CHAPTER 19
BLESSED ARE THE PEACEMAKERS

BLESSED ARE THE PEACEMAKERS, FOR THEY SHALL BE CALLED THE SONS OF GOD. (MATTHEW 5:9 NKJV)

The image of a peacemaker must have been somewhat foreign to the multitude listening to Jesus' Sermon on the Mount. The majority of the Old Testament outlines how the children of Israel had been heavily involved in wars and periods of time that would in no way be described as peaceful. Even during the time they were in Egypt, the Israelites were under the harsh rule of others, which again would not fall into what would typically be thought of as a peaceful situation. What's more, at the time of Christ, the Jews were under Roman occupation and rule. Peace was not a concept with which they had a real experience. An important question to consider is, do we?

In Matthew 5:9 Jesus used a word found nowhere else in the New Testament—peacemaker. When we think of peacemakers, we may think of someone who serves as an ambassador to work out treaties between warring nations. But Jesus was describing more than someone who serves as an emissary to promote the cessation of fighting. *Peacemaker* in Matthew 5:9 is a compound word ultimately describing someone who authors or creates a state of tranquility, and to some extent contentment, with and within all relationships. This idea of true peace, of harmony between different groups, was a foreign concept in Jesus' day, and in truth it remains so today.

As we have seen previously, peace is a fruit of the Spirit. So here, Jesus continued to describe the working of the Holy Spirit as we move through the beatitudes. Once we are "justified by faith, we have peace with God through our Lord Jesus Christ" (Romans 5:1 ESV). In fact, in Ephesians 2:14 we are told Christ "Himself is our peace." In 2 Timothy 2:22, Paul encouraged Timothy to pursue, among other things, "peace, along with those who call on the Lord out of a pure heart" (NIV). There, the words of Paul to Timothy tie this beatitude regarding peacemakers directly to the one that preceded it regarding those with a pure heart. Is this coincidental? Undoubtedly it is not. A pure heart created by the Holy Spirit will manifest peace in the heart of the believer, and the believer will become a peacemaker.

To be peacemakers, we must first know what peace is. We cannot create something we know nothing about. We have already discussed anxiety as a real issue in our culture. To be at peace, we have to rest solely in the fact that we are God's and whatever our story is, it is about His glory, not us and ours. When we take ourselves out of the equation and rest in Him, we begin to know peace. His peace will manifest itself in our lives and will compel us to share it with others. This will lead us to make peace.

Jesus said those who author peace—the peacemakers—would be called sons of God. Here, a son of God is one God has esteemed as a son, someone who has been born again (Luke 20:36). It is God who calls the peacemakers sons of God. He is the author of the call. He decides who receives the call to make peace in His name because it's all about His glory. However, a true peacemaker is a foreign concept to the natural order of things. It is not our nature to author harmony between anyone, except when it benefits us. When the world sees someone who is truly a peacemaker in the manner Christ described, it is so alien as to be obviously from God, and those who manifest such character would be called sons of God.

CHAPTER 20
BLESSED ARE THOSE WHO ARE PERSECUTED

BLESSED ARE THOSE WHO ARE PERSECUTED FOR RIGHTEOUSNESS SAKE,

FOR THEIRS IS THE KINGDOM OF HEAVEN. (MATTHEW 5:10 NKJV)

We previously discussed persecution in the chapter on praying. We do not like to think about persecution. We certainly do not think of being persecuted as a desirable thing. It is not a comfortable or peaceful thought, which makes this beatitude in Matthew 5:10 striking when it follows immediately after the one regarding peacemakers.

The Lord has told us we will be persecuted. It is a given that if we follow Him, persecution will happen. In John 15:20, He told the disciples, "If they persecuted Me, they will persecute you also" (NIV). It should be expected. Persecution is evidence of a Christlike life; however, we do not really want it, do we?

This beatitude comes at the end of the list of eight general Beatitudes, those not addressed specifically to the disciples. As we have seen, the Beatitudes can be seen as Jesus' condensation of the gospel and the resultant outgrowth occurring as a consequence of faith—sanctification. This last beatitude then expresses what is to be expected when all of the other Beatitudes have been realized in the life of a believer. At that point, the world will realize a believer is a follower of Christ and as a result, the world will hate the believer (John 15:19). Essentially, the point hidden here is if we are not being persecuted, we are not enough like Christ for the world to realize we belong to Him.

The word translated as *persecuted* has meanings pointing toward a root in the idea of running. The image in the word is to inflict persecution upon someone to the point he would want to flee. Have I ever been persecuted like this? I have, but it had nothing to do with righteousness. It had to do with being picked on because, as a kid, I was obese. I definitely know what it's like to be singled out and harassed to the point that I would want to run away from the harassment; I did run away from the persecution any chance I got. But that's not what this beatitude is about. Similarly, I can read the words of Paul in 2 Corinthians 4:8–9 and find great encouragement when he says, "We are hard pressed on every side, but not crushed; perplexed, but not in despair; persecuted, but not abandoned; struck down, but not destroyed" (NIV).

I can find encouragement in that verse right up until I realize I do not really know what Paul is talking about. For the sake of my faith, I have never been struck down or persecuted. For the sake of my faith, I have not really been hard-pressed from every angle, and I have not been perplexed to any significant degree. These words from Paul describe what he had been going through and what he had endured.

How often have I been in some circumstance, whether of my own making or otherwise, and invoked these words about being hard pressed? What are the situations in which these words are invoked in today's church? I've heard them invoked because someone was in the hospital as a result of crashing their car … while speeding. I've heard them invoked because someone who smoked for forty years finally developed cancer and was in the hospital in bad shape. There are a host of other similar circumstances where these verses and others addressing persecution have been recited. But Jesus was not talking specifically about any of those sorts of situations, and the way we so often invoke the persecution role cheapens the real sacrifices and persecution of those Christians, past and present, who have been and are being truly persecuted.

This beatitude is about the faithfulness of God to uphold believers who are persecuted for their righteousness. That is not to say God is not faithful in those other situations—He is always faithful. But pulling the persecution card for anything and everything that does not go our way is illegitimate, especially when we have played a major role in the outcome. When we do that, we are making it about us and not about God.

Jesus brings the Beatitudes full circle with Matthew 5:10. He ends with the promise of "for theirs is the kingdom of heaven," which is where He began in Matthew 5:3 when He spoke about the poor in spirit. The image we worked through for the poor in spirit is one of someone so spiritually bankrupt as to be cowering, terrified in his own spiritual destitution. Similarly, one who is persecuted, at least in a physical sense, may end up in a state of cowering and fear. In this regard, the two are brought together, giving the Beatitudes a sense of a cyclical growth process.

CHAPTER 21
BLESSED ARE YOU THE DISCIPLES

BLESSED ARE YOU WHEN THEY REVILE AND PERSECUTE YOU, AND SAY ALL KINDS OF EVIL AGAINST YOU FALSELY FOR MY SAKE. (MATTHEW 5:11 NKJV)

In the first eight beatitudes, Jesus did not address specifically any particular group in the multitude. Those first eight outlined in Matthew 5:3–10 were general to everyone. However, with the beatitude in Matthew 5:11, Jesus made a shift from a general beatitude regarding "those" who were nonspecific believers to a specific beatitude directed toward the disciples. In Matthew 5:11–12, Jesus used "you," as He was directing His comments to the disciples. He did not say *"if* they revile and persecute you," He said, "when." He was springing straight off of Matthew 5:10 to tell the disciples directly they would suffer persecution. Jesus told the disciples they should consider it a blessing when people reviled or insulted them; when people persecuted them; and when people said every possible kind of evil words against them. Is that our attitude? Is that the attitude of our churches?

Jesus concluded this beatitude with the phrase "for My sake." It is important that the persecution Christ was promising would be persecution suffered because of or on account of the disciples' belief and relationship with Christ. The disciples were to expect persecution as a result of their knowing Him and living their life for Him. This is again consistent with His words in John 15:20—they were to expect to be persecuted. What's more, they were to consider it a blessing.

Do you consider it a blessing when people lie about you and say all sorts of evil things against you because you believe in Jesus Christ? Or have you ever had that happen? Jesus wasn't talking about once or twice; He was talking about an ongoing persecution. He was not talking about someone making fun of your shirt or your Christian music. He was talking about legitimate, unending persecution. Why haven't we had that happen, and is it a good thing we haven't had it happen?

We live in a completely different culture and social arena than the disciples did. It seems today no one can say anything without someone figuring out a way to have his or her feelings hurt. So much of what is or is not said in our society is driven by political correctness. Where is political correctness in Matthew 5:11? In fact, this beatitude seems to say to us that we should not want people to be politically correct with regard to how they address our faith in Jesus Christ. Is this beatitude the antithesis of political correctness? Jesus said it is a blessed scenario when others tell evil lies about us and persecute and insult us for our faith in Him. If we agree with Jesus, why are we afraid of this occurring in our lives, or why do we complain about it when it does? Should we not celebrate it and thank God for His working in our lives in such a way as to make us the recipients of true persecution? Should we not be thankful we resemble Christ enough to evoke such a response from the world? If we disagree with Jesus here, then do "we have the mind of Christ" Paul spoke of in 1 Corinthians 2:16?

In 1 Peter 4:14, Peter wrote, "If you are reproached for the name of Christ, blessed *are you,* for the Spirit of glory and of God rests upon you. On their part He is blasphemed, but on your part He is glorified" (NKJV). In the end, it is to God's honor and glory when we are treated in the manner Jesus describes in Matthew 5:11. If we don't want to suffer persecution and slandering, are we not again stealing from God's glory?.

CHAPTER 22
REJOICE AND BE GLAD WHEN YOU ARE PERSECUTED

REJOICE AND BE EXCEEDINGLY GLAD, FOR GREAT IS YOUR REWARD IN HEAVEN, FOR SO THEY PERSECUTED THE PROPHETS WHO WERE BEFORE YOU. (MATTHEW 5:12 NKJV)

Though it is not a beatitude, Matthew 5:12 concludes the Beatitudes portion of Jesus' Sermon on the Mount, and as in verse 11, it is directed specifically to the disciples. This is the only verse in the Beatitudes not beginning with or even containing the word *blessed*; however, it is of utmost importance in the consideration of what Jesus was conveying in the Beatitudes as He described what it means to be truly blessed. This is a direct continuation of His words in Matthew 5:11, and all of the same points regarding that verse apply here.

Continuing with the premise that we should consider it a good thing when we are persecuted and slandered for our faith, it is important to notice Christ's tone in this verse. He began by saying, "Rejoice and be exceedingly glad." There is a celebratory quality to His instruction. In fact, this ultimately is a command from Jesus that we should rejoice and be glad when we are persecuted for His sake. He directed us to consider the eternal consequences of our own persecution when He said, "great is your reward in heaven." As with the entirety of the Beatitudes, the blessings the Lord was describing are eternal, spiritual blessings. Any persecution or unpleasant circumstances we may experience in this life should be disregarded as temporary and counted as loss when compared to our eternal reward in heaven. The apostle Paul spoke to this point in Philippians.

> More than that, I count all things to be loss in view of the surpassing value of knowing Christ Jesus my Lord, for whom I

have suffered the loss of all things, and count them but rubbish so that I may gain Christ, and may be found in Him, not having a righteousness of my own derived from *the* Law, but that which is through faith in Christ, the righteousness which *comes* from God on the basis of faith, that I may know Him and the power of His resurrection and the fellowship of His sufferings, being conformed to His death; in order that I may attain to the resurrection from the dead. (Philippians 3:8–11 NASB)

Jesus was admonishing His disciples to remember any earthly persecution, reviling, or slandering would be temporary and of incomparable insignificance in the light of God's eternal glory. In the midst of persecution, remembering the reality of our salvation and eternity can be difficult, which is likely why Christ reiterated it to the disciples. To this end, we would benefit from consistent meditation on His words in Matthew 5:11–12.

SECTION III
MAKING IT NOT ABOUT US

CHAPTER 23
A BEAUTIFUL INTERPLAY

The first section of this book was aimed at revealing that we all have areas in our lives where we put God second ... or third ... or last—we all are proud idolaters. When no one is around, if we stop to admit it, we aren't as holy as we like to think. We don't have a leg to stand on when it comes to our own righteousness. Our righteousness, that is anything we generate within ourselves as a means of hoping to satisfy God's requirement for righteousness, is filth in the sight of God. That's what the first section of this book is meant to help us remember—even when we think we have it right, we may well have it wrong.

The reality of our sinfulness can be overwhelming if we don't understand the gospel of Christ. Jesus spoke to this in Matthew 13 when He told the parable of the sower. In that parable, as in the case of anyone hearing the gospel, there are four possible outcomes when we are faced with the truth of the gospel of Jesus Christ: we turn from it or reject it outright because we cannot grasp any portion of it, or because we realize we cannot, in and of ourselves, achieve the righteousness God requires and our pride will not accept that; we accept it superficially but do not let it become real in our lives so that at the first sign of uncertainty we abandon it; we accept it and it begins to manifest in our lives up until the point it conflicts with things we hold more dearly; or we accept it and are completely changed by it—the gospel of Jesus Christ becomes who we are. These are the options Jesus outlines for those hearing the gospel.

To look at all of the requirements of the Law and think that, according to the words of Jesus in Matthew 5:20, our righteousness must exceed that of the Pharisees if we want to enter the kingdom of heaven is a scary proposition. It's an impossibly daunting task. But guess what? That's the whole point of it. We cannot meet those requirements by ourselves. We don't have the ability, even on our best days, to attain to what is required for righteousness before God. We all fail and fall short. That can be overwhelming.

I have mentioned earlier in the book that I grew up going to church. I started when I was a week old and was there nearly every time the doors were open. I'm thankful I had that experience. I'm thankful people poured into me as I was growing up so I would know who God is and all the stories of the Christian faith. I knew all of the stuff I was supposed to know, or so I thought. I was young when I came to the understanding I was a sinner and Jesus died for me. I didn't want to go to hell and Jesus was the way to go to heaven. It seemed like a pretty cut-and-dried choice to me. So I prayed to become a Christian. I still remember the scene in the living room at our house, saying the prayer to "ask Jesus into my heart." I knew what it meant, but I didn't really know what it meant. You know what I mean?

Growing up, I remember learning the dos and don'ts. I remember learning the importance of having a relationship with Jesus and how I was to follow Him. This was all happening in my life about the same time Nancy Reagan was telling all of us kids to "Just Say No." There were a lot of discussions and cautionary tales that were framed in what I now see as legalism. Was I a believer in Jesus Christ? Yes. Did I know the full implication of the gospel of Jesus Christ? No. Based on what I see in our "Christian culture," a lot of people don't. I knew I was forgiven, in a sense. But I didn't really know what that meant. There was always this underlying mentality that I had to live up to some sort of standard, that I had to check a box for praying and reading the Bible and singing "Just As I Am"[55] at the end of every church service. Where did it come from? Did someone specifically tell me that? No. Did God tell me that? No. In some sense, I watched others and then I told myself that was the way it was supposed to be. I didn't realize it, but I was being good and trying to do all of the right things to make sure God was happy with me. Making the checklist of works came to me naturally, as it does to all of us. We all want to have some contribution, some meaningful part, in our own salvation. We want it to be about us and our accomplishment, our overcoming of our own sin.

Looking back on my youth, I often get overwhelmed at my lack of understanding of the gospel. There was something I missed out on completely. The thing that I missed out on is so fundamental, so foundational to the gospel that without getting that part, you really cannot say you understand the gospel at all. What part was it? Brace yourself ... it was *grace*.

"What! You didn't understand grace!" If I am honest with myself, I didn't. Was it there? Sure, it was there somewhere, but I missed it. It wasn't that I missed what grace meant. No, it wasn't that simple. I missed the whole concept. I don't even remember it at all. I learned all sorts of things about God and the Bible. I was the fastest draw on Bible drills. I was the best at reciting verses. When someone asked a question in Sunday school, I had a legitimate answer that wasn't "Jesus" or "God" or "Because the Bible says so." I knew all that stuff in and out, or so I thought, and I missed *the* fundamental part of the whole thing—grace.

How did I miss grace? I had sung "Amazing Grace"[56] thousands of times and knew it forward and backward. But I didn't really understand what it was about. How in the world did that happen? If I think about it, I suspect it was because I was too busy caught up in memorizing Isaiah 53:5, Micah 6:8, or Romans 6:23. I was too busy doing things. I was more like Martha when I should've been like Mary (Luke 10:38–42). I was getting to know *about* Jesus without really getting to know Jesus.

What happened? What changed that helped me to see? The answer is not really straightforward. For me, it was a process, but there was definitely a culmination. I was involved in Christian organizations during college. We went on short-term mission trips and met multiple times a week to sing, study the Bible, and develop meaningful friendships. Those experiences helped prepare me for the revelation of grace. How did that revelation come about?

In 1998 I heard a song by Rich Mullins and the Ragamuffin Band. The song was entitled "My Deliverer,"[57] and it quickly became pretty popular on Christian radio. I liked the song, but I was intrigued by the name of the "Ragamuffin Band." When I investigated it, I learned that it came from the title of a book by a guy named Brennan Manning. That was interesting enough, but as I recall it didn't really spur me to investigate the book any further. A few months later, a friend recommended Manning's book, *The Ragamuffin Gospel*,[58] to me. So I went to the local bookstore and bought it. Little did I know my whole world, the framework of my faith, and everything I thought I knew about God was about to be completely rocked.

My whole life I had been around grace but never really knew of it. I never got a taste of what it meant. When I began reading Brennan Manning's *The Ragamuffin Gospel*, I was suddenly overwhelmed by the reality of God's grace and what it meant. It was like I was standing at the foot of a dam that exploded and all of it came rushing down on me. As I read across each page I became more and more aware of what Jesus Christ had given me; of what He continues to give me; of what I didn't earn and never could. I could've recited Ephesians 2:8–9 to you from the time I was an early teen.

> For by grace you have been saved through faith, and that not of yourselves; *it is* the gift of God, not of works, lest anyone should boast. (Ephesians 2:8–9 NKJV)

I didn't really get it though. It didn't click for me until I read *The Ragamuffin Gospel* and God used it to peel the scales off of my eyes. Did I have faith in Jesus Christ—that He had died to save me and that I had to believe on His sacrifice for my righteousness? Yes, but I didn't understand the whole story. In an instant I went from looking at a black and white drawing of my salvation to being dropped in the middle of a three-dimensional, Technicolor world of salvation by the grace of Jesus Christ. It was, and still is, overwhelming.

The thing about grace is you can't earn it. If you could earn it, it wouldn't be grace; it would be payment. That can be hard to swallow for some people. Our natural inclination—our carnal nature—is to want to think God's favor, His forgiveness,

His love, and His grace are given to us because we are special or because we have somehow earned it. We want to have some control in the story. But if we stop to think about what would be required to earn God's favor, we see the impossibility of the proposition.

What did God require to save mankind from our sinful state? He required the life of His one and only Son, Jesus Christ. If He didn't require that, He wouldn't have sent Jesus for that purpose. Jesus' death was the mechanism by which we could be reconciled to God. Now here's the question:

> What good act or lifetime of good acts could I possibly perform
> that would be worth the life of the one and only Son of God?

Think about how ridiculous it would be to stand before God while running through a list of the "good things" we had done in the hopes that giving some sandwiches to homeless guys or not sleeping with our neighbor's wife would be enough for God to say, "You know, you're right. That was worth My only Son coming to earth, living a sinless life, being mocked, beaten, crucified, and separated from Me. Yeah that was worth it. Great job!" When you think of it in that regard, doesn't it seem absolutely ridiculous? Isn't that what our tendency is, though?

We want to feel like we have made a contribution to our salvation and that we are rewarded for it. Could that be why we keep score? In the back of our minds, aren't we keeping score on everyone else because if we are ahead of them in the count it means we have earned God's favor? When we are ahead in the count, don't we feel like we deserve His favor? But grace isn't about keeping score. It is not about how much good we do; it's about how good God is. The gospel is the story of God pouring out His unbounded grace on us in spite of us.

As I was reading *The Ragamuffin Gospel*, I was struck by the reality that God cannot love me more than He does already. He loves me as much as it is possible to love me. There's nothing I can do to make Him love me more, and so I don't have to keep score anymore of all the good things I do and that others don't. Conversely, God cannot love me less than He does already. His love for me will not decrease. There's nothing I can do to make Him love me less, so I don't have to keep track of all of the bad things I do either. That realization was an epiphany for me. The light switch went on, and I was left dumbfounded and in awe of the real grace of God. I continue to be to this day.

Once I realized what God's grace was and accepted what it meant in my life, I realized I am truly free. I'm free to not check boxes. I'm free to not worry about where I fall short. I'm free to not worry about where everyone else falls short. I'm free to not loathe myself. I'm free to love everyone without fear his or her moral bankruptcy will stain my self-righteousness. I'm free to celebrate that God has made me righteous—that I am a new creation in Him and His goodness, not in anything

I have done. I am free to serve Him with reckless abandon. I'm free to walk in the good works He has prepared for me, not because I'm trying to earn something but because I love Him and want to honor Him.

Coming face-to-face with the scandalous grace of God in Jesus Christ changes people. It changes people to the core of their souls. It's the kind of change needed for us to make it not about us. To be able to come to grips with the reality that it's all about God and His glory, we must come to terms with the fact it's not about us and ours. We have to come to terms with the reality that apart from God and His grace, we are nothing. Accepting that reality is the first step. What's the next?

I've met a lot of people who worry about being "good enough." They want to keep up with the spiritual Joneses, and if they feel like they aren't keeping up, it's as though their entire spiritual underpinning is snatched from beneath them. They cannot fathom a God who would ever love or even accept them since they aren't the most righteous, wise, or compassionate. Even in their humiliated state, they are the center of their attention; God is superfluous to the conversation because the conversation is about them. Though the two seem diametrically opposed, the perpetually self-deprecating saint is no different than the arrogant and self-righteous Pharisee—both have their full attention on their own spiritual position and not on the glory of God. When our focus is on our own spiritual worth, whether we see ourselves as wanting or in abundance, we are placing the focus on ourselves and taking it off of God, which robs Him of glory and us of grace.

A personal willingness to deny ourselves is necessary to truly comprehend the magnitude of God's grace. When we deny ourselves, we are admitting our lack of importance. We are acknowledging we have nothing of any worth to offer. In that moment, we are able to let go of all of the baggage and fear of spiritual failure. We are able to dive deep into the center of God's love and grace without concern of being good enough or holy enough.

Denying myself means I not only subjugate my will to God's, which is certainly denial, but it also means I deny any things about me I have held as important. For me to deny myself requires I tear down the façades of personal greatness and success I have built. The scaffolds and buttresses of my pride and ego must be torn down. Any accomplishment I think I have made or contribution I have to give has to be seen as what it is—trifling when placed before Elohim. There is nothing of worth I have to offer God. He has no need of anything I could possibly produce or place before Him. In spite of that reality, He seeks a relationship with me. He has taken on flesh, borne my sin, carried my cross, and died in my place when I had nothing of worth to give Him. He has seen me fail to the best of my ability in my own striving and contriving. Yet He pursues me with a ravenous love, not because I am faithful but because He is. If I do not or cannot deny myself, I will not have the opportunity to see God's amazing grace for what it truly is. By maintaining my self-worth, pride, or dignity, I miss out on what His grace really means.

As discussed in the first section of this book, when Jesus said in the ninth chapter of Luke that anyone who would follow after Him must deny himself, the idea in the word deny was *to forget one even exists*. To actually follow after Jesus is to do so with reckless abandon, without consideration of ourselves in the least. Jesus was relieving us of any special talent, skills, or worth we might think we bring to the table so we could follow Him wholly. When we hang on to our pride or accomplishments, our self-worth or personal spiritual success, we fail to follow the command of Christ, and we miss out on the greatness of grace because we carry with us something by which we hope to lay claim to that grace. Denying myself means relinquishing any claim I have to my own goodness, my own accomplishments, my own worth.

If I'm not willing to deny myself, then I'm not willing to know the riches and depth, the overwhelming abundance, of God's grace. To begin to experience the magnitude of His grace, I have to admit my spiritual destitution in the same manner as the "poor in spirit" in the Beatitudes. I have to admit I'm an utter failure with nothing to bring to the table but filthy rags. This is not to be confused with mourning my inadequacies but rather recognizing them and leaving them be. I have to turn away from myself, whether my shortcomings or my successes, and turn toward God wholeheartedly. In a sense, I have to submit to a spiritual amnesia so I forget all I am and all I have done and focus on Christ alone in His glory. It is from this attitude that Paul wrote in Philippians,

> Brethren, I do not regard myself as having laid hold of *it* yet; but one thing *I do:* forgetting what *lies* behind and reaching forward to what *lies* ahead, I press on toward the goal for the prize of the upward call of God in Christ Jesus. (Philippians 3:13–14 NASB)

Paul had both tried to destroy Christ's church and later had accomplished great things to promote it. Yet he saw those things as rubbish. He was not looking at anything He had done but was focused on the glory of the Lord. He was neither lamenting his failures, nor lauding his accomplishments. Rather, he denied himself, left everything—the great and the grievous—behind, and moved toward Jesus Christ. In the moment when one comes to a place of complete, open denial of self, the profound reality of grace can be revealed. With this in mind, let's explore grace and self-denial a little further.

CHAPTER 24
CLINGING TO WORTHLESS IDOLS

THOSE WHO CLING TO WORTHLESS IDOLS FORFEIT THE GRACE THAT COULD BE THEIRS. (JONAH 2:8 NIV)

The translation of Jonah 2:8 in the New International Version is my favorite verse in the Bible. It sums up the entirety of the gospel for me. There is so much to the verse, not the least of which is a bit of irony. The verse comes near the end of Jonah's prayer from within the great fish, and he is seemingly repenting for having disobeyed the command of God to go to Nineveh.

As a refresher, Jonah was commanded to go to Nineveh, the capital city of Israel's archenemy Assyria, to warn the Ninevites their wickedness had stirred God to punish them. Jonah defied the command of God and went in the opposite direction because he had no desire to warn the Ninevites of their impending doom—being an upstanding Jew, he relished the idea of some Old Testament retribution upon the enemies of Israel (Jonah 4:2). Ultimately, he ended up swallowed by a large fish after he was tossed overboard in a tempestuous storm. It was while he was in the gullet of the fish that Jonah prayed his prayer, and shortly thereafter he was regurgitated out onto land. When God told Jonah to go to Nineveh a second time, he went.

In the third chapter of the book of Jonah, the prophet warned the people of Nineveh of God's imminent wrath, and the warning was heard all the way to the level of the king. The people of Nineveh, undoubtedly much to Jonah's surprise, heeded his words, repented of their sin, and prayed to God for compassion. "When God saw what they did and how they turned from their evil ways, he relented and did not bring on them the destruction he had threatened" (Jonah 3:10 NIV).

The people of Nineveh, who had worshipped idols and lived in flagrant immorality, turned to God. Jonah's warnings were a success. The people had listened and repented. He must have been glad, right? Wrong. In fact, Jonah was so angry that the city of Nineveh would not be destroyed he prayed, "Now, LORD, take away my life, for it is better for me to die than to live" (Jonah 4:3 NIV). How's that for a shining example of grace and love on Jonah's part?

The irony of the story is that even though Jonah was praying about those who cling to worthless idols, he was the one who was clinging to the worthless idol of Israel's chosen status. He was happily self-righteous and liked the idea that the Assyrian capital of "more than a hundred and twenty thousand people" (Jonah 4:11) would be laid waste. Jonah was clinging to his own self-worth when he could've been receiving the outpouring of God's grace.

Are we the same way? How often do we compare ourselves to others and find that we come out ahead in our own calculations? How often do we assign spiritual scores to ourselves and others? In those situations we don't really want grace, do we? We don't want to think we are all bankrupt and in need of equal measures of God's gracious forgiveness. Don't we want a scorecard? Don't we want to be able to look at the tallies and say to ourselves that we have come out ahead? If there is a scorecard, I can make sure I am deserving of God's favor—I can make sure I come out ahead. The scorecard makes me matter, at least in my estimation. Grace tears any hope of our worthiness away from us. Our worthiness is exposed for what it is—a worthless idol detracting from the glory of God.

Grace and Mercy

If you've been around the Christian community very long, you have probably heard someone discuss the difference between grace and mercy. The explanation usually goes something like this: grace is when we are given something (gift) we do not deserve, and mercy is when we are not given something (punishment) we do deserve. This little explanation of the differences between the two concepts is helpful for understanding, in a superficial manner, what the two are. However, this is a fairly artificial separation because it gives the impression that grace lives *over here* and mercy lives *over there*, and the two do not come together. But is that true? If we look at the source of grace and mercy, are the two separate?

As it pertains to the actions of Jesus, I cannot think of a time when grace and mercy were not working in concert. Zacchaeus did not deserve Jesus' friendship and the grace of having dinner with the Lord but rather deserved condemnation for his deceitful practices. In grace he received the former, and in mercy he did not receive the latter. The Pharisees did not deserve the grace of Jesus' teaching and patience, but rather they deserved the Lord's wrath as they tested, tried, and condemned Him. In reality, Jesus' presence as "God with us" is the embodiment of grace and mercy being manifest in flesh. All with whom He interacted were given what they did not deserve—the presence of God Incarnate. Conversely, He bestowed mercy on those same people because He did not give them what they deserved—condemnation and death. When it comes to God, grace and mercy are inseparable. His mercy is an extension of His grace and vice versa. Why then do we separate the two?

Separating grace and mercy allows me to allocate them as I see fit to whomever I see fit, whether myself or someone else. I can say, "This person will receive mercy," and "That person will receive grace." In the artificial separation, I am able to maintain the position as self-appointed judge, giving mercy to those I do not necessarily like and reserving grace for those I do like. We separate mercy and grace because it gives us power. In reality, to receive grace means we also receive mercy. God imputes the righteousness of Christ upon us by grace (Romans 5:17) and mercifully withholds the condemnation we deserve (Romans 8:1). We have to be willing to receive them both, and we cannot be offended when someone else is the recipient.

When I was in early elementary school—kindergarten to about second grade— we always had a big piece of poster board hanging in our classroom with a grid and everyone's names on it. The grid kept up with our behavior. If we maintained good behavior, or as my grandmother would say, "deportment," we would receive a shiny gold star in the little square beneath the given date. This way we could look to the board and see who was a little angel and who was not. If we received enough gold stars by the end of a given period, we would get a prize. If we did not receive enough gold stars, our parents would be notified and "a conference" would be held.

Some of the children in my class struggled to maintain their deportment. As a totally fabricated example, it was difficult for some children to stop talking when there were so many other children around to listen. The teachers of my children have witnessed this same phenomenon, and I'm pretty sure the kids must have inherited it from my wife. Nevertheless, there were those of us who did not receive as many stars as some of the others. Meanwhile, there were others, almost always the little girls in the class, who received stars for nearly every day. By the end of the grading period, certain classmates would have a trove of stars that ran off of the poster board and across the wall, occasionally bending around corners, while other more gregarious children, perhaps, or those prone to disruptive behaviors, would be left with only a handful of the coveted stars. While the children with stellar deportment frolicked to and fro in perpetual beams of sunlight playing with their prizes, those with few stars sat cowering in a cloud of terror, knowing soon enough a conference would be requested with our—I mean their—parents. Both groups deserved what was coming to us, and we knew it.

What if the outcome of the behavior board was changed? Imagine for a minute a different scenario from that which unfolded during my childhood. Imagine yourself as a talkative first grader with a couple of stars and a looming parent-teacher conference to discuss your poor behavior. What would you do if on the last day of the grading period the teacher announced no one's parents would be notified of their children's poor behavior? How excited would you be to find that out? That's mercy. In that moment, you did not receive the punishment for what you had done. But what if we take the scenario a step further? How would you respond if on the last day of the grading period the teacher walked to the board and filled up every spot on your behavior grid and then walked over and gave you the prize you did not earn? Would it leave you a bit dumbfounded and wondering why things had happened that way? That's grace. That's receiving a gift you could not earn.

In assuming the perspective of the child who had a problem with deportment, it's not hard to appreciate and revel in mercy and grace. What if we take the perspective of the well-behaved children? Imagine yourself being the child with exceptional behavior with a line of stars stretching across the board, along the wall, and off down the hallway toward the third-grade classrooms. You're the kid everyone in the school knows is the best behaved … perhaps even in the whole world. Would it bother you if you heard the teacher announce no one's parents would be notified for the need of a conference to discuss lackluster behavior? The thought of that does not bother me. Sure, there are the bullies who I want to get what's coming to them, but at the end of the day, it would not upset me if they did not receive their due. I am okay with them receiving mercy. I suspect you would likely feel the same way—mercy's okay.

But what if the teacher pulled a completely crazy stunt? What if she walked to the board and began giving stars to those kids—the talkative ones, the ones shooting spit wads in my well-groomed hair, the ones making armpit noises when they are supposed to be reading *See Pug Run*, the ones rubbing nose goblins on my oh-so-neatly-written alphabet—the ones who were supposed to be punished? What if she just kept giving them stars until they stretched across the board, along the wall, and off down the hallway toward the third-grade classrooms? What if she gave them the same number of stars you, as the best-behaved kid in the galaxy, had? Would that bother you? If I were honest, it would bother me, quite a lot. Why is this scenario bothersome?

If I boil it down, it's because I want to be elevated. I want to be better than everyone else. It's okay if people don't get condemned, but it is something else for them to be made as good as I am. If they are as good as me, then I am not special, and I really want to be special. It's a special, worthless idol to me. It's what I can hold up to God to say, "See. I'm worthy." If that's taken away, what do I have?

I think this scenario gets to the root of why a lot of people in the church are scared of grace. It's easy enough to disguise our fear in a concern over someone's spiritual well-being. We certainly wouldn't want someone rushing out and living a derelict life because he has been blinded by grace. To this end, we always feel the need for the obligate recitation of Paul's statement in Romans 6:1–2, "What shall we say then? Shall we continue in sin that grace may abound? Certainly not!" (NKJV). We are afraid if someone realizes what grace means, he is going to go crazy with wild living—sex, drugs, and rock and roll. Reciting this portion of Romans as a means of suppressing grace is a complete misunderstanding of not only what Paul was saying but also of the effect of grace. Grace changes people.

Grace, real grace, comes from God. It's His to give; there's no place in the New Testament where grace is given from someone other than God. While we may facilitate the receiving of grace when we speak words of edification (Ephesians 4:29), we do not give grace. It is God reaching down to place upon us the righteousness and goodness we cannot earn. When that happens—when the hand of God touches us in our spiritual desolation—we are changed. Our entire reality is reformed. We are left humbled at the throne of God.

The response of the sinner, the spiritually destitute, the defiled and broken, to grace is awe and marveling, but it is also a desire to be transformed by it. It is a matter of perspective. When those who see themselves as worthless and shameful receive grace it creates a desire to want to live up to it. In Titus, Paul wrote that God's grace, which in this instance is the incarnate Christ, "has appeared, bringing salvation to all men, instructing us to deny ungodliness and worldly desires and to live sensibly, righteously and godly in the present age" (Titus 2:11–12 NASB). The response to grace is righteousness, not spiritual anarchy, as some in the church would have us believe. As a talkative kid with few stars, being given stars I did not earn would make me want to live up to that, but it would also make me believe I could. Up to the point of grace, it was clear I could not obtain good deportment. I could not earn the stars for good behavior, and so there was no reason to even attempt to behave. Grace changes that.

Sadly, the response of the self-righteous to grace is vastly different from the penitent sinner. The self-righteous person, or Pharisee, lives a life aimed at attaining righteousness through maintenance of all rules, regulations, and requirements. By his own estimation, the self-righteous person is able to be "good enough" through religious devotion to the rules. In the mind of the self-righteous, he is deserving of any good things he receives; in a very real sense, he sees no reason for grace because he has earned it. Because of this, the response of the self-righteous to grace is one of fear or even anger.

Remember the scenario of being the kid with all of the stars? The thought of others getting the same reward I was going to get was upsetting. Why? Because I was "better" than they were. I deserved the reward and they did not. In such a situation, my inclination is to stop my good behavior and start behaving like all of the kids who were breaking the rules. Why should I bother obeying all of the rules if it does not get me anything extra? My self-righteousness creates a response to grace opposite of what it should be when I am humbled. I become angry and cry, "Foul!" I don't want someone else getting the glory I think I have earned. It's not fair … and that's the very attitude Jesus was addressing in the parable of the workers in Matthew 20:1–16. When in my self-righteousness I raise the fairness argument, Jesus looks at me and asks, "Is it not lawful for me to do what I wish with what is my own? Or is your eye envious because I am generous?" (Matthew 20:15 NASB).

Do I really want grace? As the self-righteous members of the church, do we really want to espouse the incomprehensible riches of the grace of God, even for ourselves? We don't want grace. We want to keep score. We want to be able to point to those good things we have done and say, "See. I'm worthy. I'm deserving." When the meaningfulness of our collection of stars is taken away by God's outpouring of grace, what do we have left? We like the idea of mercy, but the idea of grace is scary. While at once freeing, it also tears away the worthless idols we have set up to make us feel important, worthy, or deserving.

This may seem obvious, but to get away from clinging to worthless idols, we have to admit we have them and that we cling to them. For those of us who are heavily invested in Christianity, making those admissions can be a lot harder than it seems. We have to be willing to admit we have vain idols strewn throughout our lives. Not only that, we have to confess that those idols take all sorts of forms, whether godly or ungodly, and often it is the former. We have to recognize that we have developed a keen ability to disguise idols as things that could otherwise be seen as God-honoring. We also have to be honest enough to concede that we have allowed those idols to usurp the rightful position of God. In those situations, we have to tear down the idols, even when they could otherwise be honoring to God.

In the first section of the book, we walked through a number of ways we put ourselves first. We have dressed them up in ways to keep from having to face up to the truth, and whether we want to admit it or not, those things are idols—things we put in front of God. We cling to them tenaciously because we think they give us something we crave.

The first worthless idol we came upon was our view of our own importance. This idol is tantamount to pride, and all others flow from it. We cannot fathom the possibility we are not integral to God's story. It's an offensive idea to us because our pride gets injured. Why do we guard our pride so much? Isn't our pride really the whole problem anyway? If we could stop trying to protect our pride, everything would be changed. All of our shortcomings and failures—all of our sins—are the direct result of our pride. We put ourselves over God. We find every opportunity to put people below us. It's all a part of the charade of making us feel better about ourselves.

In 2 Samuel, the ark of the covenant was returned to Jerusalem. When the ark was brought into the city, David was dancing "with all of his might." He was ecstatic that the ark was being returned to its rightful place because it symbolized the presence of God. David was overwhelmed with worshipping in God's presence to the point of being completely lost in dancing, jumping, and twirling about. What's more, he began stripping off his clothes! David, the king of Israel, was dancing around in the nude.

Think about that scene for a moment. Think about the ruler of the country dancing around like a lunatic. This was the same David who was known as a mighty warrior, whom the people of Israel respected. How must his foolish display have looked to others? Surely they must have stood there aghast at the spectacle. We know for one that his wife, Michal, "despised him in her heart" because of his display (2 Samuel 6:16 NKJV). How did David respond to the criticism foisted upon him? Did he apologize for his behavior or for offending others? David's words speak great truth into our discussion: "And I will be even more undignified than this, and will be humble in my own sight" (2 Samuel 6:22a NKJV). David did not apologize. He went so far as to say that if Michal waited around a little while, she would see him be even more embarrassing to her reputation.

The heart of the issue comes in that David said he would be humble in his own sight. He was not concerned about what others thought of him. He was not worried about his reputation or public position. He was ecstatic in the presence of the Lord, and out of that he celebrated. David surrendered the idol of self-importance, of his vaunted reputation and position of power, and humbled himself before God. In so doing in that moment, he worshipped in spirit and truth. Had he done anything else, had he attempted to worship in some other manner, it would have been offensive to God.

There are those of us who do not have the luxury of positions of power or great public reputations. We do not have to worry about keeping up our highly regarded reputations, or so we say. In those situations, we don't have to worry about being led astray by such idols, right? Hopefully after reading the book this far, you realized what a lie that is. We can bend any situation to fit our needs for self-service. I can say I have relinquished all worldly position or possessions to serve the Lord. But I can also make certain that everyone knows what a great sacrifice I have made to live such an austere life. It's easy to become "the most humble person I know" then. In truth, I am seeking glory in my feigned self-sacrifice. I gain recognition by my sacrificial position. When I do, I have simply traded one manifestation of my pride in my position and reputation for another.

How do we get away from pride? How can we turn from the myriad ways we put ourselves ahead of everyone else, including God? We have to get rid of the idols—all of the idols. We have to be willing to deny ourselves completely and be ready for whatever it is God wants for us and from us. For some it is austerity, for some it is wealth. For some it is preaching the gospel in closed countries, for others it is being the hands and feet of Christ to the unlovable here at home. Whatever the case, God will be stretching you and changing you to be more like Jesus. But this is more than lip service. It's more than the feel-good, I'm-going-to-get-my-act-together-and-finally-live-for-God-forsaking-all-others sensation you get when you hear someone speak about the life-changing events they have seen as missionaries in the far reaches of the world. It's burning the idols, leaving it all behind for whatever it is God really wants from you, and basking in His glorious grace as He makes you more like Jesus Christ. Is that what you really want? Are you willing to count all things—all the idols, all the comfort, all the reputation or power or recognition—as loss for the sake of knowing Christ?

I thought I had come to the close of this chapter, but the words of a hymn from my youth keeping ringing in my head, and I feel compelled to include it. If you know the song, I would encourage you to read these words as if for the first time and ask yourself if they are true for you. If you don't know the song, now is a great time to get to know it. Are these words really true in your life? Do you live a life that someone on the outside looking in could say, without equivocation, you would rather have Jesus than anything? Do you live a life that God would say you would rather have Jesus? If not, it's time to deny yourself and start burning the idols.

I'd Rather Have Jesus
Rhea F. Miller, 1922
I'd rather have Jesus than silver or gold;
I'd rather be His than have riches untold;
I'd rather have Jesus than houses or lands;
I'd rather be led by His nail-pierced hand

> Refrain:
> Than to be the king of a vast domain
> And be held in sin's dread sway;
> I'd rather have Jesus than anything
> This world affords today.

I'd rather have Jesus than men's applause;
I'd rather be faithful to His dear cause;
I'd rather have Jesus than worldwide fame;
I'd rather be true to His holy name
He's fairer than lilies of rarest bloom;
He's sweeter than honey from out the comb;
He's all that my hungering spirit needs;
I'd rather have Jesus and let Him lead

CHAPTER 25
DENYING OURSELVES

THEN HE SAID TO THEM ALL, "IF ANYONE DESIRES TO COME AFTER ME, LET HIM DENY HIMSELF, AND TAKE UP HIS CROSS DAILY, AND FOLLOW ME." (LUKE 9:23 NKJV)

"**D**eny yourself ..." Those words echo in my head as I try to come to terms with what Jesus meant by them. He said if I want to follow Him, I have to completely dissociate from myself, my interests, and my desires for anything that is not of Him. All of those things, all the deceitful things my pride conjures up—how good and upstanding I am; my feigned piety; my importance to my church; the money I give; the "worship" I present under my own stipulations—have to be forfeited for what they are. I have to come to a place where I have admitted I am the poor in spirit who Christ talked about in Matthew 5:3.

Contrary to what our society would like to believe, there's only one way we can follow Jesus—completely. When Jesus said we must deny ourselves, He was speaking of a complete and utter denial. There was no halfway or almost. There was no "pretty good." It was "forget yourself entirely, take up your cross, and follow Me." He said if I'm unwilling to forget everyone and everything, myself included, then I'm unworthy to be His disciple.

In the first section of this book, we explored a number of ways we fail to deny ourselves. We are experts at disguising our self-interests with the clothes of humility and service or Pharisaical religiosity. We are corrupt, even those who would profess to follow the Lord. How do we deny ourselves if we are corrupt? How can we ever live up to Christ's model, to God's righteous requirements? In truth, we can't, and that's where grace comes in.

What does it mean, from a practical standpoint, to deny myself? It seems paradoxical, but to deny myself requires that I admit certain things. I have to admit things that are unpleasing to my ego. I have to own up to things to which I would rather not own up. In a very real sense, I have to be willing to surrender those attributes I have that make me feel entitled or worthy. I must forfeit my pride and "count all things loss for the excellence of the knowledge of Christ Jesus my Lord" (Philippians 3:8 NKJV).

In the book's first chapter, I explored the mistake we make of assuming we are of integral importance to God's story, to His plan. When we deny ourselves, we relinquish any claim to our own importance. This acceptance of the reality of our actual position moves us toward the place where we can be able to realize the greatness of God and the magnitude of what His grace means. But it is not easy for us to come to such a place. In fact, it often takes major work on the part of the Holy Spirit to bring us to such a place.

For a significant percentage of people in the American church, subjugating ourselves is terribly difficult. A portion of the history of this was explored in chapter 3, which discussed our rights. We are constantly bombarded with messages that stroke our ego and inflate our self-worth. The entire marketing industry is based around our innate response to such caressing of our psyches. As a result, we have a difficult time going against the grain of our carnal desires and the messages we get from society at large. Denying ourselves is hard in America.

For some people, denying themselves is easy, or maybe it is better stated that it is not terribly hard to abase themselves from a materialistic point of view. There are those of us who relish the opportunity to deny themselves in a materialistic sort of way. These folks are usually referred to as ascetics. They celebrate being liberated from the worldly materialism that consumes others—they have reached some sort of higher plane that has allowed them to give up various and sundry material things, with the exception of their MacBooks, overly priced handmade shoes, and coffees. In reality, they have traded one idol for another, both of which have their origins in self-gratification.

What if we denied ourselves in specific circumstances? It's easy to say we are of no importance. It is easy to say we deny ourselves in large, sweeping terms. But when we get down to the nuts and bolts of it, it is often not as easy as we would like to think. For instance, what does it look like to deny ourselves with regard to our church? Perhaps denying myself means that I teach a Sunday school class for first graders. Conversely, it could mean giving up teaching a Sunday school class because it inflates my self-worth. What about worship services? To deny myself may mean that I'm willing to give up a style of music because I have made it an idol.

What does denying myself look like in my marriage; with my kids; in my church; at my place of work; while driving down the highway; when sitting and waiting at the doctor's office; when my drink is not refilled as quickly as I would like; when I want to pass judgment on someone else because it inflates my ego; when I want to overeat; when I want to complain about my taxes; or when I want to defend my rights? What does it look like in those nitty-gritty, day-in and day-out situations we all face? In truth, it varies with different people. The issue at play is that denying ourselves can look different for different people. For some, it may be buying a non-luxury car, whereas for others it may be *not* living an ascetic lifestyle. It depends on how pride manifests in each believer's life.

A question that we all must answer is this: *Am I willing to do everything required to deny myself?*

I mentioned earlier in the book that I grew up in the church. Perhaps because of my aptitude with Scripture memorization and having the ability to answer Sunday school questions with something other than "Jesus," there were a number of people who thought I would grow up to be a pastor. To some people, that may be flattering, but for me it was scary. It wasn't scary because of some fear of standing up and giving sermons or anything like that. The idea of being a pastor was scary to me because I love science, and I wanted to do something I saw as academically rigorous, fun, and rewarding. In my context at the time, I did not see being a pastor as any of those things at all. I didn't want to do it—at all. Any time some elder saint would comment about my potential to be a pastor, I would cringe inside. In my head I was yelling, "Stop saying that!" I did not want it to be true. The idea of being a pastor held no appeal to me, and I had "bigger plans," whatever they were.

In reality, the idea of being a pastor scared me because, in my experience to that point, a number of the pastors I had met did not seem as intellectually inclined or curious as I was. It was lost on me that they had incredible faith, knew the Word and could rightly divide it, and spoke truth into the lives of the people they served. I totally overlooked that at that point in my life. Further, in my experience to that point, pastors were always scraping by, driving vans that were forever breaking down, and living in dilapidated houses subsidized or owned by the little congregations they served. I knew what it was to live in the lower end of the economic spectrum. I had no desire to stay there forever. I had no desire for my own kids to one day have to endure the financial hardships I did. The thought of that scared me because I wanted "more" out of life.

All of those thoughts, those fears and self-centered ideas, lay tucked away, or more accurately were walled off in a deep, dark place like Fortunato in Poe's *Cask of Amontillado*.[59] I hid them and did my best to forget those things because I was afraid that God might actually want me to be a pastor, or worse a missionary to some foreign land. Did I feel "called" to that? No, but neither did I entreat God to find out if He might want me to pursue such a thing. I didn't want to risk giving Him any ideas.

Being Willing

With a year left before completing medical school, my wife and I were married. A week after returning from our honeymoon, we decided it would be a good idea to serve as chaperones for our church youth group's summer camp at Centrifuge in Greeneville, South Carolina. It was trying for all of the reasons being youth chaperones can be trying, but it was a great, life-changing week and God revealed Himself wonderfully to us. During the week my new bride, though she had always said she had faith in Christ, realized she had not and truly came to faith; she was saved while serving as a chaperone on the youth trip! It was a wonderful trip right up to the last night.

As we filed into the auditorium on the last night, the music was pumping and the atmosphere was electrified—everyone was excited. I took my seat and was watching a slide presentation on the big screen at the front of the auditorium. It was a simple format with pictures flashing up of various people doing things, and then the screen would flash with words one at a time: time, money, talent ... This went on for a minute or two, and then the final slide was a black screen with white lettering with the question: "What are you willing to give?" That slide, those words, hit me in the gut like a sledgehammer. I sat in stunned silence, breathless. It was as though God stuck His finger on my chest, pinned me to the seat, and said, "What are you really willing to give? You know that fear, that doubt you've been hiding, the thing you thought you could keep from Me? I know about it. I know your heart and that little dark place you've tried to keep from Me, never mentioning it to anyone out of the fear I would demand it of you. Well, it's time to come clean. What are you *really* willing to give?"

In that moment, I broke. The wall I had built around my fear collapsed. In my heart, as tears burst forth from my eyes, I cried out, finally, "Everything!" After years of carrying around that fear I had so tidily hidden away, I finally was able to release it. In that instant, I surrendered to whatever God would ask of me. I was tired of hiding it. I threw down the weight of that dark, prideful secret and stood before God, willing to do whatever He would ask, whatever it meant, whatever the consequences. In that moment of utter surrender, of denying myself, I had never felt so free.

To come to a place to say, "Everything," I had to be willing to turn my back on everything I thought defined me. I had to lay it all—that is all of what I saw as myself—at God's feet and say, "Here am I, Lord, send me" (Isaiah 6:8). After having that watershed event occur, what did I do? I immediately assumed my new bride and I were going to be called to serve as missionaries in some faraway land like India, the place I had previously served during a short-term trip. As it turned out, doing so was not what God wanted. He wanted me to be *willing* to go. He had other plans that He continues to work out in the life of our family, all of which were impacted by my finally surrendering.

Where did I make my mistake? There were plenty of them, but the one that stands out to me the most was that I was not honest with God. I was dishonest out of a fear of what He might demand of my life. I expected that God did not want for me what I wanted. I had decided it would be bad for me if I were to take on a career path as a pastor or missionary. In reality, I had decided God did not want what I saw as best for me, because on some level I doubted His goodness. That's the dark reality of that scenario as it played out in my life. I was willing to deny myself up to a point, which is exactly what Christ *does not want*. I have to be willing to deny it all, to submit my whole life, whether the monumental or the mundane, to His will. If I am not willing to do the thing Jesus said is required to follow Him, that being denying myself *in toto*, then how can I call myself a follower of Christ?

After having come through such a defining moment in my faith, have I conquered denying myself? No, not at all really. I still put myself above others. I still lack a servant's heart. I still want my church to operate the way I want it to operate. I still think my erudition is profound. I still have a long, long way to go. But I can say honestly that I am willing to go there. I am willing to sacrifice whatever I am asked for the sake of knowing Christ and serving Him.

It is imperative for us to come to the point where we can say that we are willing to do anything the Lord asks, and then when He asks, we have to do it. Are you willing to say that it's not about you and mean it? Look in the eyes of the person in your mirror and be honest with yourself. Are you willing to give up those places you think you have hidden from God?

Are you willing …? Are you willing to praise God in silence during a worship service if it means His glory is manifest to more people? Are you willing to drive a nondescript car if it means that you crucify your own sense of entitlement? Are you willing to love your wife as Christ loved the church if it means giving up golf to support her endeavors? Are you willing to submit yourself to your husband if it means you surrender your own importance? Are you willing to stop defending rights you gave up to Christ's lordship? Are you willing to stop condemning others and start to love those you castigate if it means that they will come to know God and the truth can be spoken into their lives? Are you willing to care for widows and orphans if it means disrupting your family and creating a financial situation that requires sacrifice? Are you willing to live at a higher standard if it means surrendering the pride you treasure from your asceticism? Are you willing to admit your sins are as despicable as those of anyone else, even if it means losing your position in others' eyes? We all harbor things—idols—we think we have disguised and hidden from God, others, and ourselves. We grossly overestimate the effectiveness of our camouflage. To follow Christ's command and deny ourselves, we have to admit the truth and surrender *everything*. It is in surrendering, in being truthful, that we cast off the burden and are liberated.

Denying myself is unnatural. It's not the way things work in our world. We do not have the innate ability to deny ourselves. I have to depend on the Holy Spirit working in me to bring me to the place where I can deny myself. Without the Holy Spirit working in me, no amount of good works will give me the ability to deny myself. We need only examine the case of the rich, young ruler to see this. Here was a man who, according to his own words at least, had kept all of the Law throughout his entire life. If anyone was in a position to be able to deny himself, based on works, this was the man who should have been able to do it. But we know that when Jesus told him that if he wanted to be perfect he had to sell everything he had and give it to the poor, the young ruler "went away sad because he was wealthy" (Mark 10:17:31 NKJV). Unless the Holy Spirit works in our hearts in everything we harbor, neither can we deny ourselves.

If we want to come to a place where we make it about God, where we are not seeking our own glory, and where we deny ourselves, it is imperative that we pray accordingly. When I pray, it is easy to pray nonspecific things like, "God help me to be a godly man." That is well and good, but it does not do much for helping me grow in faith or in my relationship with Jesus Christ. Instead, if I want the Holy Spirit to actualize change in me, it is more effective to pray in a specific manner. If I am being honest with God and myself—after all, there are no secrets in the relationship no matter what I may think—then praying in a deliberate, candid, and fervent way is more effectual (James 5:16). Also, if we take Christ's prayer in Gethsemane from Matthew 26 as a model, we should ask and seek God's will in the circumstance.

If I am content to hide my idol behind a mask, my prayers will usually belie my action. For instance, if I want to move to an affluent neighborhood, I might pray, "God, please help me to find the home You would have for us in Rich Man's Court." We impose our will on God and skip right to the expectation that He is going to answer our prayer based on our desire. This sort of approach is drastically different from the prayer arising from the surrendered heart.

When my heart is surrendered and I deny myself, everything about my relationship with the Lord is different, including the type of prayers I pray. I am more inclined to pray, "God, please show me Your desire for where we should live. Show us the place that will bring You the most glory." In this type of prayer, the focus is on God being glorified, not on my materialism and comfort being satisfied. Prayer like this carries a significant risk, at least as the world sees risk. What if God were to answer that we should sell our house, move into an apartment, and use the extra money to support clean drinking water endeavors in Africa? What if God were to tell us we should stay where we are and not be "rewarded" with a palatial home with all the accouterments? Would that be satisfying?

In chapter 10, I discussed how there are those people who are resolute that their calling is to not have to undertake any sort of material sacrifice. While this is oddly fascinating and completely antithetical with the New Testament, it makes one wonder about the type of prayers those folks are offering to God. Are they praying out of a surrendered heart? Are they praying, "God, would You have me sell everything I have, give it to the poor, and follow You?"

Until that night as a chaperone at Centrifuge, I did not pray out of a surrendered heart, and truthfully, there are times when I still do not. My prayers were so often marked by, "God, please bless me as I ..." When I surrender, when I deny myself, my prayers are more like, "God, what do You want for my family? What do You want for my career? What would You have me to do that brings You the most glory?" If I believe God is good and that He is for me, then I have nothing to fear when it comes to surrendered prayer. The prayers of the self-denied believer are prayers earnestly seeking after God's will. They are the prayers of the liberated heart, and they will be answered in a positive manner.

> Now this is the confidence that we have in Him, that if we ask
> anything according to His will, He hears us. And if we know that
> He hears us, whatever we ask, we know that we have the petitions
> that we have asked of Him. (1 John 5:14–15 NKJV)

Do you want to surrender? Do you want to deny yourself and live a life aimed at glorifying God alone? If you don't, can you admit you should want to deny yourself? It is not something you can do on your own, but it is something the Holy Spirit is willing and able to work out in you. If you don't want to deny yourself, pray that you would have the desire. Seek God and ask Him to give you a heart willing to be surrendered. The following is an example of a prayer that may help you to pray for the desire to deny yourself.

> Father God,
> May Your will be done in my life.
> I admit I do not have the desire to deny myself.
> There are things I have idolized.
> There are things I place above You.
> I have followed my desires and not Yours.
> Holy Spirit, would You work in me to give me the desire to deny myself?
> Would you show me my idols and give me a love for God that exceeds those things?
> Please forgive me for these sins that crowd You out of my life.
> Please give me the faith to want to surrender everything to You and Your will. Amen

If you already want to surrender but know you have not, then praying that God would give you the strength and faith to deny yourself is the next step. He has told us if we want to follow Him, we must deny ourselves. We also know, as we have read in James 5:14, if we pray in accordance with His will, it will happen. Therefore, when we pray that God would help us to deny ourselves for His glory, expect He will honor those prayers. Here's an example of such a prayer:

Father God,
Be glorified in my life.
I admit I have held out things from You.
I admit there are things I put before You.
Please forgive me for that sin.
Please forgive me for doubting Your goodness.
God, I want to deny myself and follow You wholeheartedly.
Please help me to surrender everything to You.
Would you please work in me, Holy Spirit, to reveal those things
I put before God?
Would You give me the strength and faith to put You above
everything else, and to remove anything I would put before You?
Please give me the grace to live this prayer out every day, for Your
glory. Amen

If I want to follow after Jesus wholeheartedly, I have no choice but to deny myself and all of my desires apart from Him. But it is by the power of the Holy Spirit that I can deny myself in the first place. When I ask the Holy Spirit to work in my heart to produce self-denial, I must expect it will happen. God wants us to know Him and glorify Him. If we are going to have the relationship with Him that comes only through Jesus Christ, then we must deny ourselves; we must surrender completely. Whether spiritual, material, or social, we must be willing to sacrifice everything for the sake of Christ.

If there is something getting in the way of my surrender to God, something that glorifies me and not Him, then I must be willing to remove it, no matter how seemingly valuable it is. If I am seeking and receiving glory for something, it must be removed from my life. Mankind is easily addicted to vainglory, and it must be treated like any addiction. We can take the best of things and find a way to pervert them into our own glorification. This is how we see evangelists caught up in ostentatious living, or worship leaders who are prima donnas—even though what they are doing can bring honor to God, it has become about them. An alcoholic cannot have another drink; in the same manner, one who glorifies himself through what should be God-honoring, should no longer undertake that endeavor.

Every part of my life is to be a sacrifice to God. I am to live in perpetual surrender to the lordship of Jesus Christ. To do so, I must completely surrender everything that is not for His glory. In Romans Paul admonished us to do this and gave us the key to continuing to live in such a yielded manner.

I beseech you therefore, brethren, by the mercies of God, that you present your bodies a living sacrifice, holy, acceptable to God, *which is* your reasonable service. And do not be conformed to this world, but be transformed by the renewing of your mind, that you may prove what *is* that good and acceptable and perfect will of God. (Romans 12:1–2 NKJV)

According to Paul, once we have denied ourselves, it is imperative that we renew our minds to the point of being completely transformed. The word translated as transformed is *metamorphoō*, which is the same word from which we get the word metamorphosis. It is the same word used to describe the change Christ underwent at the transfiguration. This is an undeniable change that is to occur in us, and it comes about as we deny ourselves, as we sacrifice our entire lives to the will of God.

Perhaps you are convinced you are denying yourself and taking up your cross daily. If you are, that's great. If you have surrendered everything, then I have a challenge for you. Think about the thing you would least want to do, the thing you are convinced you are *not* called to do. Once you have figured out what it is, pray about it. Ask God if He would have you do that very thing you do not want to be called to do. Perhaps it is serving as a missionary in the wilds of South America. Maybe it's worshipping in a manner that makes you uncomfortable. It could be it's moving to a part of town you don't believe is the place for you. Maybe it's taking a less-glamorous job. Whatever it is, ask God if He would have you do it. If you cannot or will not pray in such a manner, then you have not surrendered everything; you're holding out on God. Be willing to lay it all out at God's feet and pray, not just once but multiple times. It may be you find God begins to work in your heart to change your view on whatever the issue is. He may not call you to undertake whatever it is, but He will definitely work in you to change your perspective on it. Go ahead—give it a try.

When we deny ourselves, we surrender everything about us. We leave behind the good and the bad to move forward after Christ. In the complete denial of self, I must admit there is nothing good I have done or have the capacity to do. That admission is imperative in the salvation experience. We are saved solely through the work of Christ and His grace. I am the ultimate spiritual failure with nothing of worth to offer. That's what denying myself means—that admittance. When I arrive at that place, the place of the poor in spirit, then I am ready to receive God's overwhelming grace, and in that, I have come full circle. In that, it becomes not about me, but about God and His glory … and that is what it's all about.

*A*CKNOWLEDGMENTS

Writing a book, no matter the subject matter, is a mountainous undertaking. It requires a great deal of thought, study, motivation, energy, and time on the part of the author. However, the task would never come to fruition without the support and encouragement of others. God builds us with the hands of others, and it is here I want to acknowledge some who have built me.

First, I thank my wife for her constant encouragement and support. Your self-sacrifice and servant's heart humble me daily. I cannot thank God enough for you and our marriage. I do not deserve you, but I want to spend every day trying to.

Second, to the faithful people in the little church in the hollow where I grew up, thank you. You poured God's Word into me and showed me what it means to be faithful. It's been a long time coming, but I hope you can see some of the fruit of your labor here in mine.

Bob McGann, you have been instrumental in this writing. When I first entertained the idea of writing this book, you were the first to encourage me to pursue it. From day one you have given me support and feedback on the manuscript, not because you had to but because, as my brother and friend, you wanted to. I cannot convey the depth of my appreciation to you.

John Spadafora, thank you for your thoughtful review of the manuscript. It is a better product to the Lord's glory as a result of your input. Thank you also for being a great encouragement to me, and for being someone I can look to who is further along the road than I am. I appreciate your heart and witness.

To my friend, Paul, whose last name I leave out because he would want it that way, your servant's heart is something I continue to learn from and am convicted by. Thank you for showing me what it looks like to be the anus in the body of Christ. There are so many reasons why I thank God that He placed us across the street from you guys. You have been an encouragement and example so many times when you did not know it. Thank you for your friendship and love.

To the men in the Tuesday-morning Bible study, thank you for giving me the opportunity to study God's Word with you. It has been a delight. The entirety of section II of the book is the direct result of our studies, and I look forward to whatever else God has for us.

There are so many who have unknowingly or knowingly contributed to my spiritual development throughout my life, and I cannot name them all. This work is a direct result of all of the efforts of untold numbers of people. God has been glorified through you.

Notes

Introduction

1.   Cloverton. "God Help Me To Be." *Patterns*. Cloverton, 2013. CD.

Chapter 1

2.   Tolkien, JRR. The Lord of the Rings: The Fellowship of the Ring. Boston, MA. Houghton Mifflin. 1994.
3.   Stanford University. (2010, July 29). *Locke's Political Philosophy*. Retrieved January 10, 2014, from Stanford Encyclopedia of Philosophy: http://plato. stanford.edu/entries/locke-political/

Chapter 2

4.   Ogden CL, Carroll MD, Kit BK, Flegal KM. (2012) Prevalence of Obesity in the United States, 2009-2010. National Centers for Health Statistics Data Brief. No. 82. Retrieved January 11, 2014 from http://www.cdc.gov/obesity/data/ adult.html
5.   Wilson L. (2013) How big is a house? Average house size by country. Retrieved on January 11, 2014 from http://shrinkthatfootprint.com/how-big-is-a-house.
6.   Self Storage Association. (2013, November 22). *Self Storage Association Fact Sheet*. Retrieved January 11, 2014, from http://www.selfstorage.org/ssa/Content/ NavigationMenu/AboutSSA/FactSheet/default.htm.
7.   National Accounts Main Aggregates Database. (2013 December) United Nations Statistics Division. Retrieved January 12, 2014 from http://unstats. un.org/unsd/snaama/resQuery.asp
8.   Greed [Def. 1] (n.d.) In *The Free Dictionary*, Retrieved January 10, 2014, from http://www.thefreedictionary.com/greed.
9.   Harris Interactive Inc. (2013) The 2013 Consumer Financial Literacy Survey. The National Foundation for Credit Counseling. Retrieved March 18, 2014 from https://active.nfcc.org/newsroom/financialliteracy/files2013/ nfcc nbpca 2013%20financialliteracy survey datasheet key%20 findings 032913.pdf
10. Experian. (2013, November). *The Fourth Annual State of Credit*. Retrieved January 12, 2014, from Experian: http://press.experian.com/United-States/

Press-Release/experians-state-of-credit-report-finds-millennials-struggling-the-most-with-debt-management.aspx

11. C. Smith, M. O. Emerson, P. Snell, *Passing the Plate.* (New York: Oxford University Press, 2009).

12. Barna Group. (2013, April 13). *American Donor Trends.* Retrieved January 12, 2014, from Barna Group: https://www.barna.org/barna-update/culture/606-american-donor-trends#. UyhCtyf-DU.

Chapter 3

13. *Aparneomai* [Def. 1a]. (n.d) In *The Blue Letter Bible.* Retrieved January 14, 2014, from http://www.blueletterbible.org/lang/lexicon/lexicon. cfm?Strongs=G533&t=NKJV

Chapter 4

14. Heber, R; Dykes, JB. *Holy, Holy, Holy.* The Baptist Hymnal. Nashville, TN: Genevox, 1991. Pg 2

15. Tozer, A.W. (2009) The Purpose of Man: Designed to Worship. Ventura, CA. Gospel Light Worldwide. Pg. 71.

Chapter 5

16. Vanderkam, L. (Autumn 2012) The Paperback Quest for Joy: America's unique love affair with self-help books". Retrieved on January 18, 2014 from *City Journal* (New York: Manhattan Institute for Policy Research) at http://www. city-journal.org/2012/22_4_self-help-books.html

Chapter 6

17. National Institute of Mental Health. (2005). *Any Anxiety Disorder Among Adults.* Retrieved January 19, 2014, from National Institute of Mental Health: http:// www.nimh.nih.gov/health/topics/anxiety-disorders/index.shtml

18. Anxiety [Def. 1]. (n.d.). In Dictionary.com, Retrieved January 19, 2014, from http://dictionary.reference.com/browse/anxiety.

19. Phelps, E.A.; Ling, S.; Carrasco, M. *Emotion facilitates perception and potentiates the perceptual benefits of attention.* Psychol Sci 2006;17(4):292-9.

20. von Leupoldt, A.; Dahme, B. *The impact of emotions on symptom perception in patients with asthma and healthy controls.* Psychophysiol 2013;50(1):1-4.

21. Moody-Stuart, K. (1879) Brownlow North, Records and Recollections. London. Hodder and Stoughton. Pg 138.

22. The Barna Group. (2002 February 12) Americans are most likely to base truth on feelings. Retrieved on January 19, 2014 from https://www.barna.org/barna-update/article/5-barna-update/67-americans-are-most-likely-to-base-truth-on-feelings#.Uymlqtyf-DW.

Chapter 7

23. Relevant [Def. 2]. (n.d.). In Your Dictionary, Retrieved January 20, 2014 from http://www.yourdictionary.com/relevant.

24. Cacioppo, J; Patrick, W. (2008) *Loneliness: Human Nature and the Need for Social Connection*, New York, NY. W.W. Norton & Co.

25. The Barna Group. (2013 April 30) Christians: More Like Jesus or Pharisees? Retrieved on January 20, 2014 from https://www.barna.org/barna-update/faith-spirituality/611-christians-more-like-jesus-or-pharisees#.Uym4P9yf-DU

26. Smith, C; Emerson, M.O.; Snell P. (2009) Passing the Plate. New York, NY. Oxford University Press USA

27. Ambassador [Def. 1]. (n.d.). In Dictionary.com, Retrieved January 23, 2014 from http://dictionary.reference.com/browse/ambassador.

28. Tozer, A.W. (2009) Reclaiming Christianity: A Call to Authentic Faith. Ventura, CA. Regal. Pg. 18.

29. Hartford Institute for Religion Research. (2012). *Fast Facts About American Religion*. Retrieved January 21, 2014, from Hartford Institute for Religion Research: http://hirr.hartsem.edu/research/fastfacts/fast_facts.html#denom

Chapter 8

30. Hartford Institute for Religion Research. (2012). *Fast Facts About American Religion*. Retrieved January 21, 2014, from Hartford Institute for Religion Research: http://hirr.hartsem.edu/research/fastfacts/fast_facts.html#denom

31. Fullerton, W.Y. (1966) Charles Haddon Spurgeon: A Biography. Chicago, IL. Moody Press.

Chapter 9

32. National Marriage and Divorce Rate Trends. (2013) National Vital Statistics System of the Centers for Disease Control and Prevention. Retrieved on January 11, 2014 from http://www.cdc.gov/nchs/nvss/marriage_divorce_tables.htm

33. The Barna Group. (2008 March 31) New Marriage and Divorce Statistics Released. Retrieved on January 11, 2014 from https://www.barna.org/barna-update/article/15-familykids/42-new-marriage-and-divorce-statistics-released#.UynUU9yf-DU

34. Number of Jobs Held, Labor Market Activity, and Earnings Growth Among the Youngest Baby Boomers: Results from a Longitudinal Survey. (2012 July 25) U.S. Department of Labor Bureau of Labor Statistics Press Release. Retrieved on January 23, 2014 from http://www.bls.gov/news.release/pdf/nlsoy.pdf

35. The Barna Group. (2008 March 31) New Marriage and Divorce Statistics Released. Retrieved on January 11, 2014, from https://www.barna.org/barna-update/article/15-familykids/42-new-marriage-and-divorce-statistics-released#. UynUU9yf-DU.

36. Notare, T; McCord, H.R. (2012) Marriage and the Family in the United States: Resources for Society. United States Conference of Catholic Bishops. Retrieved on January 23, 2014 from http://www.usccb.org/issues-and-action/marriage-and-family/marriage/upload/Marriage-and-Family-in-the-US.pdf

Chapter 10

37. Bonhoeffer, D. (1995) The Cost of Discipleship. New York, NY. Touchstone. Pg. 63.

38. Ibid.

39. Ibid., 89.

40. Ibid., 80.

41. Ibid.

Chapter 11

42. Bonhoeffer, D. (1995) The Cost of Discipleship. New York, NY. Touchstone. Pg. 91.

43. Ibid.

44. Yun, B. (2008) Living Water. Grand Rapids, MI. Zondervan. Pg. 215.

45. Wurmbrand, R. (2004) Tortured for Christ. London. Hodder and Stoughton. Pg. 105.

46. Ripken, N. (2013) The Insanity of God. Nashville. B&H. Pg. 263.

47. Ibid., 286.

Chapter 12

48. United States Department of Health and Human Services. (2014, February). *Federal Poverty Guidelines*. Retrieved March 18, 2014, from United States Department of Health and Human Services: http://www.familiesusa.org/resources/tools-for-advocates/guides/federal-poverty-guidelines.html

49. Gallup World. (2013, December 16). *Worldwide, Median Household Income About $10,000*. Retrieved March 18, 2014, from Gallup World: http://www.gallup.com/poll/166211/worldwide-median-household-income-000.aspx

50. Bongaarts, J. (2001). *Household Size and Composition in the Developing World*. Retrieved March 18, 2014, from Population Council: http://www.popcouncil. us/pdfs/wp/144.pdf

51. *Chariots of Fire*. Dir. Hugh Hudson. Twentieth Century-Fox, 1981. Film.

52. McCasland, D. *Eric Liddell: Pure Gold*. Grand Rapids, MI: Discovery House Publishers, 2001. Book.

53. Liddell, E. *The Disciplines of the Christian Life*. New York, NY: Ballantine Books, 1985. Book.

Chapter 14

54. Chrysostom, St. John. *Homilies on the Gospel of Matthew*, Homily XV.4 circa 390.

Chapter 23

55. Elliott, C; Bradbury, W.B. *Just As I Am*. The Baptist Hymnal. Nashville, TN: LifeWay Worship, 2008. Pg. 435.

56. Newton, J; Excell, E.O. *Amazing Grace*. The Baptist Hymnal. Nashville, TN: Genevox, 1991. Pg. 330.

57. The Ragamuffin Band. "My Deliverer" *The Jesus Record*. Sony, 1998. CD.

58. Manning, B. *The Ragamuffin Gospel*. New York, NY: Doubleday, 2000. Book.

Chapter 25

59. Poe, E.A. "The Cask of Amontillado." *Godey's Lady's Book*. November 1846: 33(5):216-218. Print.

$\mathscr{A}$PPENDIX

Notes on Greek Etymology for Matthew 5:3–11 in Section II

The original Greek words and definitions used throughout the book, including in section II, were accessed via the Blue Letter Bible website (http://www.blueletterbible.org), an independent entity that utilizes the Strong's system of Hebrew and Greek. Permission for the use of information from the website was directly obtained from Sowing Circle, the producers of the Blue Letter Bible website.

5:3

"Poor in spirit" is a phrase derived from two Greek words, *ptōchos*, which is translated as *poor*, and *pneuma*, which is translated as *spirit*. The word *ptōchos* means something without any worth; something completely without any desirable value. It is derived from *ptosso*, meaning "to crouch," which is akin to *ptoeō*, which means "to be terrified."

The word translated *kingdom* is *basileia*, which refers to the power and authority to rule, especially regarding the territory subject to the rule of a king.

The Greek word translated as *heaven* in this verse is *ouranos*, which refers to that place above the stars where God dwells

5:4

The word *mourn* that is used in Matthew 5:4 is *pentheō*, which is fairly straightforward—it means to *mourn* or to *lament*.

The word translated as *comforted* in Matthew 5:4 is a compound word, *parakaleō*. The word carries a number of definitions, including *to comfort, console, encourage*, and *teach*. If we further break down *parakaleō* into the two words from which it is composed, we get *para* and *kaleō*. *Para* means *from, of, at, by, beside*, or *near*. *Kaleō* means *to call or invite*, but it also can mean *to call by name*. So the image that is being conveyed here in *parakaleō* is that of an intimate, personal relationship.

5:5

The Greek word that is translated as *meek* in Matthew 5:5 is *praÿs*, which carries a fairly straightforward meaning, that of *meekness* or *gentleness of spirit*. A notable thing about the word *praÿs* is what it is lacking, that being self-assertiveness, self-interest, or self-aggrandizement.

The Greek verb translated as *inherit* is the word *klēronomeō*, which means *to receive an allotted portion as via inheritance*. The verb may be better understood when the noun from which it is derived, *klēronomos*, is considered. *Klēronomos* is a person that is *an heir*.

5:6

The word translated as *hunger* in Matthew 5:6 is *peinaō*, which carries some interesting origins and associations with English. The word means *to suffer need* or *be hungry*. It also means *to crave ardently* or *to seek with eager desire*. However, if we look into our own language, we find a trail back to *peinaō* that furthers our understanding.

The origin of the English word *pine*, meaning *to long for painfully*, can be traced to similar origins as *peinaō*. In middle English, the word was "pinen," which meant *to torment, torture,* or *to be in pain*. In old English, the word was "pin," meaning *to torture*. In Latin, the word was "poena," meaning *punishment*. In Roman mythology, Poena was the spirit of punishment and the attendant of punishment to Nemesis, the goddess of divine retribution.

In a manner similar to hunger, the word for thirst, *dipsaō*, paints a greater picture than what we usually think of. *Dipsaō* carries the meaning of *to suffer thirst* or *suffer from thirst*. The suffering in this word is a real part of the word's meaning. The word also involves those whose thirst is so great as to be painful—they eagerly long for refreshment.

The word translated as righteousness is *dikaiosynē*, and it is a noun that carries with it a quality of *virtue, integrity, rightness, correctness of thinking, feeling, and acting*. This we condense into righteousness, but it is multifaceted, including rightness with God but also rightness in acting toward our fellow man and in our dealings with ourselves.

The final word in this beatitude is seemingly straightforward, but as we have seen with the others, there is much more to it than we would first think. The word translated as *filled* is *chortazō*, meaning *to fill* or *satisfy the desire of one*. One common usage of the word was *to feed herbs, grass, or hay*—that is, to fatten animals with food. The root word of *chortazō* is *chortos*, which is *the place where grass grows and animals graze*.

5:7

The word translated as *merciful* is the Greek word *eleēmōn*, which is completely straightforward and simply means *merciful*. The roots of *eleēmōn* help to give us a better picture of what Jesus really meant in this beatitude. *Eleeō* means *to have mercy on, to help the afflicted*, or *to bring help to the wretched*. This helps us to get a better image of what is being said by the Lord; however, if we take one step further in looking into mercy, the image will become even clearer. The Greek word here translated as *mercy* is the word *eleos*. The primary definition of *eleos* embodies the image of *kindness or goodwill toward the miserable and the afflicted, joined with a desire to help them.*

5:8

The word translated as *pure* in Matthew 5:8 is the word *katharos*. This is actually the word from which we derive the English words *catharsis* and *cathartic*. These English words carry the image of something being made clean, which is a part of *katharos*. *Katharos* does mean *to be clean* or *to be pure*, but there are further categories to which the word was applied.

The Hebrew word *tahowr* is translated as *clean* in Psalm 51:10 can also be translated as *pure*, and carries the same dimensions as the Greek word *katharos* we covered already.

The word translated as *see* in Matthew 5:8 is the Greek word *optanomai*, which means *to look at* or *to behold*, but can also mean *to allow oneself to be seen* or *to appear*.

5:9

The word translated as *peacemaker* in Matthew 5:9 is the compound word *eirēnopoios*, and it is found nowhere else in the Bible. The individual words that make up *eirēnopoios* are *eirēnē* and *poieō*. *Eirēnē* is translated as peace but is applied to a number of settings from national tranquility; harmony between individuals; safety, security, and prosperity; and the peace of the Messiah. Ultimately, *eirēnē* conveys *a state of complete tranquility* and to some extent, a sense of *contentment with and within all relationships*, whether with God, our fellow man, or the state.

The word *poieō*, which is the *maker* portion of peacemaker, carries a number of different meanings that fall under the primary definitions of *to make* or *to do*. Within the context of *to make*, two definitions that come with *poieō* are *to be the authors of, the cause*, and *to make a thing out of something.*

In this beatitude the word *huios*, meaning *son* or *children*, is coupled with the word *theos,* meaning God, to indicate *those that God esteems as sons*

5:10

The Greek word *diōkō* is translated in Matthew 5:10 as *persecuted*. The word carries multiple definitions all of which point toward a root in the idea of running. On one hand, some of the definitions are in regard to chasing after something, as in pursuing something. It can be taken in a hostile and nonhostile manner. Conversely, the word can mean *to drive away*, or *to make to run away*. In the case of the beatitude Jesus was speaking, the applicable definitions include *to drive away* or *to make to flee*, or *to harass, trouble, or mistreat one.*

5:11

The word translated as *revile* is the Greek word *oneidizō*, which is translated as *insult* in some Bible versions. We have already covered *diōkō*, the word for persecute, in the previous beatitude, and it is the same here in Matthew 5:11. The word translated as *all kinds* is the word *pas*. This word can be in regard to an individual thing or a collective, and it conveys the meaning of *each and every, everything*, or *all*. For the sake of this beatitude, it is likely best conveyed as *every possible kind.*

There are two words Jesus used that are translated as *evil* in Matthew 5:11. The first word was *ponēros*, which in this context means *something ethically evil* or *wicked*. The second word in the original text, which is essentially dropped out of English translations, is *rhēma*, which means *that which is or has been uttered by the living voice, thing spoken*, or *word*. *Rhēma* is most often translated simply as *word*. This is different from the Greek word *eipon*, which occurs in the same verse and is translated as "say."

The word *heneka*, which is translated as *sake* here, also includes the meaning of *on account of, for*, and *for the cause of.*

CPSIA information can be obtained at www.ICGtesting.com
Printed in the USA
LVOW07s0231270215

428598LV00001B/156/P